CO

✓ KU-535-073

ATLAS OF EUROPE

HarperCollins*Publishers*

HarperCollins Publishers
P O Box, Glasgow G4 0NB

First published as *MiniAtlas Europe* by Bartholomew, 1992.
First published in Gem format, 1993

© Bartholomew 1993

Illustration (pp vi-vii) and 'New Republics' city
   maps (pp 137-139) © Times Books
Maps (pp 4-79) and city plans (pp 90-136) © Hallwag
'New Republics' maps (pp 82-88) © HarperCollins

Bartholomew is a Division of HarperCollins Publishers

Reprint 10 9 8 7 6 5 4 3 2 1 0

ISBN 0 00 470278 6

Printed in Italy

CONTENTS

MAPS

NEW REPUBLICS
(Formerly USSR in Europe)

CITY PLANS

INDEX

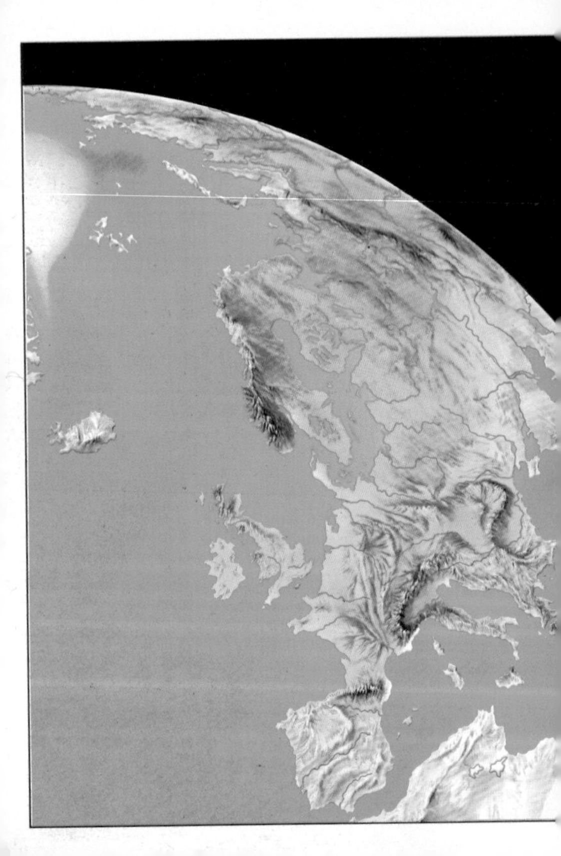

EUROPE

Momentous events have been taking place throughout Europe, with major political upheavals resulting from the decline of communism in favour of a free market economy.

The Iron Curtain has been drawn back; the Berlin Wall demolished; the Soviet Union has broken up; other countries have split, and two have been reunified. These events have necessitated a complete redrawing of the map of Europe. It now shows a unified Germany, the independent Baltic States of Estonia, Latvia and Lithuania, the new states of Slovenia, Croatia and Bosnia & Herzegovina, and latterly Macedonia; and the separate states of Slovakia and the Czech Republic. The future political stability of these emerging nations has still to be established with secure boundaries - further changes cannot be ruled out.

At the same time, the European Community (EC) strives towards even greater economic, monetary, social and political unity. The establishment ot the 'Single Market', in 1992 swept away many of the trade barriers for the 344 million people and trade within the Member States. The enlargement of the EC is also on the 'new Europe' agenda, with membership of other states under consideration.

This, then is the dynamic new Europe of today, stretching as it does from the Atlantic to the Urals, from the Arctic to the Caucasus, covering over 10 million square kilometres and now comprising over 40 countries. In a small way, this compact Gem Atlas portrays the diversity and richness of this continent, through the detailed 'MAPS' of its many countries and regions, a section on the 'NEW REPUBLICS' of the former USSR in Europe and finally the large scale 'CITY PLANS' of its great capitals and major towns.

Official Country Identification

A Austria
AL Albania
AND Andorra
B Belgium
BG Bulgaria
CH Switzerland
D Germany
DK Denmark
E Spain
EW Estonia
F France
FL Liechtenstein
GB United Kingdom
GR Greece
H Hungary
I Italy
IRL Ireland
IS Iceland
L Luxembourg
LR Latvia
LT Lithuania
M Malta
MC Monaco
N Norway
NL Netherlands
P Portugal
PL Poland
R Romania
RSM San Marino
S Sweden
SF Finland
TR Turkey
V Vatican
YU Yugoslavia

New Country Abbreviation

AR Armenia
AZ Azerbaijan
BE Belorussia
BOS Bosnia-Herzegovina
CRO Croatia
CZ Czech Republic
G Georgia
MAC Macedonia
MO Moldavia
RF Russian Federation
SL Slovakia
SLO Slovenia
U Ukraine

Reykjavik IS

N S

Oslo

DK

Copenha

IRL Dublin GB

Birmingham Hamburg

London NL Amsterdam Berlin

Brussels B Rotterdam D

Bonn

Paris L Frankfurt Pra

Vienna C

F Berne FL Munich A

Lyon Milan Ljubljana SL

Turin Zagreb

AND RSM

Marseille MC I

P Barcelona V Rome

Lisbon Madrid E Naples

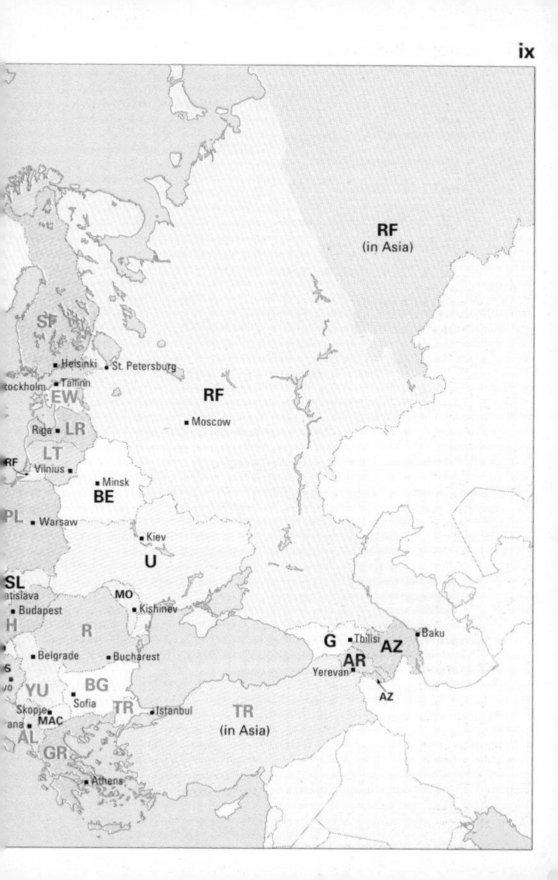
RF
(in Asia)
SF
Helsinki
St. Petersburg
Tallinn
EW
RF
Moscow
Riga
LR
LT
RF
Vilnius
Minsk
BE
PL
Warsaw
Kiev
U
SL
Budapest
MO
Kishinev
R
Belgrade
Bucharest
BG
YU
Sofia
Skopje
MAC
AL
TR
Istanbul
TR
(in Asia)
GR
Athens
G
Tbilisi
AZ
Baku
AR
Yerevan
AZ

x Europe, Economic Groupings

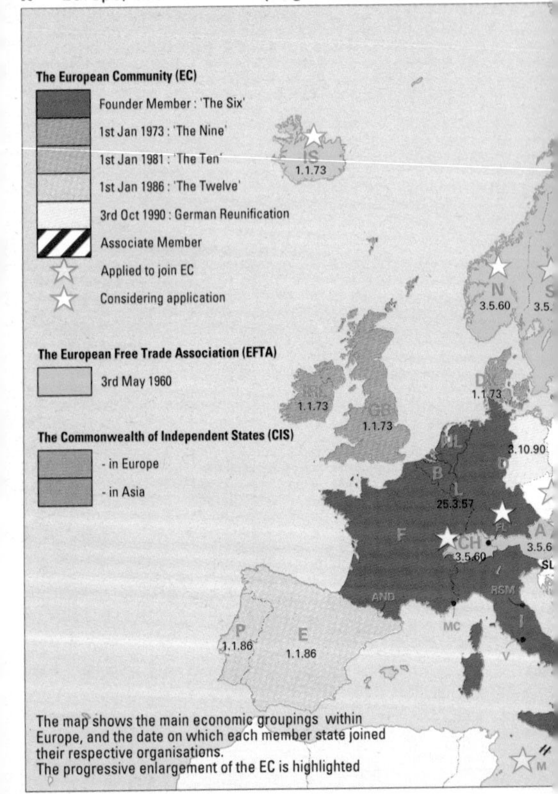

The European Community (EC)

- Founder Member : 'The Six'
- 1st Jan 1973 : 'The Nine'
- 1st Jan 1981 : 'The Ten'
- 1st Jan 1986 : 'The Twelve'
- 3rd Oct 1990 : German Reunification
- Associate Member
- ☆ Applied to join EC
- ☆ Considering application

The European Free Trade Association (EFTA)

- 3rd May 1960

The Commonwealth of Independent States (CIS)

- in Europe
- in Asia

The map shows the main economic groupings within
Europe, and the date on which each member state joined
their respective organisations.
The progressive enlargement of the EC is highlighted

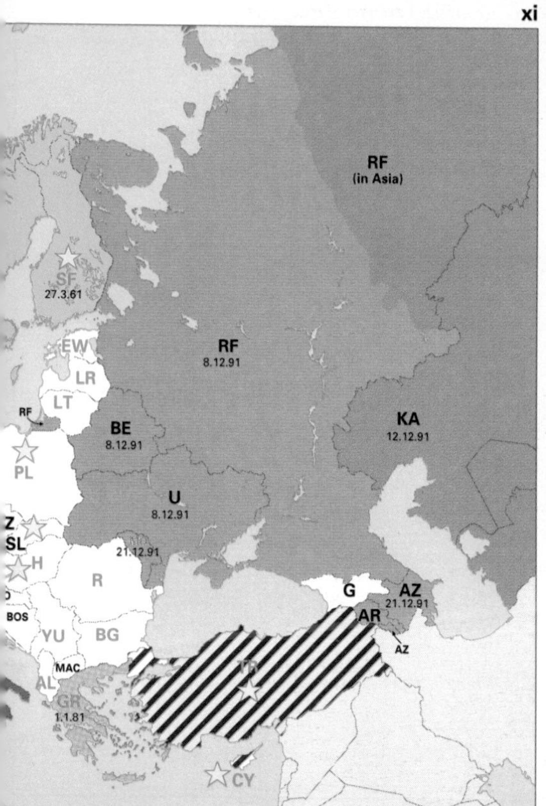
RF
(in Asia)
SF
27.3.61
EW
LR
LT
RF
RF
8.12.91
BE
8.12.91
KA
12.12.91
PL
U
8.12.91
Z
SL
H
21.12.91
R
G
AZ
21.12.91
AR
BOS
YU
BG
AZ
MAC
AL
TR
GR
1.1.81
CY

	COUNTRY	CAPITAL CITY	POPULATION in millions, 1989	AREA in sq. km	MAIN LANGUAGES	CURRENCY
A	AUSTRIA	Wien (Vienna)	7.6	83 849	German	schilling
AL	ALBANIA	Tirane (Tirana)	3.2	28 748	Albanian	lek
AND	ANDORRA	Andorra la Vella	0.05	464	Catalan,French, Spanish	franc, peseta
B	BELGIUM	Bruxelles (Brussels)	9.8	30 513	French, Dutch, German	franc
BG	BULGARIA	Sofija (Sofia)	9.0	110 912	Bulgarian	lev
CH	SWITZERLAND	Bern (Berne)	6.6	41 288	German, French, Italian	franc
D	GERMANY	Berlin/Bonn	77.6	356 755	German	mark
DK	DENMARK	København (Copenhagen)	5.1	43 069	Danish	krone
E	SPAIN	Madrid	39.1	504 782	Spanish, Catalan, Basque	peseta
EW	ESTONIA	Tallinn	1.6	45 000	Estonian, Russian	rouble
F	FRANCE	Paris	56.0	547 026	French	franc
FL	LIECHTENSTEIN	Vaduz	0.03	160	German, Alemannic dialect	franc
GB	UNITED KINGDOM	London	57.1	244 046	English, Welsh, Gaelic	pound
GR	GREECE	Athinai (Athens)	10.0	131 944	Greek	drachma
H	HUNGARY	Budapest	10.6	93 030	Magyar	forint
I	ITALY	Roma (Rome)	57.1	301 225	Italian	lira
IRL	IRELAND	Dublin	3.7	70 283	English, Irish	punt
IS	ICELAND	Reykjavik	0.3	103 000	Icelandic	krona
L	LUXEMBOURG	Luxembourg	0.4	2 586	French, German	franc
LR	LATVIA	Riga	2.7	64 000	Latvian, Russian	rouble
LT	LITHUANIA	Vilnius	3.7	65 000	Lithuanian, Russian	rouble
M	MALTA	Valletta	0.4	316	Maltese, English	pound
MC	MONACO	Monaco-Ville	0.03	1.9	French, Monegasque	franc
N	NORWAY	Oslo	4.2	324 219	Norwegian	krone
NL	NETHERLANDS	Amsterdam	14.9	40 844	Dutch	guilder
P	PORTUGAL	Lisboa (Lisbon)	10.3	92 082	Portuguese	escudo
PL	POLAND	Warszawa (Warsaw)	38.2	312 677	Polish	zloty
R	ROMANIA	București (Bucharest)	23.2	237 500	Romanian	leu
RSM	SAN MARINO	San Marino	0.02	61	Italian	lira
S	SWEDEN	Stockholm	8.4	449 964	Swedish	krona
SF	FINLAND	Helsinki	5.0	337 032	Finnish, Swedish	mark
TR	TURKEY	Ankara	54.8	780 576	Turkish	lira
V	VATICAN CITY	Cità del Vaticano	0.01	0.4	Latin, Italian	lira
YU	YUGOSLAVIA	Beograd (Belgrade)	10.6	91 285	Serbo-Croat	dinar
AR	ARMENIA	Yerevan	3.3	30 000	Armenian, Russian	rouble
AZ	AZERBAIJAN	Baku	7.1	87 000	Azerbaijani, Russian	rouble
BE	BELORUSSIA	Minsk	10.3	208 000	Belorussian, Russian	rouble
BOS	BOSNIA-HERZEGOVINA	Sarajevo	4.4	51 130	Serbo-Croat	dinar
CRO	CROATIA	Zagreb	4.7	56 540	Serbo-Croat	dinar
CZ	CZECH REP	Praha (Prague)	10.3	78 864	Czech	koruna
G	GEORGIA	Tbilisi	5.5	70 000	Georgian, Russian	rouble
MAC	MACEDONIA	Skopje	2.09	25 713	Macedonian	dinar
MO	MOLDAVIA	Kishinev	4.4	34 000	Romanian, Russian	rouble
RF	RUSSIAN FEDERATION	Moskva (Moscow)	148.0	17 075 000	Russian	rouble
SL	SLOVAKIA	Bratislava	5.3	49 035	Slovak	koruna
SLO	SLOVENIA	Ljubljana	1.9	7 815	Slovene, Serbo-Croat	dinar
U	UKRAINE	Kiyev (Kiev)	51.8	604 000	Ukrainian, Russian	rouble

MAPS

KEY TO MAP SYMBOLS

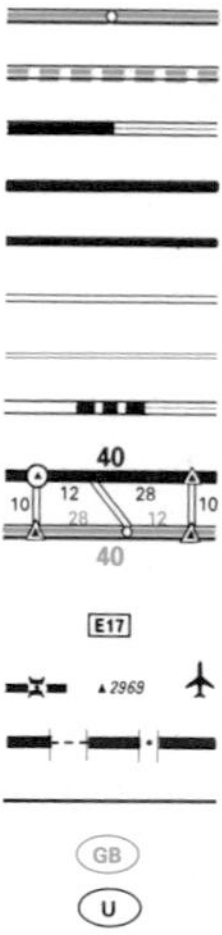

	Motorway with interchange
	Motorway under construction
	Dual carriageway
	Primary road
	Main road
	Secondary road
	Other road
	Roads under construction
40 / 10 12 28 28 12 10 / 40	Distances in kilometres
E17	European road numbers
✈ ▲2969	Pass, height in metres, airport
	Car ferry
	National boundary
GB	Official National Identification Letters
U	New Country Abbreviations

Scale 1 : 4 070 555

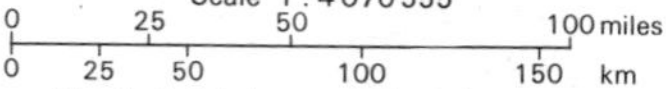

```
0       25        50                    100 miles
0    25    50         100         150    km
    64 miles to 1 inch     41 km to 1 cm
```

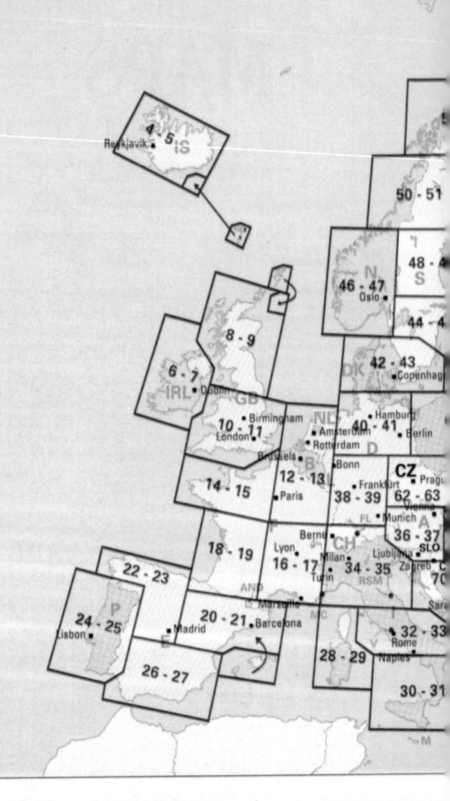
4 - 5
IS
Reykjavik
50 - 51
46 - 47
N
Oslo
48 -
S
44 -
8 - 9
6 - 7
IRL
Dublin
GB
42 - 43
DK
Copenhag
Birmingham
10 - 11
London
NL
Amsterdam
Rotterdam
40 - 41
Hamburg
Berlin
D
Brussels
B
Bonn
CZ
Prague
14 - 15
12 - 13
Paris
Frankfurt
38 - 39
62 - 63
Vienna
FL
Munich
A
36 - 37
18 - 19
Berne
CH
Lyon
16 - 17
Milan
Turin
34 - 35
Ljubljana
SLO
Zagreb
RSM
22 - 23
AND
Marseille
P
24 - 25
Lisbon
20 - 21
Madrid
Barcelona
E
MC
I
32 - 33
Rome
V
28 - 29
Naples
26 - 27
30 - 31
M

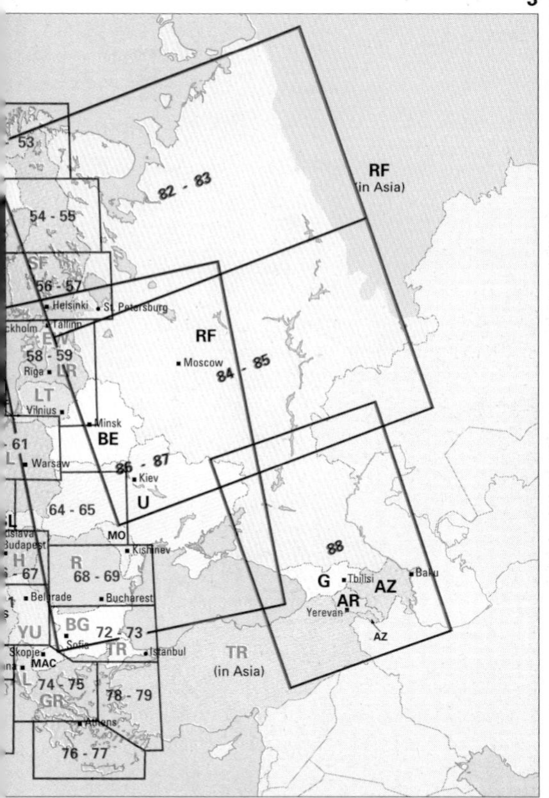

53
82 - 83
RF
(in Asia)
54 - 55
SF
56 - 57
Helsinki
St. Petersburg
Tallinn
EW
58 - 59
Riga
LR
LT
Vilnius
RF
Moscow
84 - 85
Minsk
BE
61
Warsaw
86 - 87
Kiev
U
64 - 65
MO
Budapest
Kishinev
H
67
R
68 - 69
88
G
Tbilisi
Baku
AZ
AR
Yerevan
AZ
Belgrade
Bucharest
YU
BG
72 - 73
Sofia
TR
Istanbul
TR
(in Asia)
Skopje
MAC
74 - 75
GR
78 - 79
Athens
76 - 77

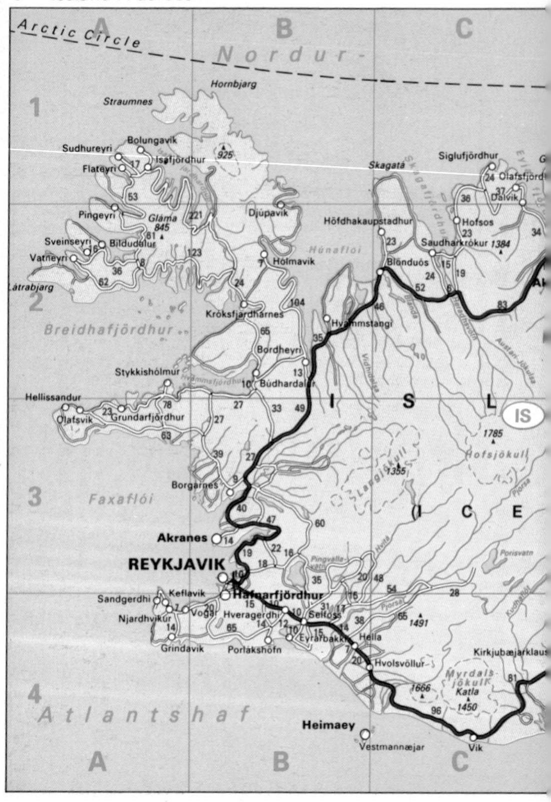
Arctic Circle
Nordur-
Hornbjarg
Straumnes
Bolungavik
Sudhureyri
Ísafjördhur
Flateyri
Skagatá
Siglufjördhur
Ólafsfjördh
Dalvik
Pingeyri
Gláma
845
Djúpavik
Höfdhakaupstadhur
Hofsos
Sveinseyri
Bildudalur
Saudhárkrókur
1384
Vatneyri
Húnaflói
Hólmavik
Blönduós
Látrabjarg
Króksfjardharnes
Hvammstangi
Breidhafjördhur
Bordheyri
Stykkishólmur
Búdhardalur
Hellissandur
I S L
IS
Ólafsvik
Grundarfjördhur
1785
Hofsjökull
Langjökull
1355
Borgarnes
Faxaflói
I C E
Akranes
REYKJAVIK
Keflavik
Hafnarfjördhur
Sandgerdhi
Vogar
Hveragerdhi
Selfoss
Njardhvikur
Eyrarbakki
Hella
1491
Grindavik
Porlákshöfn
Hvolsvöllur
Kirkjubæjarklaus
Myrdalsjökull
Katla
1666
1450
Atlantshaf
Heimaey
Vestmannæjar
Vik
A B C
1 2 3 4

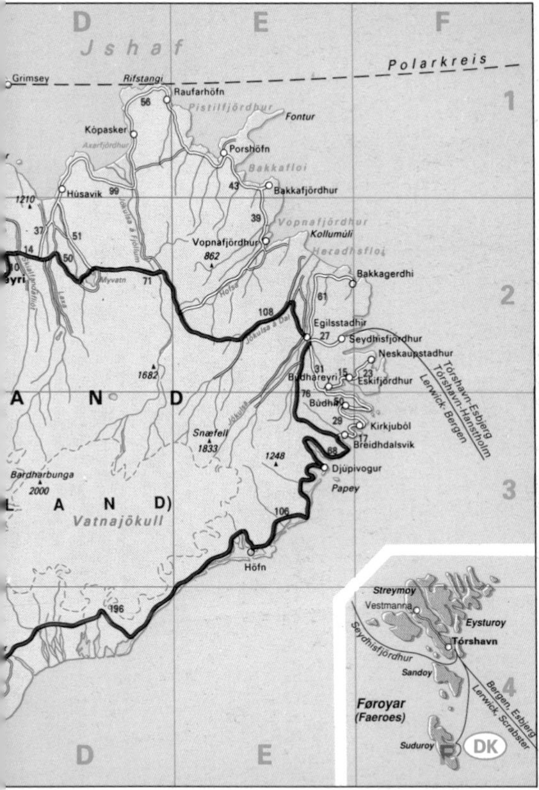

D E F

J s h a f

Polarkreis

Grimsey Rifstangi Raufarhöfn

1

56 *Pistilfjördhur* Fontur

Kópasker Þórshöfn

Axarfjördhur *Bakkaflói*

1210 Húsavik 99 43 Bakkafjördhur

37 51 39 *Vopnafjördhur*

14 50 Vopnafjördhur *Kollumúli*

yri Mývatn 71 862 *Heradhsflói*

108 Bakkagerdhi

61

2

27 Egilsstadhir

Seydhisfjördhur Tórshavn–Esbjerg
Torshavn–Hanstholm

1682 31 Neskaupstadhur

76 Budhareyri 15 23 Eskifjördhur

A N D Búdhir 29 Kirkjuból

Snæfell 17 Breidhdalsvik

1833 58

Bardharbunga *1248* Djúpivogur

2000 Papey

L A N D) 106

Vatnajökull

Höfn

196

3

Streymoy

Vestmanna *Eysturoy*

Seydhisfjördhur Tórshavn

Bergen, Esbjerg
Lerwick–Scrabster

Sandoy

Føroyar
(Faeroes)

4

Suduroy DK

D E

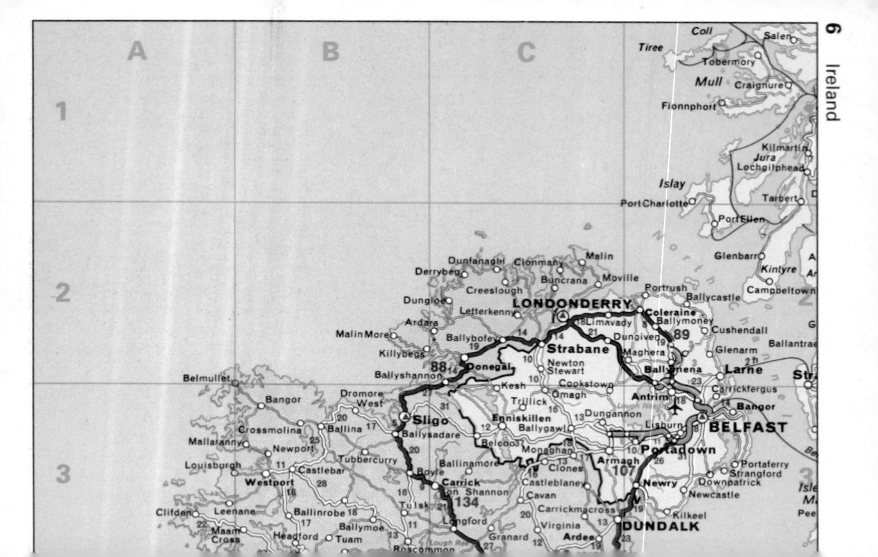
A
B
C
1
2
3
Coll
Tiree
Salen
Tobermory
Mull
Craignure
Fionnphort
Kilmartin
Jura
Lochgilphead
Islay
Port Charlotte
Tarbert
Port Ellen
Glenbarr
Kintyre
Campbeltown
Malin
Dunfanaghi
Clonmany
Derrybeg
Buncrana
Moville
Creeslough
Portrush
Ballycastle
Dungloe
LONDONDERRY
Coleraine
Letterkenny
Limavady
Ballymoney
Ardara
Cushendall
Malin More
Ballybofey
Dungiven
89
Killybegs
Strabane
Maghera
Glenarm
Ballantrae
88
Donegal
Newton Stewart
Ballymena
Larne
Ballyshannon
Belmullet
Kesh
Cookstown
Carrickfergus
Dromore West
Omagh
Antrim
Bangor
Bangor
Trillick
Lough Neagh
Sligo
Enniskillen
Dungannon
BELFAST
Crossmolina
Ballina
Lisburn
Ballysadare
Ballygawley
Mallaranny
Newport
Belcoo
Monaghan
Portadown
Tubbercurry
Armagh
Louisburgh
Ballinamore
Clones
107
Portaferry
Castlebar
Boyle
Strangford
Westport
Carrick on Shannon
Castleblaney
Newry
Downpatrick
Cavan
Newcastle
134
Tulsk
Clifden
Leenane
Ballinrobe
Carrickmacross
Kilkeel
Longford
Virginia
Maam Cross
Ballymoe
DUNDALK
Headford
Tuam
Granard
Ardee
Roscommon
Lough Ree

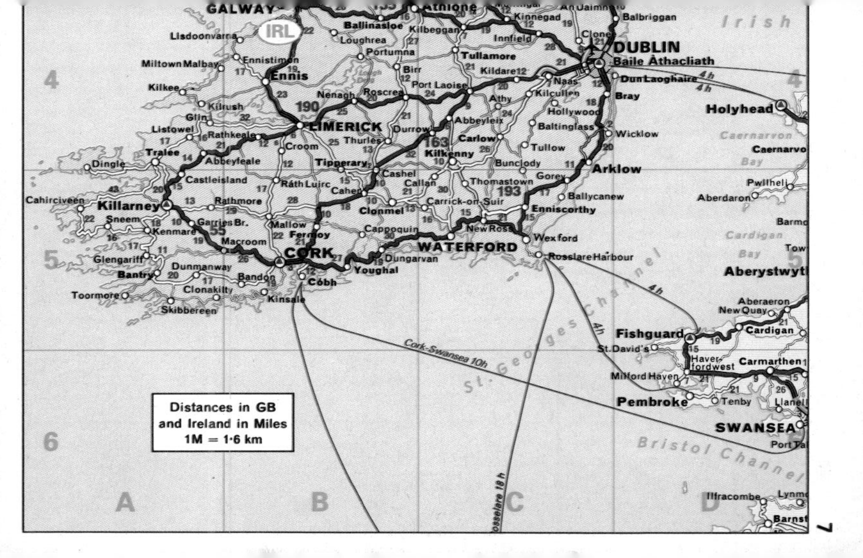
Distances in GB
and Ireland in Miles
1M = 1·6 km
IRL
GALWAY
DUBLIN
Baile Àthacliath
LIMERICK
CORK
WATERFORD
Killarney
Ennis
Ballinasloe
Loughrea
Portumna
Birr
Roscrea
Nenagh
Thurles
Tipperary
Cashel
Cahir
Clonmel
Kilkenny
Carlow
Athy
Kildare
Naas
Tullamore
Kilbeggan
Kinnegad
Innfield
Port Laoise
Abbeyleix
Durrow
Callan
Carrick-on-Suir
Thomastown
New Ross
Wexford
Rosslare Harbour
Enniscorthy
Ballycanew
Gorey
Arklow
Wicklow
Bray
Dun Laoghaire
Balbriggan
Clonee
Tullow
Bunclody
Baltinglass
Hollywood
Kilcullen
Dungarvan
Youghal
Cappoquin
Fermoy
Mallow
Cóbh
Kinsale
Bandon
Clonakilty
Skibbereen
Dunmanway
Bantry
Glengariff
Kenmare
Garries Br.
Macroom
Sneem
Cahirciveen
Dingle
Tralee
Listowel
Abbeyfeale
Castleisland
Rathmore
Croom
Ráth Luirc
Rathkeale
Glin
Kilrush
Kilkee
Miltown Malbay
Lisdoonvarna
Ennistimon
Toormore
Holyhead
Caernarvon Bay
Pwllheli
Aberdaron
Cardigan Bay
Aberaeron
New Quay
Cardigan
Fishguard
St. David's
Haverfordwest
Carmarthen
Milford Haven
Pembroke
Tenby
SWANSEA
Bristol Channel
Ilfracombe
Irish
St. Georges Channel
Cork-Swansea 10h
4h
A
B
C
D
4
5
6

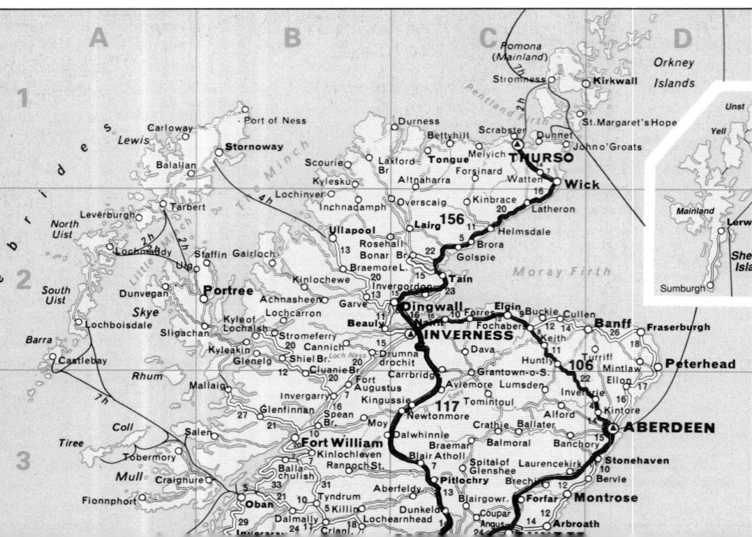
Orkney Islands
Pomona (Mainland)
Stromness
Kirkwall
St. Margaret's Hope
Shetland Islands
Unst
Yell
Mainland
Lerwick
Sumburgh
Pentland Firth
John o'Groats
Dunnet
Scrabster
THURSO
Wick
Watten
Latheron
Helmsdale
Brora
Golspie
Tain
Moray Firth
Port of Ness
Carloway
Lewis
Stornoway
Balallan
Tarbert
Leverburgh
North Uist
Lochmaddy
Hebrides
The Minch
Little Minch
Durness
Bettyhill
Melvich
Tongue
Forsinard
Altnaharra
Kinbrace
Laxford Br
Scourie
Kylesku
Lochinver
Inchnadamph
Overscaig
Lairg
156
Ullapool
Rosehall
Bonar Br.
Braemore L.
Invergordon
Dingwall
Kinlochewe
Achnasheen
Garve
Gairloch
Staffin
Uig
Portree
Dunvegan
Skye
South Uist
Lochboisdale
Sligachan
Kyle of Lochalsh
Kyleakin
Glenelg
Lochcarron
Stromeferry
Cannich
Shiel Br.
Loch Ness
Drumnadrochit
Cluanie Br.
Beauly
INVERNESS
Nairn
Forres
Elgin
Buckie
Cullen
Fochabers
Keith
Banff
Fraserburgh
Turriff
Peterhead
Mintlaw
Ellon
Huntly
106
Dava
Grantown-o-S.
Carrbridge
Aviemore
Lumsden
Inverurie
Kintore
ABERDEEN
Tomintoul
Alford
117
Spey
Kingussie
Newtonmore
Crathie
Ballater
Barra
Castlebay
Rhum
Mallaig
Invergarry
Fort Augustus
Glenfinnan
Spean Br.
Moy
Dalwhinnie
Braemar
Balmoral
Banchory
Fort William
Kinlochleven
Blair Atholl
Spital of Glenshee
Laurencekirk
Stonehaven
Bervie
Coll
Tiree
Salen
Tobermory
Mull
Craignure
Fionnphort
Ballachulish
Rannoch St.
Pitlochry
Brechin
Montrose
Oban
Tyndrum
Killin
Dalmally
Crianlarich
Aberfeldy
Dunkeld
Lochearnhead
Blairgowr.
Forfar
Coupar Angus
Arbroath
Inveraray

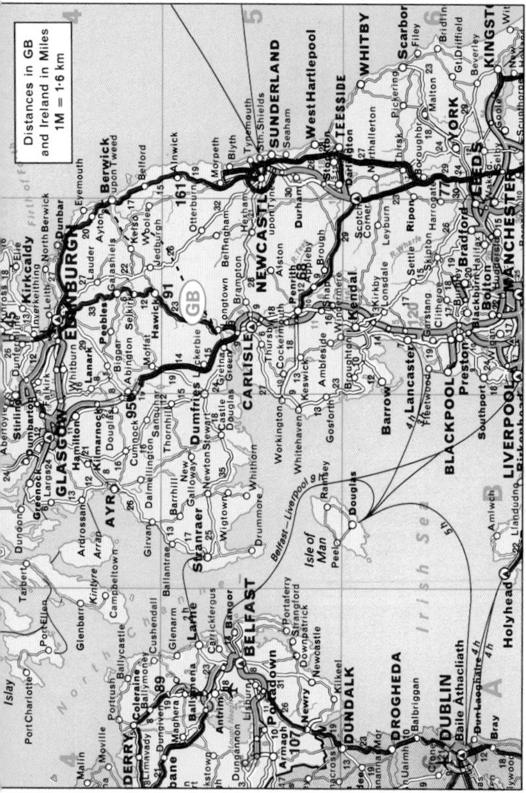

Distances in GB and Ireland in Miles
1M = 1·6 km

GB

EDINBURGH GLASGOW AYR CARLISLE Dumfries Stranraer NEWCASTLE SUNDERLAND West Hartlepool TEESSIDE WHITBY Scarborough YORK LEEDS MANCHESTER LIVERPOOL BLACKPOOL Preston Lancaster Kendal Barrow KINGSTON

Berwick upon Tweed Alnwick Morpeth Blyth Tynemouth North Shields South Shields Seaham Durham Bishop Auckland Darlington Northallerton Ripon Harrogate Bradford Halifax Bolton Southport Formby

Stirling Dunbar Eyemouth Ayton Lauder Galashiels Peebles Selkirk Hawick Jedburgh Kelso Wooler Belford Otterburn Bellingham Hexham Haltwhistle Brampton Longtown Alston Penrith Appleby Kirkby Stephen Sedbergh Settle Skipton Clitheroe Blackburn

Moffat Lockerbie Thornhill Sanquhar Cumnock New Galloway Castle Douglas Newton Stewart Wigtown Gatehouse Whithorn Workington Cockermouth Keswick Whitehaven Ambleside Gosforth Fleetwood

Glasgow Dumbarton Greenock Gourock Dunoon Largs Ardrossan Irvine Kilmarnock Hamilton Lanark Biggar Abington Douglas Strathaven

Tarbert Lochgilphead Campbeltown Girvan Ballantrae Barrhill Dalmellington Maybole

Isle of Man Douglas Peel Ramsey Castletown

BELFAST Larne Bangor Carrickfergus Newtownards Strangford Downpatrick Newcastle Kilkeel DERRY Coleraine Ballymoney Ballycastle Cushendall Glenarm Antrim Ballymena Portrush Portstewart Limavady

DUBLIN DROGHEDA DUNDALK Newry Armagh Portadown Dungannon Omagh Enniskillen Monaghan Carrickmacross Navan Balbriggan Swords Bray

Holyhead Llandudno Amlwch

Firth of Forth Solway Firth Irish Sea North Channel

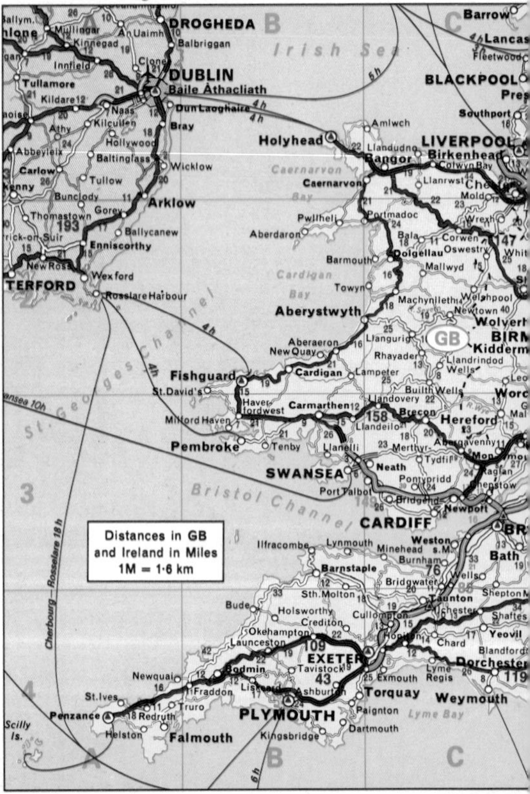

DROGHEDA **B**
Barrow **C**

Ballym. 26
Athlone
Milligan
Kinnegad
An Uaimh
Balbriggan
Innfield
Tullamore 21
Kildare 12
DUBLIN
Baile Atha Cliath
Lancas
Fleetwood
Irish Sea
6h
Clane
Naas
Kilcullen
Dun Laoghaire 4h
BLACKPOOL
Pres
Southport
Abbeyleix
Baltinglass
Carlow 26
Kenny
Bunclody
Gorey
Thomastown 193
rick-on-Suir 15
New Ross
TERFORD
Tullow
Ballycanew
Enniscorthy
Wexford
Rosslare Harbour
Bray
Wicklow
ARKLOW
Holyhead
Amlwch
Bangor
Caernarvon
Colwyn Bay
LIVERPOOL
Birkenhead
Moldo
Wrex
Caernarvon Bay
Pwllheli
Portmadoc
Llanrwst
Cardigan Bay
Aberdaron
Barmouth
Bala
Corwen
Oswestry
Dolgellau
Mallwyd
Machynlleth
Towyn
Aberystwyth
Llangurig
Llanidloes
Newtown
Wolpehool
GB
Wolver
BIRM
Kidderm
Aberaeron
New Quay
Rhayader
Llandrindod
Wells
Leo
Worc
Lampeter
Llanurig
Builth Wells
Fishguard
Cardigan
St. David's
Haverfordwest
Carmarthen 12
158
Llandovery 22
Brecon
Hereford
Mal
Milford Haven
Tenby
Llandeilo
Llanelli
Neath
Merthyr
Tydfil
Abergavenny
Raglan
Chepstow
Pembroke
SWANSEA
Port Talbot
Pontypridd
Bridgend
CARDIFF
Newport
BR
St. George's Channel 4h
Cherbourg - Rosslare 18h
Bristol Channel
Distances in GB
and Ireland in Miles
1M = 1·6 km
Ilfracombe
Lynmouth
Minehead
Weston s.M.
Burnham
Wells
Bath
Barnstaple
Bridgwater
76
Taunton
Shepton M
Sth. Molton
Cullompton
Ilchester
Shaftes
Yeovil
Bude
Holsworthy
Crediton
17
Chard
Dorchester
119
Newquai
Okehampton
Launceston
109
EXETER
Honiton
Axminster
Lyme
Regis
8
Weymouth
St. Ives
Bodmin
Tavistock
43
Exmouth
Lyme Bay
Scilly is.
Penzance
Redruth
Truro
Liskeard
Ashburton
PLYMOUTH
Torquay
Paignton
Dartmouth
Helston
Falmouth
Kingsbridge
Fraddon

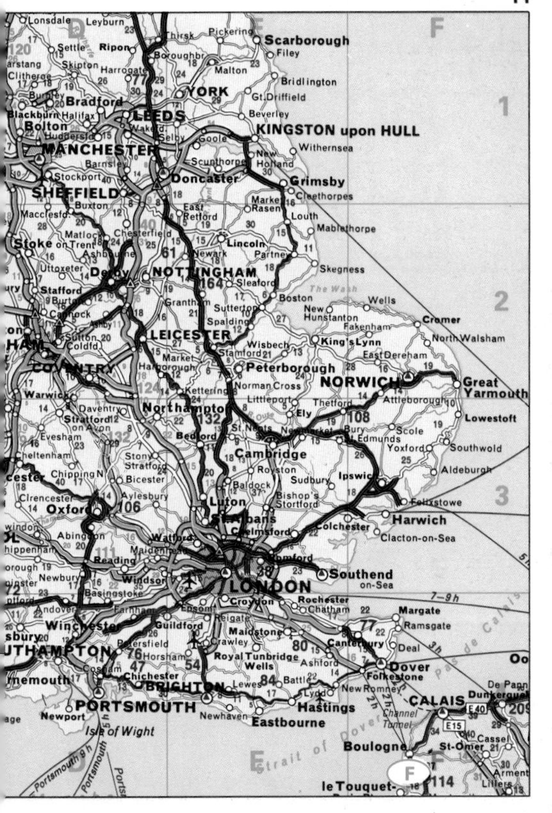
D
E
F
1
2
3
Lonsdale
Leyburn
Thirsk
Pickering
Scarborough
Filey
Settle
Ripon
Boroughbr
Malton
Skipton
Harrogate
Bridlington
Clitheroe
YORK
Burnley
Bradford
Gt.Driffield
Blackburn
Halifax
LEEDS
Beverley
Bolton
Wakefd.
Selby
Goole
KINGSTON upon HULL
Huddersfd
MANCHESTER
Withernsea
Barnsley
Scunthorpe
New Holland
Stockport
Doncaster
Grimsby
SHEFFIELD
Cleethorpes
Market Rasen
Buxton
East Retford
Louth
Macclesfd.
Mablethorpe
Matlock
Chesterfield
Lincoln
Stoke on Trent
Ashbourne
Newark
Partney
Uttoxeter
Derby
NOTTINGHAM
Skegness
Stafford
Sleaford
The Wash
Burton
Grantham
Boston
Wells
Cannock
Sutterton
New Hunstanton
Cromer
Spalding
Fakenham
Ashby
Sutton Coldfd.
LEICESTER
North Walsham
Wisbech
King's Lynn
Market Harborough
Stamford
East Dereham
COVENTRY
Peterborough
NORWICH
Great Yarmouth
Norman Cross
Kettering
Warwick
Littleport
Thetford
Attleborough
Daventry
Northampton
Ely
Lowestoft
Stratford on Avon
Bury St. Edmunds
Scole
Evesham
Bedford
St. Neots
Newmarket
Yoxford
Southwold
Cheltenham
Cambridge
Aldeburgh
Stony Stratford
Chipping N.
Bicester
Royston
Sudbury
Ipswich
Baldock
Cirencester
Aylesbury
Bishop's Stortford
Felixstowe
Oxford
Luton
Harwich
St. Albans
Chelmsford
Colchester
Abingdon
Watford
Clacton-on-Sea
Maidenhead
Reading
Romford
Newbury
Windsor
Southend on-Sea
Basingstoke
LONDON
Andover
Farnham
Croydon
Epsom
Rochester
Chatham
7–9h
Margate
Winchester
Guildford
Reigate
Maidstone
Ramsgate
Crawley
Canterbury
Deal
Petersfield
Horsham
Royal Tunbridge Wells
Ashford
Dover
Cosham
Chichester
Lewes
Battle
Folkestone
BRIGHTON
Lydd
New Romney
De Panne
PORTSMOUTH
CALAIS
Dunkerque
Newport
Newhaven
Hastings
Eastbourne
Channel Tunnel
E40
E15
Isle of Wight
Pas de Calais
Strait of Dover
Boulogne
Cassel
St-Omer
Lillers
le Touquet-
F

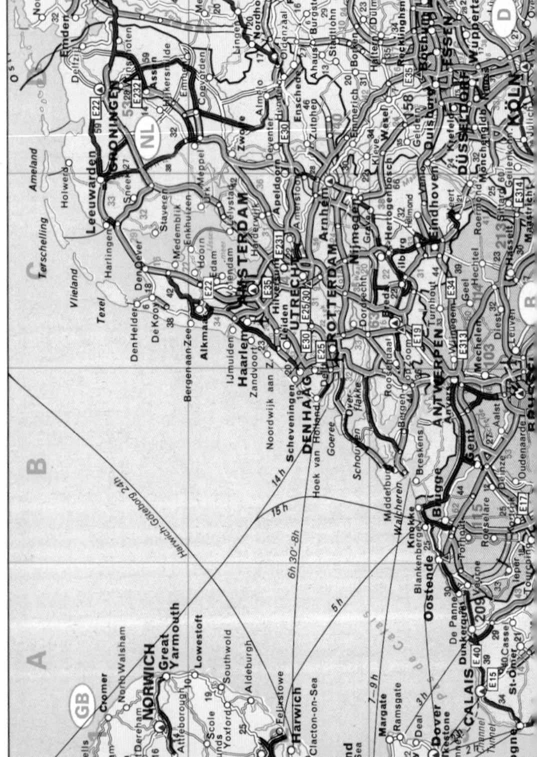
A
B
C
D
GB
NL
Cromer
North Walsham
NORWICH
Great Yarmouth
Lowestoft
Southwold
Aldeburgh
Felixstowe
Harwich
Clacton-on-Sea
Margate
Ramsgate
Deal
Dover
CALAIS
St-Omer
Cassel
Dunkerque
De Panne
Veurne
Oostende
Blankenberge
Knokke
Brugge
Gent
Aalst
Oudenaarde
Deinze
Roeselare
Tielt
Torhout
Ieper
Kortrijk
Middelburg
Walcheren
Breskens
Schouwen
Goeree
Over-flakke
Hoek van Holland
DEN HAAG
Scheveningen
Noordwijk aan Zee
Zandvoort
Haarlem
IJmuiden
Alkmaar
Bergen aan Zee
Den Helder
De Kooy
Texel
Vlieland
Terschelling
Ameland
Harlingen
Leeuwarden
Holwerd
Sneek
GRONINGEN
Delfzijl
Emden
Norden
Assen
Emmen
Coevorden
Meppel
Zwolle
Lingen
Nordhorn
Almelo
Hengelo
Enschede
Deventer
Apeldoorn
Zutphen
Arnhem
Nijmegen
Emmerich
Kleve
Wesel
Bocholt
Borken
Ahaus
Oldenzaal
Lelystad
Urk
Staveren
Enkhuizen
Medemblik
Hoorn
Edam
Volendam
AMSTERDAM
Hilversum
UTRECHT
Amersfoort
Harderwijk
Leiden
Delft
ROTTERDAM
Dordrecht
Breda
Roosendaal
Bergen op Zoom
Tilburg
's-Hertogenbosch
Eindhoven
Helmond
Weert
Roermond
Venlo
Geldern
Grave
ANTWERPEN
Anvers
Mechelen
Leuven
Diest
Geel
Turnhout
Herentals
Hasselt
Hechtel
Sittard
Geilenkirchen
Maastricht
Mönchengladbach
Krefeld
DÜSSELDORF
Duisburg
ESSEN
Bochum
Recklinghausen
Haltern
Dülmen
Wuppertal
KÖLN
Stadtlohn
Burgsteinfurt
Harwich-Göteborg 24h
14h
15h
6h 30'-8h
5h
7–9h
3h
E22
E232
E35
E231
E25/30
E30
E25
E19
E34
E313
E314
E17
E40
E15

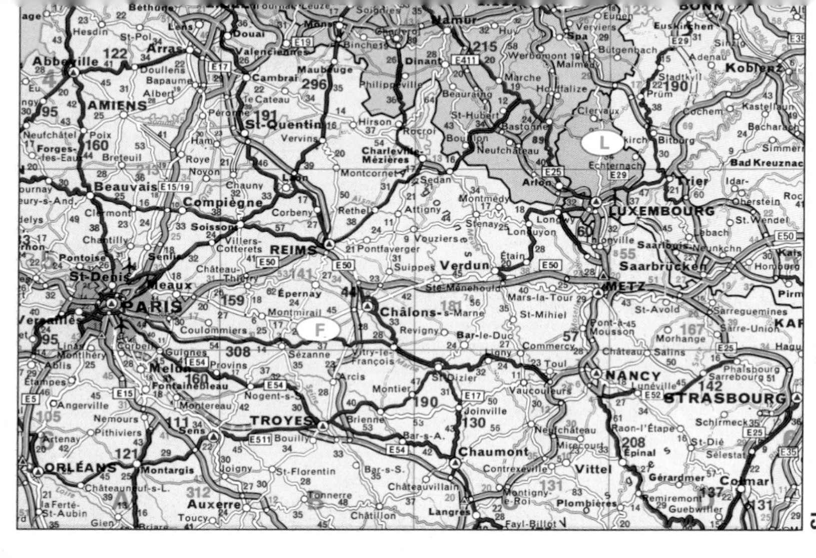

Béthune
Namur
Eupen
Verviers
Spa
Euskirchen
Hesdin
St-Pol
Lens
Douai
Mons
Binche
Huy
Bütgenbach
Adenau
Koblenz
Abbeville
Arras
Valenciennes
Dinant
Werbomont
Malmedy
Doullens
Bapaume
Albert
Cambrai
Maubeuge
Philippeville
Marche
Houffalize
Stadtkyll
Prüm
Cochem
Kastellaun
AMIENS
Le Cateau
Péronne
St-Quentin
Beauraing
St-Hubert
Bastogne
Clervaux
Bacharach
Neufchâtel
Poix
Ham
Hirson
Rocroi
Bouillon
Neufchâteau
Bitburg
Simmern
Forges-les-Eaux
Breteuil
Roye
Vervins
Charleville-Mézières
Echternach
Bad Kreuznach
Noyon
Montcornet
Sedan
Arlon
Trier
Idar-Oberstein
Beauvais
Chauny
Laon
Compiègne
Corbeny
Rethel
Attigny
Montmédy
LUXEMBOURG
Clermont
Soissons
Stenay
Longwy
Longuyon
St. Wendel
Lebach
Chantilly
Villers-Cotterets
REIMS
Vouziers
Thionville
Saarlouis
Neunkchn
Pontoise
Senlis
Pontfaverger
Suippes
Verdun
Étain
Saarbrücken
Homburg
St-Denis
Meaux
Château-Thierry
Épernay
Ste-Ménehould
METZ
PARIS
Montmirail
Châlons-s-Marne
Mars-la-Tour
St-Mihiel
St-Avold
Sarreguemines
Versailles
Coulommiers
Revigny
Bar-le-Duc
Pont-à-Mousson
Sarre-Union
Morhange
Linas
Montlhéry
Corbeil
Guignes
Sézanne
Vitry-le-François
Ligny
Commercy
Toul
Château-Salins
Ablis
Melun
Provins
Arcis
St-Dizier
Vaucouleurs
NANCY
Lunéville
Phalsbourg
Sarrebourg
Étampes
Fontainebleau
Nogent-s-S.
Montier
Joinville
STRASBOURG
Angerville
Montereau
Brienne
Nemours
TROYES
Schirmeck
Pithiviers
Sens
Bouilly
Bar-s-A.
Neufchâteau
Raon-l'Étape
St-Dié
Artenay
Mirecourt
Épinal
Sélestat
ORLÉANS
Montargis
Joigny
St-Florentin
Bar-s-S.
Chaumont
Contrexéville
Vittel
Gérardmer
Colmar
Châteauneuf-s-L.
Tonnerre
Châteauvillain
Montigny-le-Roi
Plombières
Remiremont
Guebwiller
la Ferté-St-Aubin
Auxerre
Langres
Toucy
Gien
Châtillon
Fayl-Billot

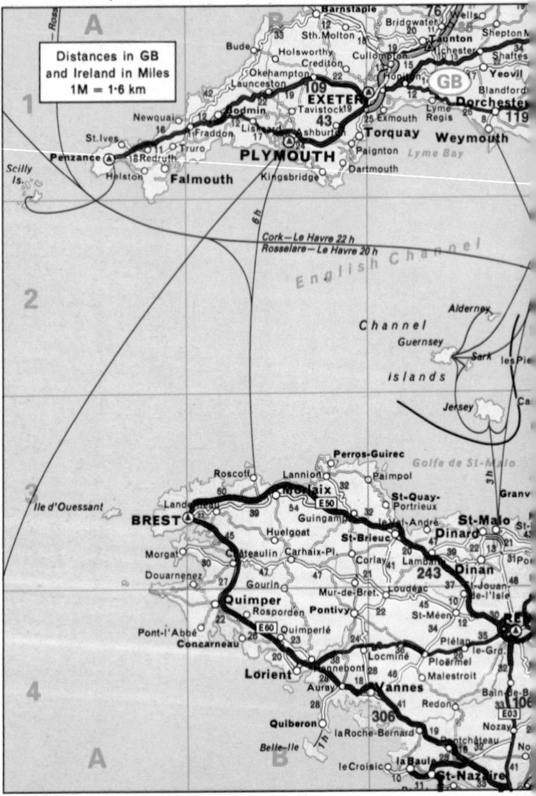

Distances in GB
and Ireland in Miles
1M = 1·6 km

Cork – Le Havre 22 h
Rosselare – Le Havre 20 h

English Channel

Channel

Alderney

Guernsey

Sark   les Pie

islands

Jersey   Ca

Scilly
Is.

St.Ives

Penzance

Helston

Redruth

Newquai

St.Fraddon

Truro

Bodmin

Lostwithiel

Launceston

Okehampton

Credition

Holsworthy

Bude

Sth.Molton

Barnstaple

Wells

Bridgwater

Shepton

TAUNTON

Chard

Ilminster

Yeovil

Blandford

Dorchester

GB

119

EXETER

Honiton

Cullompton

Tiverton

Tavistock

Ashburton

Moretonhampstead

Lyme
Regis

Weymouth

Lyme Bay

Torquay

Paignton

PLYMOUTH

Dartmouth

Kingsbridge

Falmouth

Exmouth

Golfe de St-Malo

Perros-Guirec

Paimpol

Lannion

Roscoff

Ile d'Ouessant

BREST

Landerneau

Morlaix

Guingamp

Huelgoat

Morgat

Châteaulin

Carhaix-Pl.

St-Quay-
Portrieux

Le Val-André

St-Brieuc

Corlay

Loudéac

Mûr-de-Bret.

Granv

St-Malo

Dinard

Dinan

243

Jouan

l'Isle

Douarnenez

Quimper

Gourin

Pontivy

Rosporden

Pont-l'Abbé

Concarneau

Quimperlé

Lorient

Hennebont

Auray

Locminé

St-Méen

Ploërmel

Malestroit

Plélan

Le-Gd-

E03

106

VANNES

Quiberon

Belle-Ile

la Roche-Bernard

Redon

Nozay

306

le Croisic

la Baule

St-Nazaire

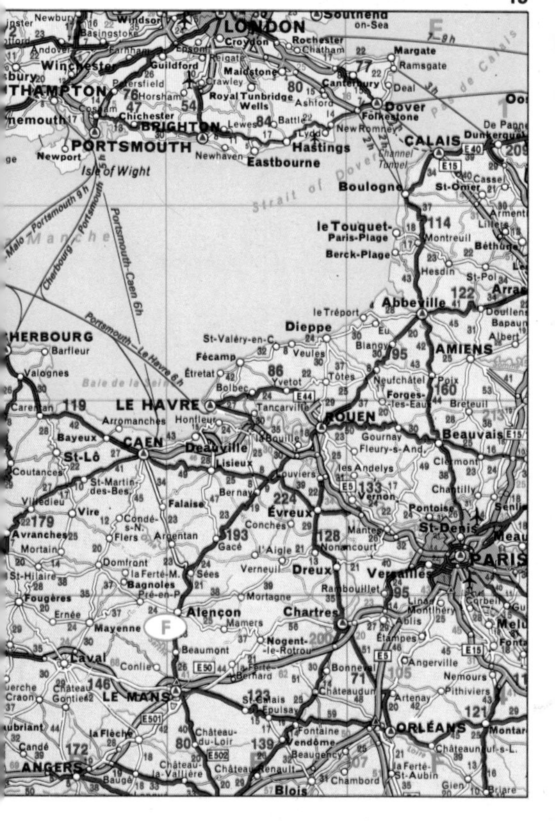

LONDON
Southend-on-Sea
Newbury
Windsor
Basingstoke
Andover
Farnham
Epsom
Croydon
Rochester
Chatham
Margate
Ramsgate
Winchester
Guildford
Reigate
Maidstone
Canterbury
Deal
Petersfield
Crawley
Horsham
Royal Tunbridge Wells
Ashford
Dover
Folkestone
Chichester
BRIGHTON
Lewes
Battle
New Romney
Lydd
Hastings
Cosham
PORTSMOUTH
Newport
Newhaven
Eastbourne
Isle of Wight
CALAIS
Dunkerque
De Panne
Pas de Calais
Channel Tunnel
Strait of Dover
Boulogne
Cassel
St-Omer
Armentières
Lillers
Béthune
le Touquet-Paris-Plage
Berck-Plage
Montreuil
Hesdin
St-Pol
Arras
Abbeville
le Tréport
Eu
Doullens
Bapaume
Albert
Dieppe
Blangy
AMIENS
St-Valéry-en-C.
Veules
Fécamp
Étretat
Yvetot
Tôtes
Neufchâtel
Poix
Bolbec
Forges-les-Eaux
Breteuil
Portsmouth 9h
Portsmouth-Caen 6h
Portsmouth–Le Havre 6h
Cherbourg–Portsmouth
Baie de la Seine
HERBOURG
Barfleur
Valognes
Carentan
LE HAVRE
Tancarville
ROUEN
Arromanches
Honfleur
Gournay
Beauvais
Bayeux
CAEN
Deauville
la Bouille
Fleury-s-And.
Clermont
St-Lô
Lisieux
Louviers
les Andelys
Chantilly
Coutances
St-Martin-des-Bes.
Bernay
Vernon
Villedieu
Falaise
Évreux
Pontoise
Senlis
Vire
Condé-s-N.
Conches
Mantes
St-Denis
Avranches
Flers
Argentan
Gacé
L'Aigle
Nonancourt
PARIS
Mortain
Domfront
Verneuil
Dreux
Versailles
St-Hilaire
la Ferté-M.
Sées
Bagnoles
Pré-en-P.
Rambouillet
Fougères
Mortagne
Linas
Montlhéry
Corbeil
Ernée
Alençon
Chartres
Ablis
Melun
Mayenne
Mamers
Étampes
Nogent-le-Rotrou
Fontainebleau
Laval
Beaumont
Angerville
Conlie
la Ferté-Bernard
Bonneval
Nemours
Château Gontier
LE MANS
Châteaudun
Pithiviers
Craon
St-Calais
Artenay
Épuisay
ORLÉANS
Montargis
la Flèche
Château-du-Loir
Fontaine
Vendôme
Châteauneuf-s-L.
Candé
Beaugency
ANGERS
Château-la-Vallière
Château-Renault
la Ferté-St-Aubin
Baugé
Chambord
Blois
Gien
Briare
E40
E15
E44
E5
E50
E501
E502
F

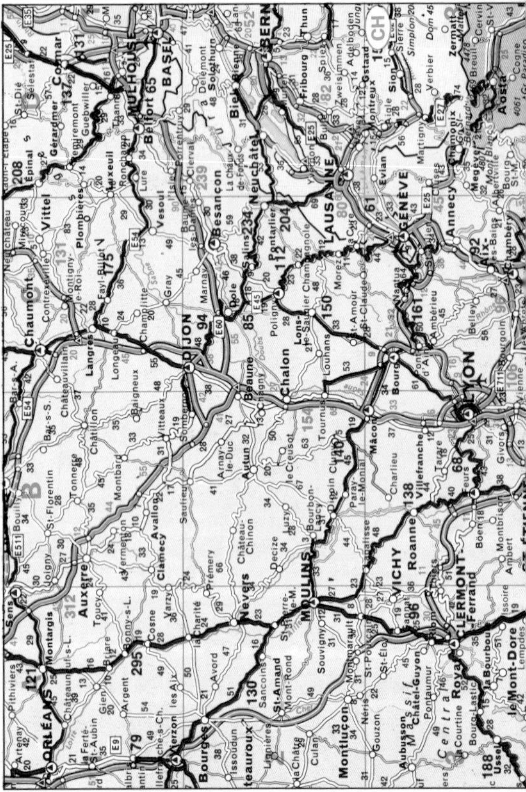

MULHOUSE · BASEL · CH · BERN · Colmar · St-Dié · Belfort 65 · Fribourg · Thun

Gérardmer · Plombières · Lure · Vesoul · Besançon 234 · Neuchâtel · LAUSANNE · GENÈVE · Annecy

Vittel · Chaumont · Langres · DIJON 94 · Dole · Beaune · Chalon · Bourg · LYON

Auxerre · Avallon · Clamecy · Autun · Le Creusot · Mâcon · Villefranche · Roanne

Nevers · MOULINS · VICHY · CLERMONT-FERRAND

ORLÉANS · Bourges · Montluçon · Mont-Dore

Châteauroux · St-Amand · Aubusson · Royat

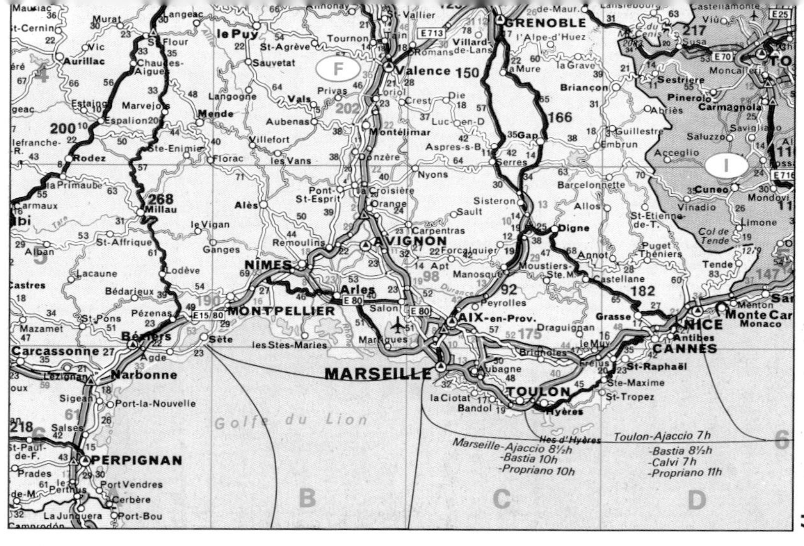
GRENOBLE
Valence 150
Villard-de-Lans
Romans
Tain
Tournon
St-Vallier
le Puy
Langeac
St-Flour
Murat
Aurillac
Vic
Chaudes-Aigues
St-Agrève
Sauvetat
Privas
Vals
Aubenas
Langogne
Mende
Marvejols
Espalion
Estaing
Rodez
Millau
Ste-Enimie
Florac
Villefort
les Vans
Montélimar
Loriol
Crest
Die
Luc-en-D
Aspres-s-B
Serres
Gap
la Mure
l'Alpe-d'Huez
la Grave
Briançon
Embrun
Guillestre
Abriès
Sestriere
Pinerolo
Carmagnola
Moncalieri
Susa
Saluzzo
Savigliano
Acceglio
Cuneo
Vinadio
Mondovi
Limone
Col de Tende
Tende
Barcelonnette
Allos
St-Etienne-de-T.
Puget-Théniers
Annot
Castellane
Digne
Sisteron
Nyons
Donzère
Pont-St-Esprit
la Croisière
Orange
Carpentras
Sault
AVIGNON
Forcalquier
Apt
Manosque
Moustiers-Ste.M.
Alès
le Vigan
Ganges
Remoulins
NÎMES
Arles
MONTPELLIER
Sète
les Stes-Maries
Salon
Martigues
AIX-en-Prov.
Peyrolles
Draguignan
Grasse
NICE
Antibes
CANNES
Menton
Monte Carlo
Monaco
St-Raphaël
Fréjus
le Muy
Brignoles
Ste-Maxime
St-Tropez
Aubagne
MARSEILLE
TOULON
la Ciotat
Bandol
Hyères
Iles d'Hyères
Durance
Rhône
Golfe du Lion
Marseille-Ajaccio 8½h
-Bastia 10h
-Propriano 10h
Toulon-Ajaccio 7h
-Bastia 8½h
-Calvi 7h
-Propriano 11h
St-Affrique
Alban
Lacaune
Lodève
Bédarieux
Pézenas
St-Pons
Mazamet
Castres
Carmaux
la Primaube
Béziers
Agde
Carcassonne
Lézignan
Narbonne
Sigean
Port-la-Nouvelle
Salses
PERPIGNAN
St-Paul-de-F.
Prades
le Perthus
Port Vendres
Cerbère
Port-Bou
La Junquera
Camprodón
E15/80
E 80
E713
E70
E25
E716
F
I
A
B
C
D
166
175
182
190
200
202
217
268
92
98

ORLÉANS

LE MANS

TOURS

ANGERS

NANTES

Blois

Saumur

Poitiers

LIMOGES

Angoulême

Bourges

Châteauroux

Montluçon

la Rochelle

les Sables-d'Olonne

la Roche-sur-Yon

Saintes

Royan

Ile de Ré

Ile d'Oléron

Ile d'Yeu

Noirmoutier

Massif Central

Gironde

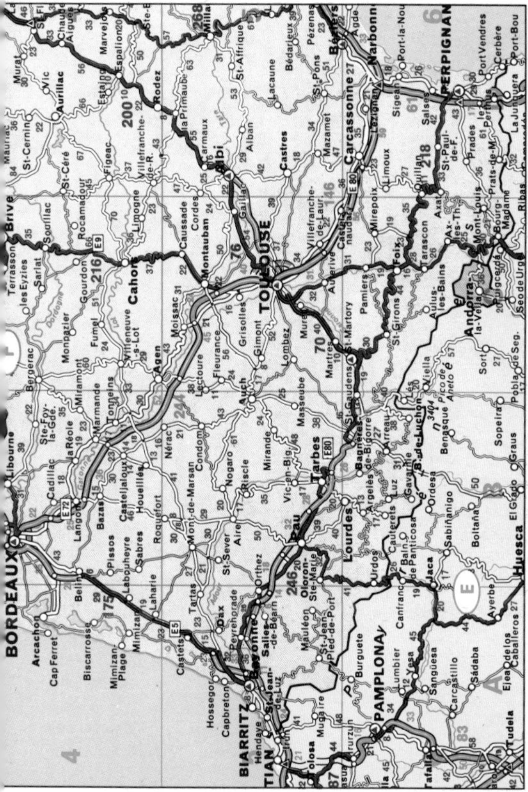

BORDEAUX

BIARRITZ

TOULOUSE

PERPIGNAN

Narbonne

Carcassonne

Andorra-la-Vella

Lourdes

Tarbes

Pau

Cahors

Montauban

Albi

Castres

Agen

Rodez

Aurillac

Brive

PAMPLONA

HUESCA

Foix

Auch

Condom

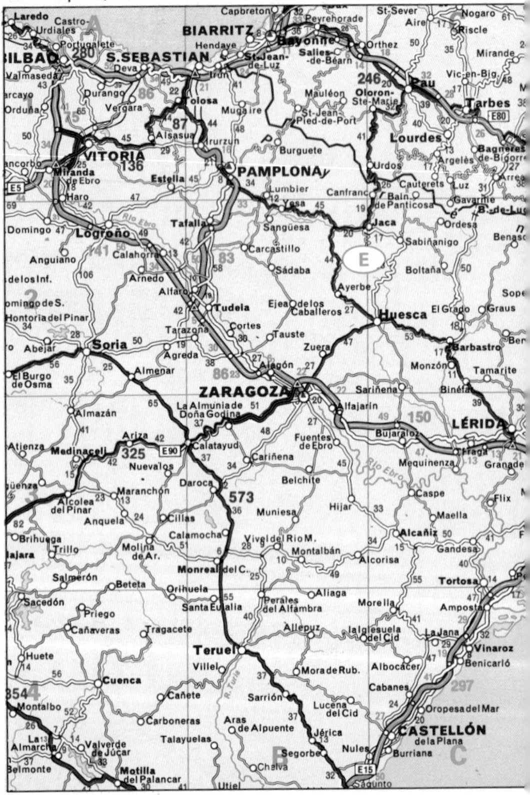

Laredo Castro-
Urdiales Capbreton St-Sever Nogaro
BIARRITZ Peyrehorade Aire Riscle
Hendaye Bayonne Salies- Orthez Mirande
BILBAO S.SEBASTIAN St-Jean- de-Béarn Vic-en-Big
Valmaseda Deva St-Luz Mauléon Pau Tarbes
arcayo Durango Vergara Tolosa Irun Ste-Marie 246 E80
Orduna Aísasua Mugaire St-Jean- Oloron- Lourdes
Pied-de-Port Argelès-Gazost Bagnères-
VITORIA 136 Alsasua Urrurzun Burguete Urdos de-Bigorre
Miranda Estella PAMPLONA Canfranc Cauterets Luz
de Ebro Lumbier Jaca Gavarnie
Haro Tafalla Sangüesa Sabiñánigo Ordesa Benas
Domingo Logroño Carcastillo Boltaña Sope
Anguiano Calahorra Sádaba Ayerbe El Grado Graus
delos Inf. Arnedo Ejea delos HUESCA Barbastro
omingo de S. Alfaro Caballeros Monzón Tamarite
Hontoria del Pinar Tudela Tauste Zuera Binéfar
Abeja Soria Agreda Cortes Alagón Sariñena LÉRIDA
Tarazona Zuera
El Burgo Almenar ZARAGOZA Alfajarín 150
de Osma La Almunia de Bujaraloz
Almazán Doña Godina Fuentes Mequinenza Fraga Grande
Atienza Ariza de Ebro Caspe
Medinaceli Calatayud Cariñena Belchite Flix
uenza Alcolea Maranchón Nuevalos Daroca Maella
del Pinar Anquela Cillas Muniesa Híjar Gandesa
Brihuega Trillo Calamocha Vivel del Rio Montalbán Alcañiz Tortosa
ajara Molina Amposta
Salmerón Beteta de Ar. Monreal del C. Perales Alcorisa Vinaroz
Sacedón Priego Orihuela del Alfambra Aliaga Morella La Jana Benicarló
Cañaveras Tragacete Santa Eulalia Allepuz Iglesuela CASTELLON
Huete del Cid de la Plana
Cuenca Teruel Villel Mora de Rub. Albocácer Cabanes Oropesa del Mar
Cañete Lucena Burriana
Montalbo Carboneras Sarrión del Cid
Las Aras Jérica Nules
Almarcha Valverde de Alpuente Talayuelas Segorbe E15
de Jucar Motilla Chelva Sagunto
Belmonte del Palancar Utiel

E

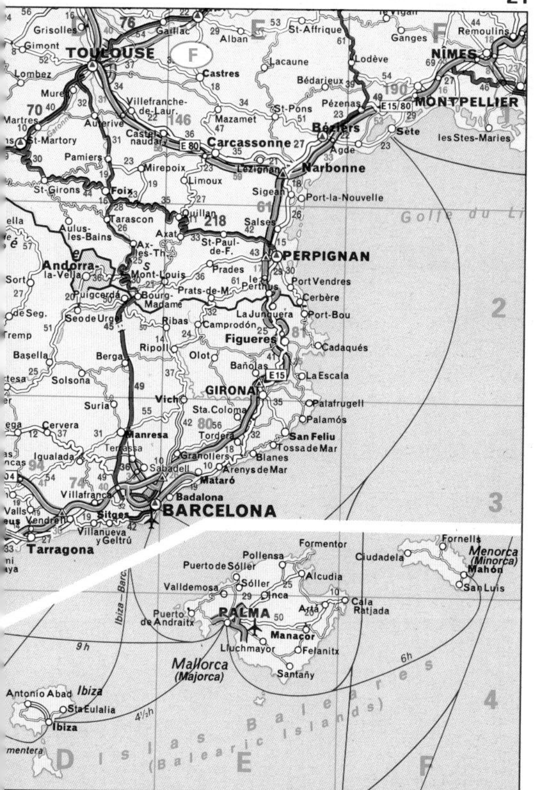

TOULOUSE
Grisolles
Gimont
Lombez
Muret
Martres
St-Martory
Auterive
Pamiers
St-Girons
Foix
Tarascon
Aulus-les-Bains
Ax-les-Th.
Andorra-la-Vella
Sort
Puigcerdá
Seo de Urgel
Tremp
Basella
Solsona
Suria
Cervera
Igualada
Villafranca
Valls
Vendrell
Tarragona
Gaillac
Alban
Castres
Villefranche-de-Laur.
Castelnaudary
Mazamet
Carcassonne
Mirepoix
Limoux
Quillan
Axat
St-Paul-de-F.
Prades
Mont-Louis
Bourg-Madame
Prats-de-M.
le Perthus
St-Affrique
Lacaune
Bédarieux
St-Pons
Pézenas
Béziers
Agde
Lézignan
Narbonne
Sigean
Port-la-Nouvelle
Salses
PERPIGNAN
Port Vendres
Cerbère
Port-Bou
La Junquera
Camprodón
Ribas
Ripoll
Berga
Olot
Figueres
Cadaqués
Bañolas
La Escala
GIRONA
Vich
Sta.Coloma
Palafrugell
Palamós
Manresa
Tordera
San Feliu
Tossa de Mar
Terrassa
Granollers
Blanes
Sabadell
Arenys de Mar
Mataró
Badalona
BARCELONA
Sitges
Villanueva y Geltrú
Lodève
Ganges
Remoulins
NÎMES
MONTPELLIER
Sète
les Stes-Maries
Golfe du Li
F
E15/80
E 80
E15
Formentor
Pollensa
Puerto de Sóller
Sóller
Alcudia
Valldemosa
Inca
Cala Ratjada
Artá
Puerto de Andraitx
PALMA
Manacor
Lluchmayor
Felanitx
Santañy
Mallorca
(Majorca)
Ciudadela
Fornells
Menorca
(Minorca)
Mahón
San Luis
Antonio Abad
Ibiza
Sta Eulalia
Ibiza
mentera
Ibiza–Barc
9 h
6h
4½h
Islas Baleares
(Balearic Islands)

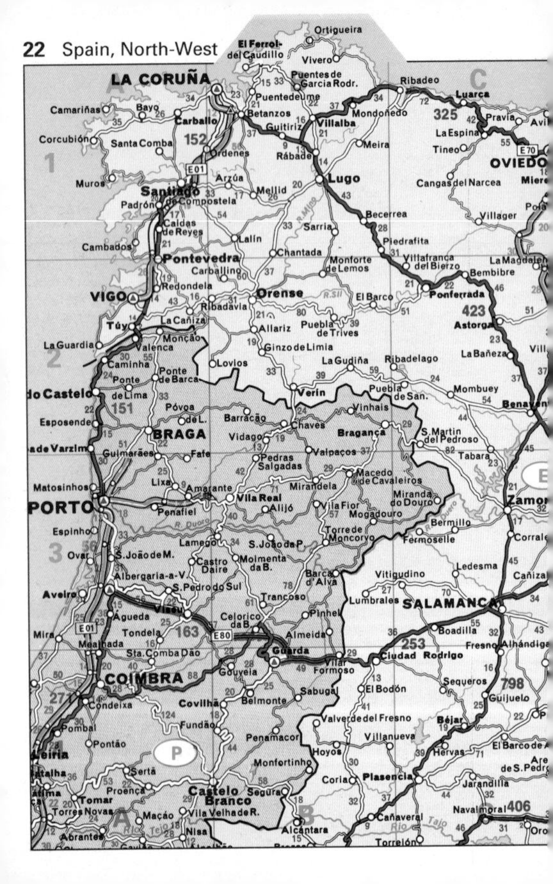
Ortigueira
El Ferrol-
del Caudillo
Vivero
Puentes de
García Rodr.
Ribadeo
Luarca
LA CORUÑA
Puentedeume
Camariñas
Bayo
Carballo
Betanzos
Guitiriz
Villalba
Mondoñedo
Pravia
La Espina
Tineo
OVIEDO
E70
Corcubión
Santa Comba
Ordenes
Meira
Rábade
Muros
E01
Arzúa
Lugo
Cangas del Narcea
Santiago
de Compostela
Mellid
Padrón
Caldas
de Reyes
Becerrea
Villager
Sarria
Lalín
Piedrafita
Cambados
Chantada
Villafranca
del Bierzo
Pontevedra
Carballino
Monforte
de Lemos
La Magdalena
Bembibre
Redondela
VIGO
Orense
Ponferrada
El Barco
Ribadavia
R. Sil
Túy
La Cañiza
Allariz
Puebla
de Trives
Astorga
Monção
La Guardia
Valença
Ginzo de Limia
La Bañeza
Caminha
Lovios
La Gudiña
Ribadelago
Ponte
de Barca
Ponte
de Lima
Verín
Puebla
de San.
Mombuey
Benavente
Póvoa
de L.
Vinhais
Esposende
Barracão
Chaves
BRAGA
Bragança
S. Martin
del Pedroso
Vidago
Valpaços
Tabara
Guimarães
Fafe
Pedras
Salgadas
Macedo
de Cavaleiros
Matosinhos
Lixa
Amarante
Mirandela
Miranda
do Douro
Zamora
PORTO
Vila Real
Alijó
Vila Flor
Penafiel
Mogadouro
R. Douro
Bermillo
Espinho
Torre de
Moncorvo
Fermoselle
Corrales
Lamego
S. João da P.
Ovar
S. João de M.
Castro
Daire
Moimenta
da B.
Ledesma
Albergaria-a-V.
Barca
d'Alva
Vitigudino
Cañizal
S. Pedro do Sul
Aveiro
Trancoso
Lumbrales
SALAMANCA
Águeda
Viseu
Pinhel
Celorico
da B.
Tondela
Mira
E01
E80
Almeida
Boadilla
Mealhada
Fresno
Alhándiga
Sta. Comba Dão
Guarda
Vilar
Formoso
Ciudad Rodrigo
Gouveia
COIMBRA
Sequeros
Belmonte
Sabugal
El Bodón
Guijuelo
Condeixa
Covilhã
Fundão
Valverde del Fresno
Béjar
Pombal
Villanueva
Penamacor
Pontão
Hoyos
Hervás
El Barco de Á.
Leiria
Monfortinho
Batalha
Sertã
Coria
Plasencia
Jarandilla
Fátima
Proença
Castelo
Branco
Segura
Tomar
Torres Novas
Mação
Vila Velha de R.
Cañaveral
Navalmoral
Abrantes
Nisa
Alcántara
Río Tajo
Torrelón
Oropesa
P
E

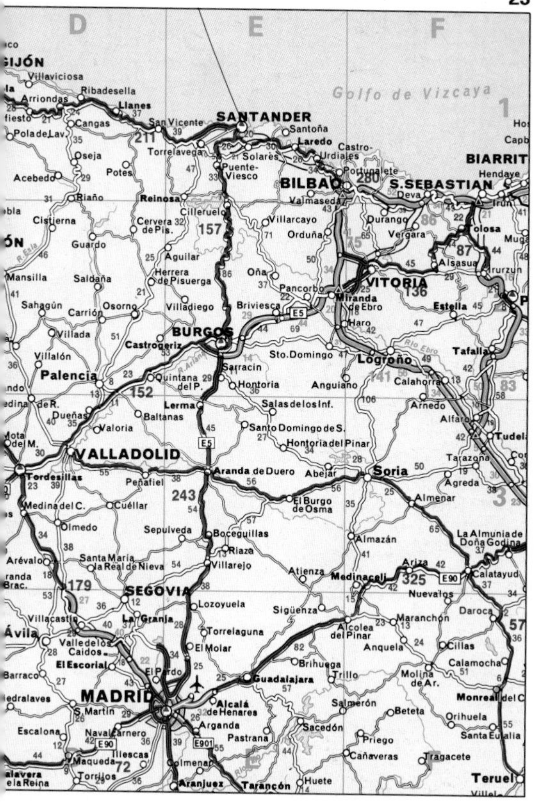
D
E
F
Golfo de Vizcaya
GIJÓN
Villaviciosa
Ribadesella
Arriondas
Llanes
Cangas
Pola de Lav.
SANTANDER
San Vicente
Santoña
Laredo
Castro-Urdiales
Torrelavega
Solares
Oseja
Potes
Puente-Viesco
Portugalete
BIARRITZ
Hendaye
Acebedo
BILBAO
S.SEBASTIAN
Riaño
Reinosa
Valmaseda
Deva
Irun
Cistierna
Cilleruelo
Villarcayo
Durango
Tolosa
Cervera de Pis.
Orduña
Vergara
Guardo
Aguilar
Alsasua
Irurzun
Mansilla
Saldaña
Herrera de Pisuerga
Oña
VITORIA
Pancorbo
Miranda de Ebro
Sahagún
Carrión
Osorno
Villadiego
Briviesca
E5
Estella
Haro
Villada
BURGOS
Castrogeriz
Villalón
Sto.Domingo
Logroño
Tafalla
Rio Ebro
Palencia
Sarracin
Quintana del P.
Hontoria
Anguiano
Calahorra
Lerma
Salas de los Inf.
Arnedo
Dueñas
Baltanas
Alfaro
Valoria
Santo Domingo de S.
Tudela
Hontoria del Pinar
Tarazona
VALLADOLID
Tordesillas
Peñafiel
Aranda de Duero
Abejar
Soria
Agreda
El Burgo de Osma
Almenar
Medina del C.
Cuéllar
Olmedo
Sepulveda
Boceguillas
Almazán
La Almunia de Doña Godina
Riaza
Arévalo
Santa Maria la Real de Nieva
Villarejo
Ariza
Calatayud
Atienza
Medinaceli
E90
SEGOVIA
Nuevalos
Lozoyuela
Sigüenza
Daroca
Villacastin
La Granja
Maranchón
Ávila
Torrelaguna
Alcolea del Pinar
Valle de los Caidos
El Molar
Anquela
Cillas
El Escorial
Brihuega
Calamocha
El Pardo
Trillo
Molina de Ar.
Guadalajara
MADRID
Alcalá de Henares
Salmerón
Monreal del C.
S.Martin
Beteta
Orihuela
Arganda
Sacedón
Escalona
Navalcarnero
Pastrana
Santa Eulalia
Priego
E90
E901
Illescas
Cañaveras
Tragacete
Maqueda
Torrijos
Aranjuez
Tarancón
Huete
Teruel
Talavera de la Reina

E

Zamora

Madr

Villarino

Benavente

Astorga

423

Ponferrada

El Barco

La Bañeza

Mombuey

Corrales

Cañiza

Madr

Aleñ

de S. Pedro

Piedra

AV.

Jandilla

406

Navalmoral

Orense

La Gudiña

Puebla de San.

Ledesma

Bermillo

SALAMANCA

253

Ciudad Rodrigo

798

Guijuelo

Béjar

Hervás

Coria

Plasencia

Vigo

Redondela

Orense

Allariz

Ginzo de Limia

Verín

Vinhais

Bragança

Macedo de Cavaleiros

Miranda do Douro

Mogadouro

Vitigudino

Lumbrales

El Bodón

Fuente del Fresno

Villanueva

Valverde del Fresno

Hoyos

Corias

Montehermoso

VIGO

Tuy

La Guardia

Caminha

Valença

Ponte da Barca

Monção

Lovios

Barcelos

Vidago

Chaves

Mirandela

Vila Flor

Torre de Moncorvo

Freixo

Figueira

Almeida

Sabugal

Penamacor

Monfortinho

Vila Velha de Ródão

Vianado Castelo

151

Esposende

Póvoa de Varzim

BRAGA

Guimarães

Fafe

Póvoa

Amarante

Vila Real

Régua

Lamego

Castro Daire

Penafiel

S. João da M.

Albergaria-a-V.

Tondela

Moimenta

Trancoso

Sta. Comba Dão

Sernancelhe

Pinhel

Celorico

Guarda

Gouveia

163

Covilhã

Fundão

Castelo Branco

P

Matosinhos

PORTO

Espinho

Ovar

Aveiro

Águeda

S. Pedro do Sul

Viseu

Mangualde

COIMBRA

Condeixa

Penacova

Belmonte

Vila Velha

Figueirada Foz

Mira

Montemor

Pombal

Tomar

Mação

Monte Redondo

Marinha Grande

Leiria

Fátima

Ourém

Torres Novas

Abrantes

Nazaré

Batalha

Alcobaça

Caldas da Rainha

Óbidos

Rio Maior

A

1   2   3

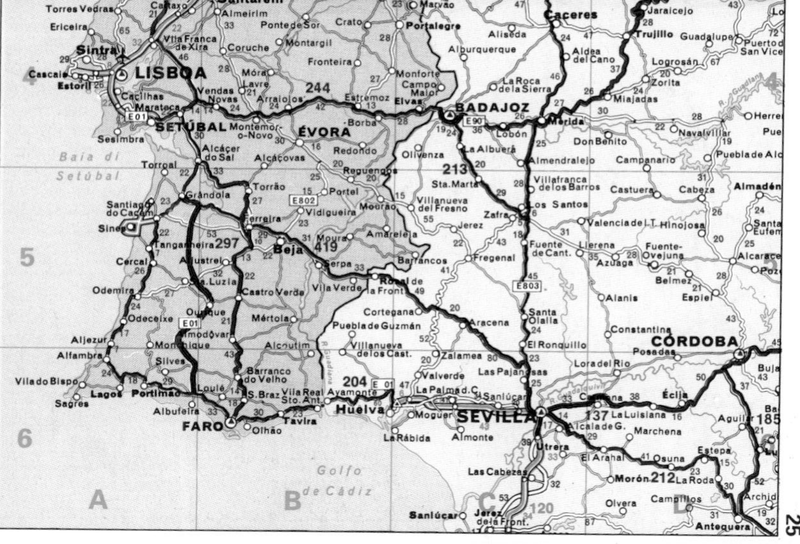
Torres Vedras
Santarém
Almeirim
Ponte de Sor
Crato
Marvão
Portalegre
Aliseda
Cáceres
Jaraicejo
Trujillo
Guadalupe
Puerto de San Vice
Ericeira
Vila Franca de Xira
Coruche
Montargil
Alburquerque
Aldea del Cano
Sintra
Fronteira
Logrosán
Zorita
Cascais
Estoril
LISBOA
Móra
Lavre
244
Monforte
Campo Maior
La Roca de la Sierra
Miajadas
Cacilhas
Vendas Novas
Arraiolos
Estremoz
Elvas
BADAJOZ
Mérida
Marateca
E01
SETÚBAL
Montemor-o-Novo
ÉVORA
Borba
E90
Lobón
Navalvillar
Herrera
Sesimbra
Redondo
Olivenza
La Albuera
Don Benito
Puebla de Alc
Baía di Setúbal
Torroal
Alcácer do Sal
Alcáçovas
Reguengos
213
Almendralejo
Campanario
Villafranca de los Barros
Castuera
Cabeza
Almadén
Grândola
Torrão
Portel
E802
Mourão
Villanueva del Fresno
Sta. Marta
Los Santos
Zafra
Santiago do Cacém
Vidigueira
Valencia de l.T.
Hinojosa
Santa Eufem
Sines
Ferreira
Moura
Amareleja
Jerez
Tanganheira
297
Beja
419
Fuente de Cant.
Llerena
Azuaga
Fuente-Ovejuna
Alcarace
Cercal
Aljustrel
Serpa
Barrancos
Fregenal
Bélmez
Odemira
Sta. Luzia
Castro Verde
Vila Verde
Rosal de la Front.
E803
Alanís
Espiel
Ourique
Mértola
Cortegana
Santa Olalla
Odeceixe
Puebla de Guzmán
Aracena
Constantina
CÓRDOBA
Aljezur
Almodôvar
Alcoutim
El Ronquillo
Alfambra
Monchique
Villanueva de los Cast.
Zalamea
Posadas
Lora del Río
Silves
Barranco do Velho
Las Pajanosas
Vila do Bispo
204
Valverde
Lagos
Portimão
Loulé
S. Braz
Vila Real Sto. Ant.
Ayamonte
La Palma d. C.
Sanlúcar
Carmona
Écija
Sagres
Albufeira
Huelva
Moguer
SEVILLA
137
La Luisiana
Aguilar
185
FARO
Olhão
Tavira
Alcalá de G.
Marchena
La Rábida
Almonte
Utrera
El Arahal
Osuna
Estepa
Golfo de Cádiz
Las Cabezas
Morón
212
La Roda
A
B
C
D
Olvera
Campillos
Archidona
Sanlúcar
Jerez de la Front.
Antequera
R. Guadiana
R. Guadalquivir
4
5
6

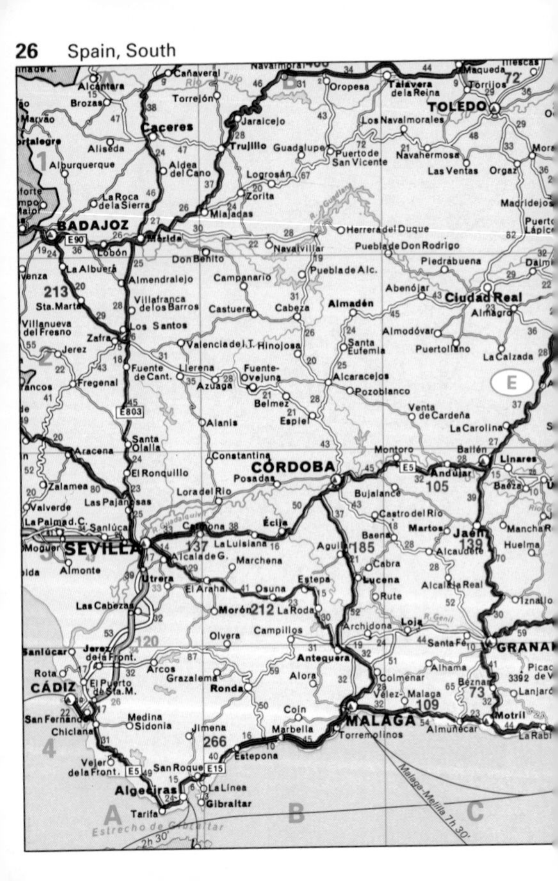
Alcántara
Brozas
Marvão
Aliseda
Alburquerque
La Roca de la Sierra
BADAJOZ
E90
Lobón
La Albuera
Almendralejo
Sta.Marta
Villanueva del Fresno
Zafra
Jerez
Fregenal
Aracena
Zalamea
Valverde
La Palma d.C.
Sanlúcar
Moguer
SEVILLA
Almonte
Las Cabezas
Sanlúcar
Jerez de la Front.
Rota
CÁDIZ
El Puerto de Sta.M.
San Fernando
Chiclana
Vejer de la Front.
E5
Algeciras
Tarifa
Estrecho de Gibraltar
Cañaveral
Río Tajo
Torrejón
Cáceres
Aldea del Cano
Mérida
Miajadas
Trujillo
Jaraicejo
Don Benito
Villafranca de los Barros
Los Santos
Fuente de Cant.
E803
Santa Olalla
El Ronquillo
Las Pajanosas
Utrera
El Arahal
Morón
Arcos
Grazalema
Ronda
Medina Sidonia
Jimena
San Roque
E15
La Línea
Gibraltar
Olvera
Campillos
Osuna
Estepa
La Roda
Marchena
Alcalá de G.
La Luisiana
Carmona
Écija
Lora del Río
Posadas
Constantina
Alanís
Llerena
Azuaga
Valencia del T.
Hinojosa
Fuente-Ovejuna
Belmez
Espiel
Castuera
Campanario
Cabeza
Zorita
Logrosán
Guadalupe
Navalmoral
Oropesa
Talavera de la Reina
Puerto de San Vicente
Los Navalmorales
Navahermosa
TOLEDO
Maqueda
Torrijos
Illescas
Las Ventas
Orgaz
Madridejos
Herrera del Duque
Navalvillar
Puebla de Alc.
Puebla de Don Rodrigo
Piedrabuena
Abenójar
Ciudad Real
Almagro
Almadén
Almodóvar
Puertollano
Santa Eufemia
Alcaracejos
Pozoblanco
La Calzada
Venta de Cardeña
La Carolina
Bailén
Linares
Montoro
CÓRDOBA
E5
Andújar
Baeza
Bujalance
Castro del Río
Martos
Jaén
Baena
Alcaudete
Aguilar
Cabra
Lucena
Rute
Alcalá la Real
Mancha R.
Huelma
Iznalloz
Archidona
Loja
Santa Fé
GRANA
Antequera
Alora
Alhama
Colmenar
Vélez-Malaga
Beznar
Lanjarón
Motril
Almuñécar
La Rabi
MALAGA
Torremolinos
Marbella
Coín
Estepona
Malaga-Melilla 7h 30'
Malaga-Melilla 7h 30'
2h 30'
R. Guadalquivir
R. Genil
R. Guadiana
213
137
212
120
266
185
105
139
109
73
72
E
A
B
C
1
2
3
4

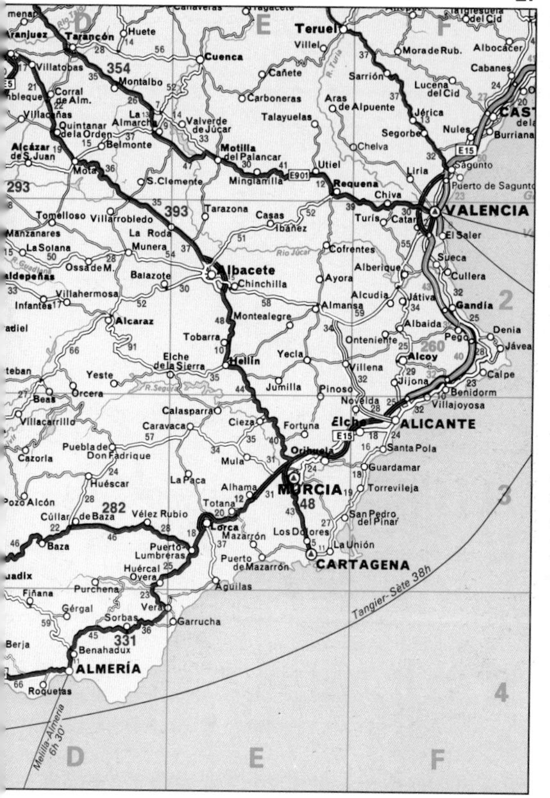
D
E
F
Teruel
Villel
Mora de Rub.
Albocácer
Aranjuez
Tarancón
Huete
Cuenca
Villatobas
354
Montalbo
Cañete
Sarrión
Cabanes
Lucena del Cid
Corral de Alm.
Carboneras
Aras de Alpuente
Villacañas
La Almarcha
Valverde de Júcar
Talayuelas
Jérica
Quintanar de la Orden
Segorbe
Nules
CAST
Burriana
Alcázar de S. Juan
Belmonte
Motilla del Palancar
Chelva
E15
Mota
Utiel
Sagunto
293
S. Clemente
Minglanilla
E901
Requena
Liria
Puerto de Sagunto
Chiva
393
Tarazona
VALENCIA
Tomelloso
Villarrobledo
Casas Ibáñez
Turís
Catarroja
Manzanares
La Roda
El Saler
La Solana
Munera
Rio Júcar
Cofrentes
Sueca
Ossa de M.
Albacete
Alberique
Cullera
Valdepeñas
Balazote
Chinchilla
Ayora
Villahermosa
Alcudia
Játiva
Gandía
2
Infantes
Almansa
Alcaraz
Montealegre
Albaida
Denia
Tobarra
Onteniente
Pego
Jávea
260
Alcoy
Elche de la Sierra
Yecla
Hellín
Villena
Yeste
Calpe
Jumilla
Jijona
Orcera
Pinoso
Benidorm
Beas
Novelda
Villajoyosa
Calasparra
Villacarrillo
Cieza
Caravaca
Fortuna
Elche
ALICANTE
E15
Puebla de Don Fadrique
Santa Pola
Cazorla
Orihuela
Mula
Guardamar
La Paca
Huéscar
MURCIA
Torrevileja
Alhama
3
Pozo Alcón
Totana
282
Cúllar de Baza
Vélez Rubio
San Pedro del Pinar
Lorca
Mazarrón
Los Dolores
Baza
La Unión
Puerto Lumbreras
Puerto de Mazarrón
CARTAGENA
Huércal Overa
Guadix
Águilas
Tangier-Sète 38h
Fiñana
Purchena
Vera
Gérgal
Garrucha
Sorbas
331
Berja
Benahadux
ALMERÍA
4
Roquetas
Melilla-Almería 6h 30'
D
E
F

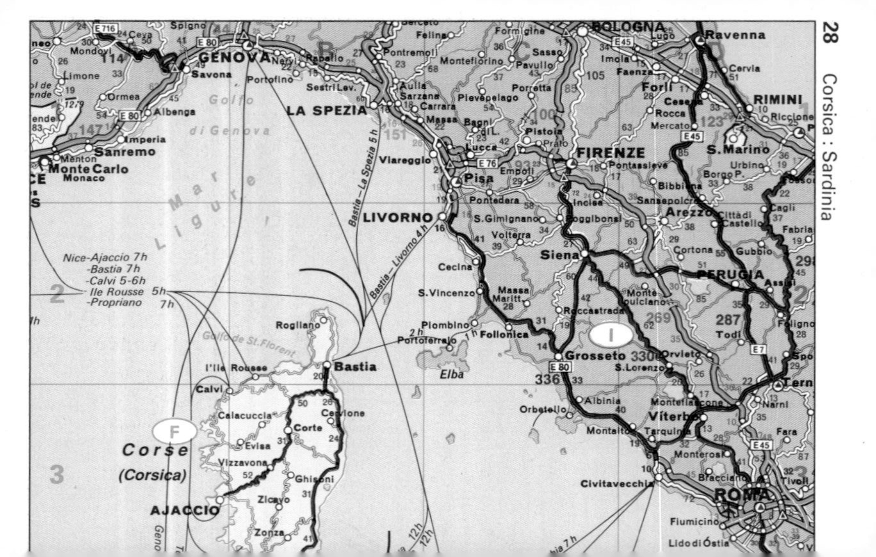
Ravenna
Cervia
RIMINI
Riccione
S.Marino
Urbino
Borgo P.
Cagli
Fabria
Gubbio
Città di Castello
Assisi
PERUGIA
Foligno
Todi
Terni
Narni
Fara
Tivoli
ROMA
Fiumicino
Lido di Ostia
Bracciano
Monterosi
Viterbo
Tarquinia
Montefiascone
Civitavecchia
Montalto
Orvieto
S.Lorenzo
Cortona
Arezzo
Sansepolcro
Bibbiena
Mercato
Rocca
Cesena
Forlì
Faenza
Imola
Lugo
BOLOGNA
Formigine
Sasso
Pavullo
Montefiorino
Porretta
Pievepelago
Pistoia
Prato
FIRENZE
Pontassieve
Incisa
Poggibonsi
Siena
Monte pulciano
Roccastrada
Grosseto
Albinia
Orbetello
Massa Maritt.
Follonica
Volterra
S.Gimignano
Empoli
Pontedera
Bagni di L.
Lucca
Pisa
Viareggio
LIVORNO
Cecina
S.Vincenzo
Piombino
Portoferraio
Elba
Massa
Carrara
Sarzana
Aulla
Pontremoli
Felina
LA SPEZIA
Sestri Lev.
Rapallo
Nervi
Portofino
GENOVA
Savona
Spigno
Ceva
Mondovi
Limone
Ormea
Albenga
Imperia
Sanremo
Menton
Monte Carlo
Monaco
Golfo di Genova
Mar Ligure
Bastia—La Spezia 5 h
Bastia—Livorno 4 h
Nice-Ajaccio 7h
-Bastia 7h
-Calvi 5-6h
-Ile Rousse 5h
-Propriano 7h
Rogliano
Golfe de St.Florent
Bastia
l'Ile Rousse
Calvi
Calacuccia
Corte
Cervione
Evisa
Vizzavona
Ghisoni
Zicavo
Zonza
AJACCIO
Corse
(Corsica)
E 716
E 80
E 45
E 76
E 7
I
F

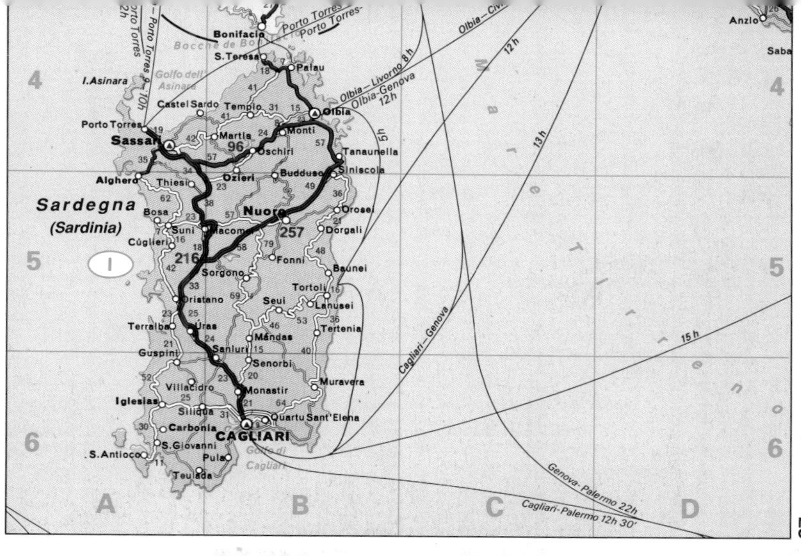
Sardegna
(Sardinia)
I
Bonifacio
Bocche de Bonifacio
Porto Torres
Porto Torres
Porto Torres 9-10h
Porto Torres
12h
S.Teresa
Palau
I.Asinara
Golfo dell' Asinara
Castel Sardo
Tempio
Olbia
Olbia–Livorno 8h
Olbia–Genova
12h
Olbia–Civ
Porto Torres
Sassari
Martis
96
Monti
Oschiri
Tanaunella
Siniscola
Alghero
Thiesi
Ozieri
Budduso
Nuoro
257
Orosei
Dorgali
Bosa
Suni
Macomer
Cúglieri
216
Fonni
Baunei
Sorgono
Tortoli
Oristano
Seui
Lanusei
Terralba
Uras
Mandas
Tertenia
Guspini
Sanluri
Senorbi
Villacidro
Monastir
Muravera
Iglesias
Siliqua
Quartu Sant'Elena
Carbonia
CAGLIARI
S.Giovanni
S.Antioco
Pula
Golfo di Cagliari
Teulada
5h
12h
13h
15h
Cagliari–Genova
Genova-Palermo 22h
Cagliari-Palermo 12h 30'
Anzio
Saba
Mare Tirreno
A
B
C
D
4
5
6

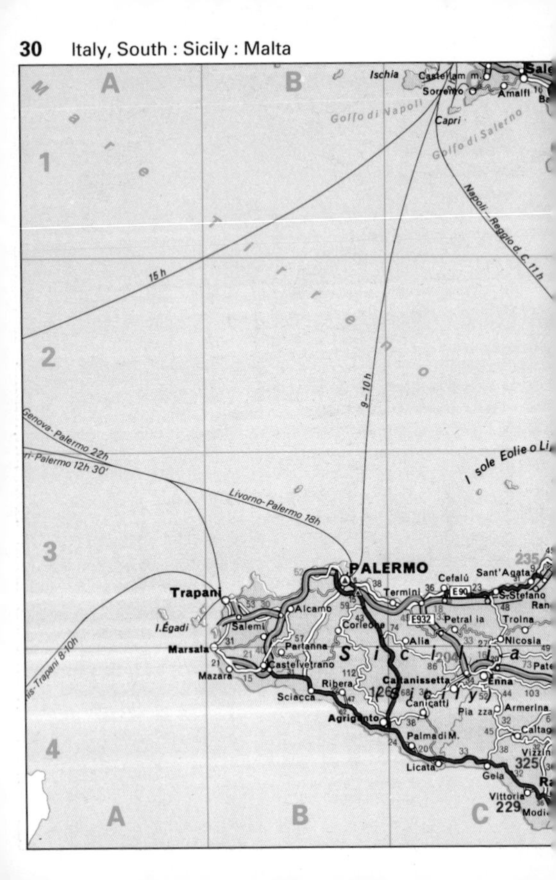
A
B
C
1
2
3
4
Mare Tirreno
Ischia
Castellam m.
Sorrento
Amalfi
Capri
Golfo di Napoli
Golfo di Salerno
Napoli–Reggio d.C. 11 h
15 h
9–10 h
Genova-Palermo 22h
Livorno-Palermo 18h
Isole Eolie o Li
PALERMO
Trapani
I.Égadi
Marsala
Mazara
Salemi
Alcamo
Partanna
Castelvetrano
Sciacca
Ribera
Agrigento
Corleone
Termini
Cefalù
Sant'Agata
S.Stefano
E90
E932
Petralia
Alia
Troina
Nicosia
Caltanissetta
Enna
Canicatti
Piazza Armerina
Palma di M.
Licata
Gela
Vittoria
Sicilia
(Sicily)

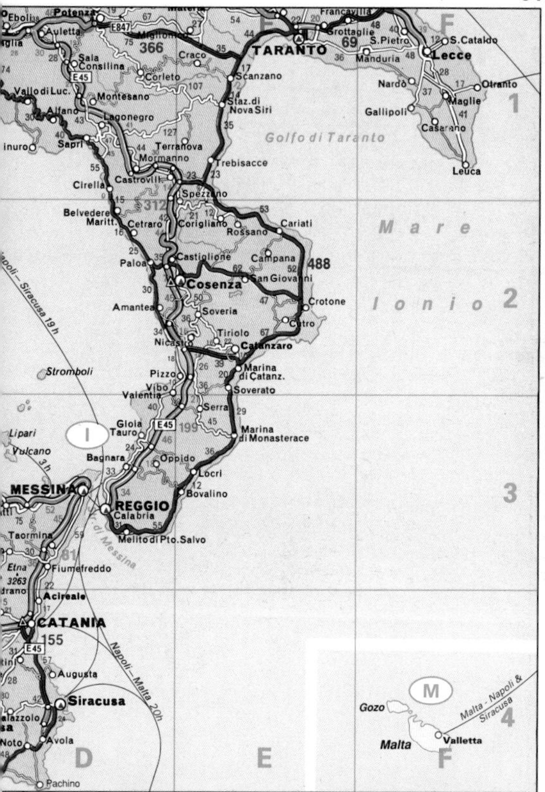
Eboli
Potenza
Auletta
E847
Miglionico
366
Sala Consilina
Craco
Corleto
E45
Vallo di Luc.
Montesano
Alfano
Lagonegro
Sapri
Terranova
Mormanno
Castrovill.
Cirella
Belvedere Maritt.
Cetraro
Paloa
Amantea
Nicastro
Pizzo
Vibo Valentia
Gioia Tauro
Bagnara
REGGIO Calabria
Melito di Pto. Salvo
MESSINA
Taormina
Fiumefreddo
Etna
3263
Acireale
CATANIA
155
E45
Augusta
Siracusa
Avola
Noto
Pachino
Stromboli
Lipari
Vulcano
I
Napoli – Siracusa 19 h
Napoli – Malta 20h
3h
Str. di Messina
TARANTO
69
Francavilla
Grottaglie
S.Pietro
Manduria
Lecce
S.Cataldo
Nardò
Otranto
Gallipoli
Maglie
Casarano
Leuca
Golfo di Taranto
Scanzano
Staz. di Nova Siri
Trebisacce
Spezzano
Corigliano
Rossano
Cariati
312
Campana
488
Castiglione
Cosenza
San Giovanni
Crotone
Soveria
Cutro
Tiriolo
Catanzaro
Marina di Catanz.
Soverato
Serra
199
Marina di Monasterace
Oppido
Locri
Bovalino
Mare Ionio
M
Gozo
Malta
Valletta
Malta - Napoli & Siracusa
D
E
F
1
2
3
4

Formigine · Sasso · Pavullo · epelago · Porretta · Pistoia

BOLOGNA · Lugo · Imola · Faenza · Forlì · Cesena · Rocca · Mercato

Ravenna · Cervia

RIMINI · Riccione · Pesaro · Fano

FIRENZE · Pontassieve · S. Marino · Urbino · Borgo P. · **ANCONA**

Empoli · Incisa · Bibbiena · Sansepolcro · Cittadi · Castello · Cagli · Fossombrone · Senigallia

Arezzo · Cortona · Gubbio · Fabriano · **Macerata** · Pto. Recanati · Iesi · Civitanova Marche

Siena · Montepulciano · **PERUGIA** · Assisi · Muccia · Tolentino · Grottammare · S. Benedetto · Porto d'Ascoli

Massa Maritt. · Roccastrada · **287** Todi · Foligno · Amandola · **Ascoli** · Arquata · Giulianova · Roseto

Follonica · Orvieto · Montefiascone · **Terni** · Narni · Posta · Teramo · Gran Sasso d'Italia 2914 · **PES**

Grosseto 330 · S. Lorenzo · **336** · Albinia · Montalto · Tarquinia · Monterosi · Rieti · **L'AQUILA** · Penne · Chieti · Lanciano

Orbetello · **Viterbo** · Bracciano · Fara · Carsoli · Avezzano · Celano · Popoli · **Sulmona** · Palena · Castel di Sangro **155**

Civitavecchia · Fiumicino · **ROMA** · Tivoli · Subiaco · Valmontone · Oricola · **I**

Lido d'Óstia · Velletri · Frosinone · Sora · Isernia · Cassino · **Capua**

Anzio · **Latina** · Priverno · Fondi · Formia

Sabaudia · **Terracina 213** Gaeta · Avella

NAPOLI · Pozzuoli · Ischia · Castellam · Sorrento · Ponza

Golfo di Gaeta

Olbia–Civitavecchia 1 h · 12 h

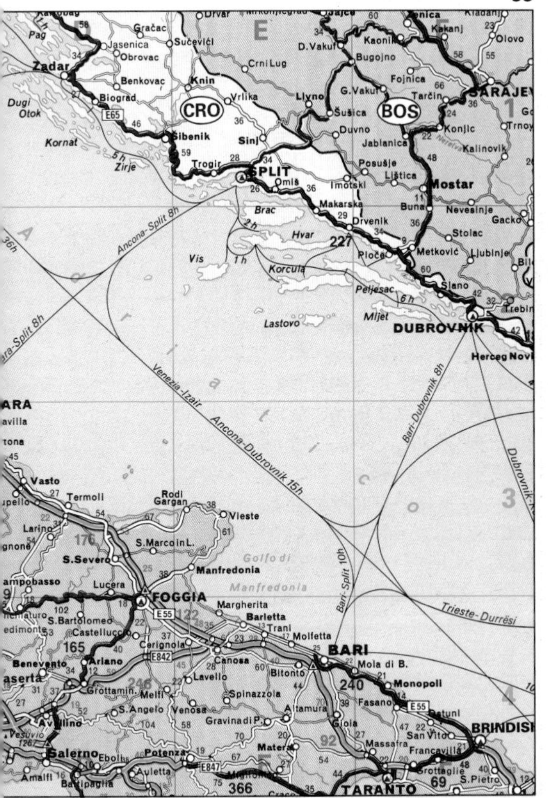
Pag
Gračac
Jasenica
Sučevići
Obrovac
Zadar
Crni Lug
Benkovac
Knin
Biograd
Vrlika
Dugi Otok
E65
CRO
Šibenik
Sinj
Kornat
Zirje
Trogir
SPLIT
Omiš
Imotski
Brac
Makarska
Hvar
Drvenik
Vis
Korcula
Ploče
Lastovo
Pelješac
Mljet
Slano
DUBROVNIK
Herceg Novi
Ancona-Split 8h
Venezia-Izair
Ancona-Dubrovnik 15h
Bari-Dubrovnik 8h
Bari-Split 10h
Trieste-Durrësi
D.Vakuf
Kaonik
Bugojno
Kakanj
Olovo
Fojnica
G.Vakuf
Tarčin
SARAJE
Livno
Šušica
BOS
Duvno
Konjic
Trnov
Jablanica
Kalinovik
Posušje
Lištica
Mostar
Buna
Nevesinje
Gacko
Stolac
Metković
Ljubinje
Trebin
ARA
avilla
tona
Vasto
Termoli
Rodi Gargan
Vieste
Larino
S.Marco in L.
S.Severo
Golfo di Manfredonia
Manfredonia
ampobasso
Lucera
FOGGIA
Margherita
S.Bartolomeo
Barletta
Trani
Molfetta
Castelluccio
Cerignola
BARI
Benevento
Ariano
E842
Canosa
Mola di B.
Bitonto
aserta
Lavello
Monopoli
Grottamin.
Melfi
Spinazzola
Fasano
Avellino
S.Angelo
Venosa
Altamura
E55
Gravina di P.
Gioia
Ostuni
BRINDISI
Vesuvio
San Vito
Massafra
Salerno
Eboli
Potenza
Matera
Francavilla
Amalfi
Battipaglia
Auletta
E847
Grottaglie
S.Pietro
TARANTO

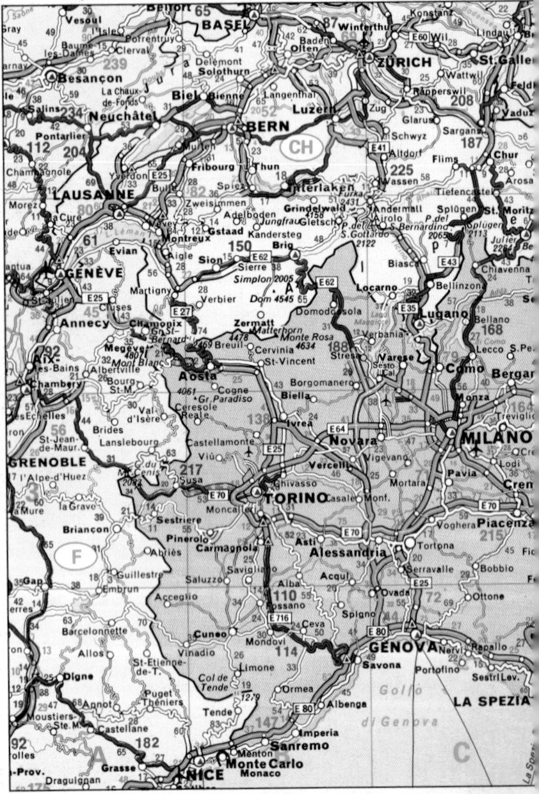

Gray
Vesoul
Belfort 65
BASEL
87 Winterthur
Konstanz
Lindau

Baume-les-Dames
Clerval
Ferrentruoy
A Delémont
Baden
Olten
E60 Wil
St. Gallen

Besançon
La Chaux-de-Fonds
239
Solothurn
Langenthal
ZÜRICH
Wattwil
Rapperswil
208
Vaduz

Pontarlier
112 204
Neuchâtel
Biel Bienne
Luzern
Zug
Glarus
Schwyz
Sargans
187
Chur

Champagnole
Yverdon E25
Fribourg
Thun
BERN
CH
E41
Altdorf
Flims
225
Arosa

Morez
LAUSANNE
Bulle
Spiez
Interlaken
Wassen
Andermatt
Tiefencastel
St. Moritz

Morteau
Zweisimmen
Adelboden
Grindelwald
Gletsch
Airolo
S. Gottardo
Splügen
2065
Juliern
2313

GENÈVE
Evian
Montreux
Gstaad
Kandersteg
150
Brig
S. Bernardino
2122
Chiavenna
E43

Annecy
Aigle
Sion
Sierre 2005
Simplon
Domodossola
Biasca
Bellinzona

Martigny
Verbier
Dom 4545
E62
Locarno
19
Lugano
Bellano

Cluses
CHAMONIX
Zermatt
Matterhorn
Monte Rosa 4634
Varese
Sesto
Como
Bergamo

Megève
Mont Blanc
4478
Breuil
Cervinia
St-Vincent
Stresa
Verbania
Lecco
S. Pe

Albertville
Gr. St. Bernard
Aosta
Cogne
Gr. Paradiso
Borgomanero
Monza
MILANO

Chambéry
Bourg St. M.
Val d'Isère
Ceresole Reale
Biella
Ivrea
Vigevano
Pavia
Crem

Les Échelles
Briançon
Lanslebourg
Castellamonte
131
Vercelli
Casale Monf.
Mortara
Lodi

GRENOBLE
l'Alpe d'Huez
Susa
217
Viù
TORINO
Chivasso
Asti
Alessandria
Tortona
Voghera
Piacenza
215

la Grave
Sestriere
Pinerolo
Moncalieri
Carmagnola
Acqui
Ovada
Serravalle
Bobbio
Ottone

Gap
Guillestre
Oulx
Saluzzo
Savigliano
Alba
110
Bra
Spigno
E80
GENOVA
Savona
Nervi
Rapallo

Embrun
Barcelonnette
Accceglio
Fossano
114
Ceva
Portofino
SestriLev.

Allos
Digne
Vinadio
Mondovì
Ormea
Albenga
Imperia
LA SPEZIA

Moustiers Ste-M.
St-Étienne-de-T.
Limone
Col de Tende 19
E80
Golfo di Genova

Annot
Castellane
182
Tende
737
147
Sanremo
C

Grasse
Draguignan
NICE
Monte Carlo
Monaco
Menton

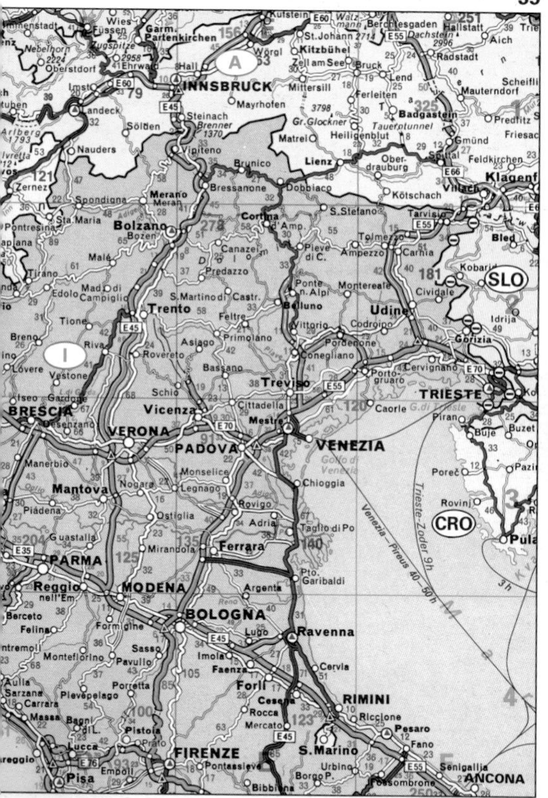

Kufstein
Wörgl
St.Johann
Kitzbühel
Zell am See
Bruck
Berchtesgaden
Hallstatt
Dachstein
2996
Aich
Radstadt
Scheifling
Mauterndorf
Füssen
Garm. Partenkirchen
Zugspitze
2958
Ehrwald
Nebelhorn
2224
Oberstdorf
Hall
INNSBRUCK
Mittersill
Lend
Ferleiten
Imst
Landeck
Mayrhofen
3798
Gr.Glockner
Badgastein
Tauerntunnel
Heiligenblut
Matrei
Gmünd
Predlitz
Steinach
Brenner
1370
Sölden
Nauders
Vipiteno
Brunico
Lienz
Ober-drauburg
Spittal
Feldkirchen
Arlberg
1793
Zernez
Merano
Meran
Bressanone
Dobbiaco
Kötschach
Villach
Klagenfurt
Spondigna
Sta.Maria
Pontresina
Bolzano
Bozen
Cortina d'Amp.
S.Stefano
Tarvisio
Tolmezzo
Bled
Canazei
Pieve di C.
Ampezzo
Carnia
Kobarid
SLO
Malè
Predazzo
Tirano
Mad. di Campiglio
Edolo
Ponte n. Alpi
Montereale
Cividale
S.Martino di Castr.
Belluno
Udine
Idrija
Trento
Feltre
Vittorio
Codroipo
Tione
Primolano
Pordenone
Gorizia
Breno
Riva
Asiago
Conegliano
Rovereto
Bassano
Cervignano
Lovere
Vestone
Porto-gruaro
Treviso
Schio
TRIESTE
Iseo
Gardone
BRESCIA
Vicenza
Cittadella
Caorle
G.di Trieste
Piran
Desenzano
Mestre
VERONA
Buje
Buzet
PADOVA
VENEZIA
Golfo di Venezia
Manerbio
Monselice
Chioggia
Poreč
Mantova
Nogara
Legnago
Rovinj
Piadena
Rovigo
CRO
Ostiglia
Adria
Taglio di Po
Guastalla
Mirandola
Ferrara
Venezia – Pireus 40 – 50h
Trieste – Zoder 9h
PARMA
Pula
Pto. Garibaldi
Reggio nell'Em.
MODENA
Argenta
BOLOGNA
Berceto
Felina
Formigine
Lugo
Ravenna
Monteflorino
Pavullo
Imola
Faenza
Cervia
Aulla
Sarzana
Carrara
Massa
Pievepelago
Porretta
Forlì
Cesena
RIMINI
Riccione
Pesaro
Fano
Bagni di L.
Pistoia
Prato
Rocca
Mercato
Lucca
S.Marino
FIRENZE
Pontassieve
Urbino
Senigallia
ANCONA
Pisa
Empoli
Borgo P.
Bibbiena
Fossombrone
E45
E55
E60
E66
E70
E35
E76
A
I

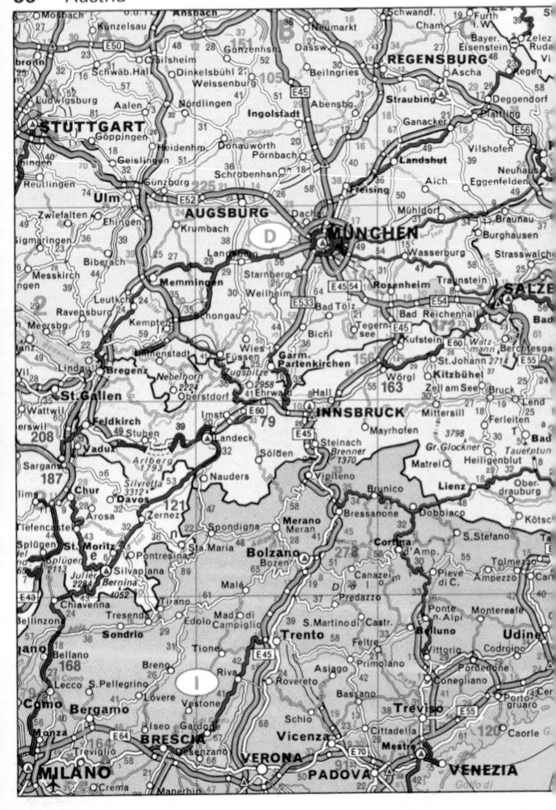
STUTTGART
Ulm
AUGSBURG
MÜNCHEN
REGENSBURG
Ingolstadt
Straubing
Landshut
Freising
Rosenheim
Memmingen
Kempten
Bregenz
St.Gallen
Feldkirch
Vaduz
Chur
Davos
St.Moritz
INNSBRUCK
Garm. Partenkirchen
Kufstein
Kitzbühel
Lienz
Landeck
Bolzano
Bozen
Merano
Meran
Bressanone
Brunico
Cortina d'Amp.
Trento
Belluno
Udine
Treviso
Vicenza
VERONA
PADOVA
VENEZIA
Mestre
BRESCIA
Bergamo
Como
MILANO
Sondrio
Chiavenna
Bellano
Lecco
Bassano
Rovereto
Riva
Feltre
Conegliano
Pordenone
Dobbiaco
Lindau
Ravensburg
Friedrichshafen
Aalen
Göppingen
Nördlingen
Donauwörth
Dachau
Starnberg
Weilheim
Bad Tölz
Füssen
Wörgl
Mittersill
Mayrhofen
Steinach
Vipiteno
Sölden
Nauders
Zernez
Arosa
Silvaplana
Pontresina
Tirano
Edolo
Tione
Rosenheim
Wasserburg
Traunstein
Bad Reichenhall
Burghausen
Braunau
Deggendorf
Plattling
Vilshofen
Eggenfelden
Mühldorf
Chiem-see
Bodensee
Arlberg 1793
Brenner 1370
Silvretta 3312
Gr.Glockner 3798
Zugspitze 2958
Nebelhorn 2224
D
I
E45
E50
E52
E54
E55
E56
E60
E64
E70
E533

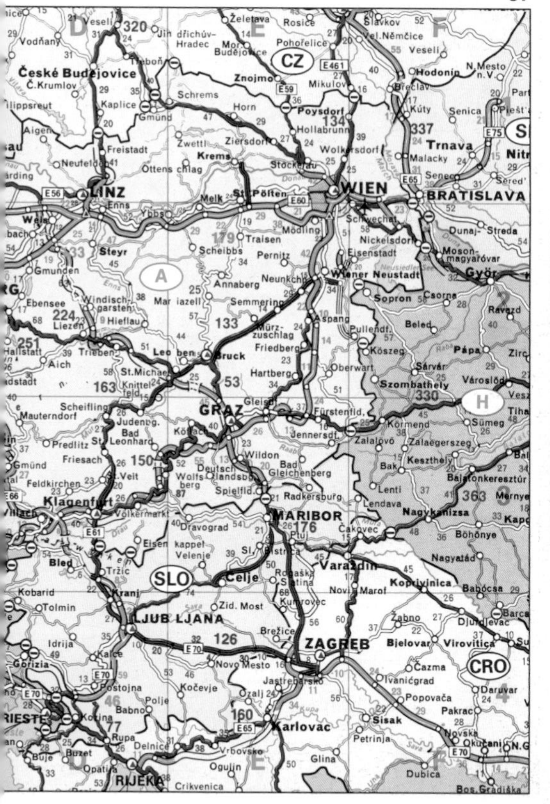
Veselí
Vodňany
České Budějovice
Č.Krumlov
Kaplice
Freistadt
Linz
Enns
Wels
Steyr
Gmunden
Ebensee
Liezen
Hieflau
Trieben
Hallstatt
Aich
St.Michael
Knittelfeld
Scheifling
Mauterndorf
Judenbg.
Bad St. Leonhard
Predlitz
Friesach
Gmünd
Feldkirchen
St.Veit
Klagenfurt
Villach
Völkermarkt
Bled
Tržic
Kranj
Kobarid
Tolmin
Ljubljana
Idrija
Kalce
Gorizia
Postojna
Trieste
Kozina
Babno Polje
Kočevje
Rupa
Delnice
Buzet
Buje
Opatija
Rijeka
Crikvenica
Vrbovsko
Ogulin
Karlovac
Jastrebarsko
Ozalj
Novo Mesto
Brežice
Kumrovec
Zid. Most
Celje
Velenje
Eisenkappel
Dravograd
Sl. Bistrica
Ptuj
Rogaška Slatina
Maribor
Spielfld.
Wolfsberg
Deutschlandsbg.
Köflach
Graz
Wildon
Bad Gleichenberg
Radkersburg
Leoben
Bruck
Mürzzuschlag
Semmering
Mariazell
Annaberg
Scheibbs
Traisen
Pernitz
Neunkchn.
Aspang
Friedberg
Hartberg
Gleisdf.
Fürstenfld.
Jennersdf.
Oberwart
Pullendf.
Köszeg
Wiener Neustadt
Eisenstadt
Mödling
Schwechat
Nickelsdorf
Wien
St.Pölten
Melk
Ybbs
Krems
Ottenschlag
Zwettl
Schrems
Gmünd
Třeboň
Jindřichův Hradec
Horn
Ziersdorf
Stockerau
Hollabrunn
Poysdorf
Wolkersdorf
Mikulov
Znojmo
Mor. Budějovice
Želetava
Rosice
Pohořelice
Slavkov
Vel.Němčice
Veselí
Hodonín
N.Mesto n.V.
Břeclav
Kúty
Senica
Piešťany
Malacky
Trnava
Senec
Sereď
Nitra
Bratislava
Dunaj. Streda
Moson-magyaróvár
Győr
Sopron
Csorna
Ravazd
Beled
Pápa
Zirc
Sárvár
Városlöd
Szombathely
Körmend
Sümeg
Zalalövő
Zalaegerszeg
Keszthely
Bak
Balatonkeresztúr
Lenti
Lendava
Nagykanizsa
Čakovec
Böhönye
Nagyatád
Varaždin
Novi Marof
Koprivnica
Babócsa
Đurđevac
Žabno
Bjelovar
Virovitica
Zagreb
Čazma
Ivanićgrad
Popovača
Daruvar
Pakrac
Sisak
Petrinja
Glina
Novska
Okučani
Dubica
Bos. Gradiška
CZ
A
SLO
H
CRO
E56
E60
E59
E461
E65
E75
E61
E70
Donau
Drau
Mur
Raab
Sava
Kupa
Una
Neusiedler See

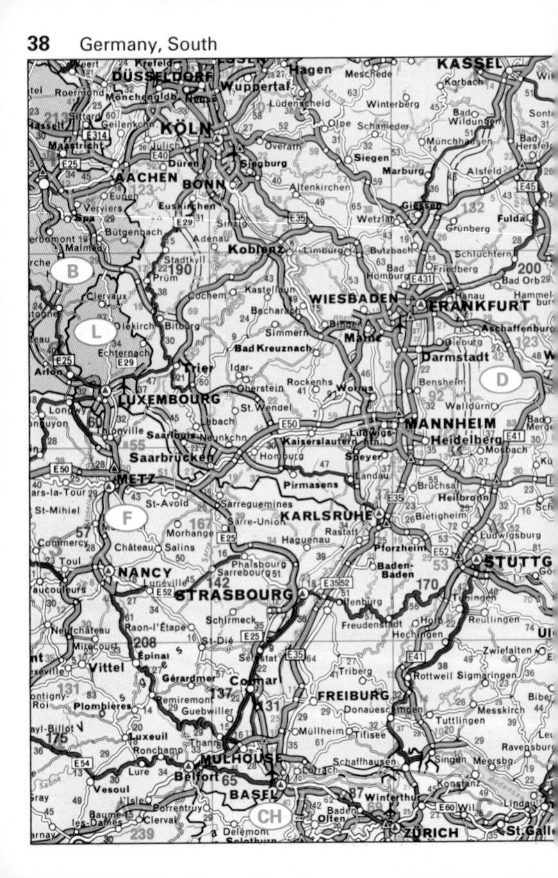
Weert
Krefeld
DÜSSELDORF
Mönchengldb.
Neuss
Wuppertal
Hagen
Meschede
KASSEL
Korbach
Roermond
Lüdenscheid
Winterberg
Sittard
Geilenkchn
KÖLN
Olpe
Schmallenberg
Bad Wildungen
Hasselt
E314
Maastricht
Jülich
Overath
Münchhausen
Bad Hersfeld
E25
E40
Düren
Siegburg
Siegen
Marburg
Alsfeld
AACHEN
BONN
Eupen
Altenkirchen
E45
Verviers
Euskirchen
Giessen
Fulda
Spa
E29
E35
Wetzlar
Grünberg
Bütgenbach
Sinzig
Adenau
Malmedy
Koblenz
Limburg
Butzbach
Schlüchtern
Stadtkyll
Bad Homburg
Friedberg
B
Prüm
E431
Bad Orb
Cochem
Kastellaun
WIESBADEN
Hanau
FRANKFURT
Clervaux
Bacharach
Bingen
Mainz
Aschaffenburg
L
Diekirch
Bitburg
Simmern
Dieburg
Echternach
Bad Kreuznach
Darmstadt
E25
E29
Arlon
Trier
Idar-Oberstein
Rockenhs
Worms
Bensheim
D
LUXEMBOURG
St. Wendel
Walldürn
Longwy
Lebach
E50
MANNHEIM
Thionville
Saarlouis
Neunkchn
Kaiserslautern
Ludwigshfn.
Heidelberg
E41
Mosbach
Saarbrücken
Homburg
Speyer
E50
METZ
Landau
Bruchsal
Pirmasens
E35
Heilbronn
Mars-la-Tour
St-Avold
Sarreguemines
St-Mihiel
F
KARLSRUHE
Bietigheim
Sarre-Union
Morhange
Rastatt
Ludwigsburg
Commercy
Château Salins
E25
Haguenau
Pforzheim
E52
Toul
Phalsbourg
STUTTG
NANCY
Sarrebourg
Baden-Baden
Lunéville
E52
E35
E52
Vaucouleurs
STRASBOURG
Offenburg
Tübingen
Schirmeck
Freudenstadt
Horb
Reutlingen
Raon-l'Étape
Hechingen
Neufchâteau
St-Dié
E25
Mirecourt
Épinal
Sélestat
E35
E41
Zwiefalten
Vittel
Triberg
Rottweil
Sigmaringen
Gérardmer
Colmar
Contigny-le-Roi
Remiremont
FREIBURG
Biberach
Plombières
Guebwiller
Donaueschingen
Messkirch
Fayl-Billot
Müllheim
Tuttlingen
Luxeuil
Titisee
Ronchamp
Thann
Ravensburg
MULHOUSE
Schaffhausen
Singen
Meersbg.
E54
Lure
Belfort
Lörrach
Konstanz
Vesoul
BASEL
Winterthur
Gray
L'Isle
Porrentruy
Baden
E60
Wil
Lindau
Baume-les-Dames
Clerval
CH
Olten
Delémont
ZÜRICH
St. Gallen

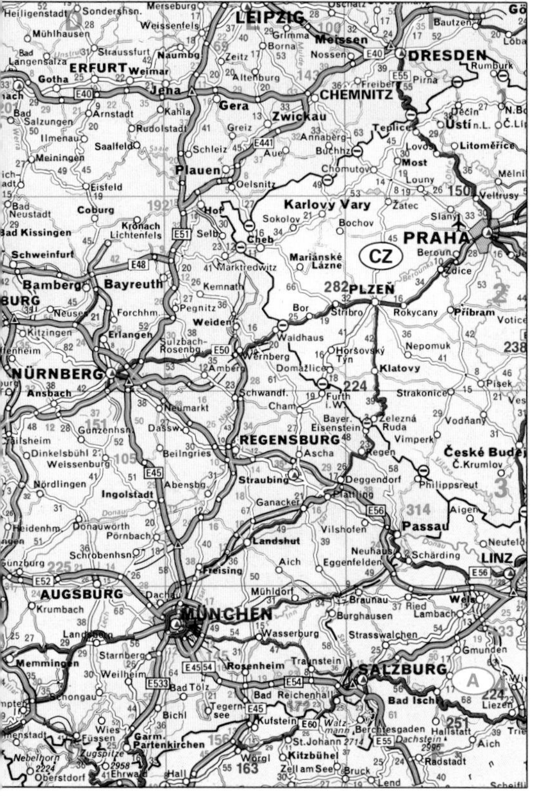
Heiligenstadt
Sondershsn.
Merseburg
LEIPZIG
Bautzen
Löba
Weissenfels
Mühlhausen
Grimma
Meissen
Bad Langensalza
Straussfurt
Naumbg.
Zeitz
Borna
Nossen
E40
DRESDEN
Rumburk
ERFURT
Weimar
Gotha
Altenburg
Freiberg
E55
Pirna
E40
Jena
CHEMNITZ
Gera
Bad Salzungen
Arnstadt
Kahla
Zwickau
Děčín
N.B.
Ústí n.L.
Č.Lí
Rudolstadt
Greiz
Annaberg
Teplice
Ilmenau
Saalfeld
Saale
Schleiz
E441
Aue
Buchhz.
Lovos
Litoměřice
Meiningen
Most
Plauen
Chomutov
Louny
Mělník
Eisfeld
Oelsnitz
Žatec
Veltrusy
Bad Neustadt
Coburg
Hof
Karlovy Vary
Slaný
Sokolov
Bochov
Kronach
Bad Kissingen
Lichtenfels
E51
Selb
Cheb
PRAHA
Schweinfurt
Mariánské Lázně
CZ
Beroun
E48
Marktredwitz
Zdice
Bamberg
Bayreuth
Kemnath
PLZEŇ
BURG
Neuses
Forchhm.
Pegnitz
Bor
Stříbro
Rokycany
Příbram
Votice
Kitzingen
Erlangen
Weiden
Waidhaus
Sulzbach-Rosenbg.
E50
Wernberg
Horšovský Týn
Nepomuk
NÜRNBERG
Amberg
Domažlice
Klatovy
Písek
Ansbach
Schwandf.
Furth i.W.
Strakonice
Neumarkt
Cham
Bayer. Eisenstein
Železná Ruda
Vodňany
Gunzenhsn.
Dassw.
REGENSBURG
Vimperk
Dinkelsbühl
Beilngries
Ascha
Regen
České Budějovice
Weissenburg
Č.Krumlov
E45
Abensbg.
Straubing
Deggendorf
Nördlingen
Ingolstadt
Philippsreut
Plattling
Ganacker
Donau
E56
Aigen
Heidenhm.
Donauwörth
Passau
Pörnbach
Vilshofen
Landshut
Neufeld
Schrobenhsn.
Neuhaus
Schärding
LINZ
Günzburg
Aich
Eggenfelden
Freising
E56
E52
AUGSBURG
Dachau
Mühldorf
Wels
Braunau
Krumbach
Ried
MÜNCHEN
Lambach
Burghausen
Landsberg
Wasserburg
Strasswalchen
Gmunden
Memmingen
Starnberg
Traunstein
Weilheim
E45
E54
Rosenheim
SALZBURG
A
E533
E54
Bad Tölz
Schongau
Bad Reichenhall
Bad Ischl
Liezen
Tegernsee
E45
Bichl
Wies
Kufstein
E60
Watzmann
Berchtesgaden
Hallstatt
Füssen
Garm.-Partenkirchen
Zugspitze
St.Johann
E55
Dachstein
Aich
Nebelhorn
Oberstdorf
Ehrwald
Wörgl
Kitzbühel
Radstadt
Hall
Zell am See
Bruck
Lend

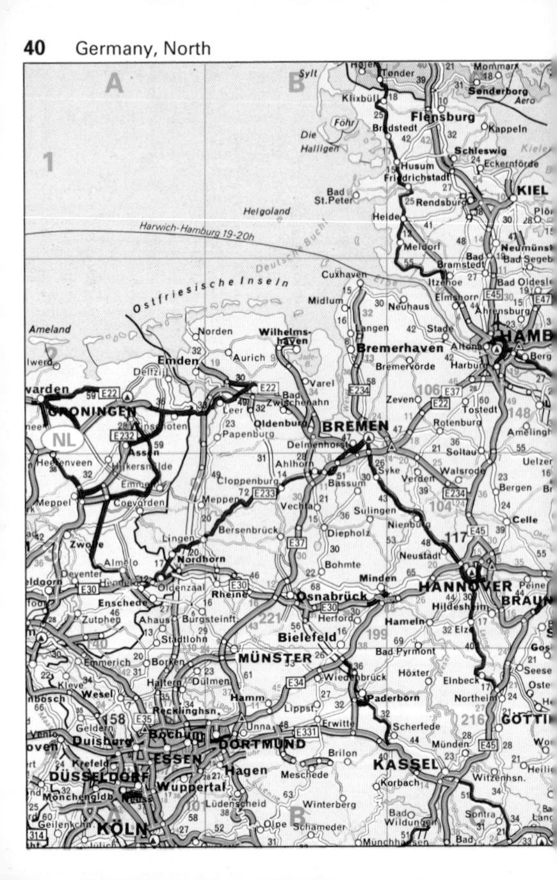
A
B
C
1
2
Sylt
Tønder
Mommark
Sønderborg
Aero
Klixbüll
Föhr
Flensburg
Kappeln
Bredstedt
Die
Halligen
Schleswig
Eckernförde
Husum
Friedrichstadt
KIEL
Bad
St.Peter
Rendsburg
Helgoland
Heide
Harwich-Hamburg 19-20h
Meldorf
Neumünster
Bad Segeberg
Deutsche Bucht
Bramstedt
Bad Oldesloe
Cuxhaven
Itzehoe
Ostfriesische Inseln
Elmshorn
Ahrensburg
Midlum
Neuhaus
Ameland
Norden
Wilhelmshaven
Langen
Stade
Bremerhaven
Altona
Emden
Aurich
Bremervörde
Harburg
Delfzijl
Varel
Leeuwarden
Bad Zwischenahn
Zeven
Tostedt
GRONINGEN
Leer
Oldenburg
BREMEN
Rotenburg
Winschoten
Papenburg
NL
Delmenhorst
Soltau
Assen
Ahlhorn
Heerenveen
Syke
Walsrode
Cloppenburg
Bassum
Verden
Bergen
Emmen
Meppel
Coevorden
Meppen
Vechta
Sulingen
Celle
Bersenbrück
Nienburg
Diepholz
Zwolle
Lingen
Neustadt
Nordhorn
Almelo
Bohmte
Deventer
Minden
HANNOVER
Hengelo
Oldenzaal
Rheine
Osnabrück
Enschede
Hildesheim
Zutphen
Ahaus
Burgsteinfurt
Herford
Hameln
Elze
Stadtlohn
Bielefeld
Bad Pyrmont
MÜNSTER
Emmerich
Borken
Höxter
Kleve
Dülmen
Wiedenbrück
Elnbeck
Haltern
Wesel
Hamm
Paderborn
Northeim
Recklinghsn.
Lippstadt
Geldern
Unna
Erwitte
Scherfede
Bochum
Duisburg
DORTMUND
Münden
ESSEN
Brilon
Krefeld
Hagen
KASSEL
DÜSSELDORF
Meschede
Witzenhsn.
Wuppertal
Korbach
Mönchengldb.
Neuss
Lüdenscheid
Winterberg
Bad Wildungen
Sontra
Gellenkchn
KÖLN
Olpe
Schameder
Münchhausen
E22
E232
E233
E234
E37
E30
E34
E35
E331
E45
E47

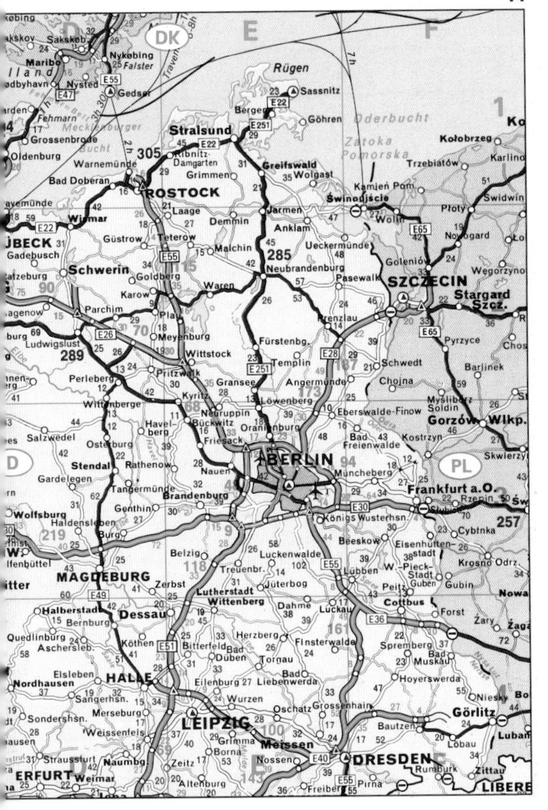
DK
E
F
D
PL
Rügen
Sassnitz
E22
Bergen
Göhren
Oderbucht
Zatoka
Pomorska
Nykøbing
Falster
Sakskøbing
Maribo
Nysted
E55
Gedser
E47
Fehmarn
Grossenbrode
Oldenburg
Warnemünde
305
Stralsund
E251
Ribnitz-Damgarten
Grimmen
Greifswald
Wolgast
Bad Doberan
ROSTOCK
Kamień Pom.
Świnoujście
Wolin
Kołobrzeg
Trzebiatów
Karlino
Swidwin
Płoty
Wismar
Laage
Teterow
Demmin
Jarmen
Anklam
Ueckermünde
E65
Nowogard
Güstrow
Malchin
285
Neubrandenburg
Pasewalk
Goleniów
SZCZECIN
Stargard Szcz.
Wegorzyno
Gadebusch
Schwerin
Goldberg
Waren
Karow
Parchim
Plau
Meyenburg
Ludwigslust
E26
289
Wittstock
Fürstenbg.
Templin
Prenzlau
E28
Schwedt
Pyrzyce
Barlinek
Perleberg
Pritzwalk
Gransee
Angermünde
Chojna
Kyritz
Löwenberg
Myślibórz
Soldin
Wittenberge
Neuruppin
Eberswalde-Finow
Gorzów Wlkp.
Havelberg
Bückwitz
Oranienburg
Bad Freienwalde
Kostrzyn
Salzwedel
Osterburg
Friesack
BERLIN
Skwierzyna
Stendal
Rathenow
Nauen
Müncheberg
Gardelegen
Tangermünde
Brandenburg
Frankfurt a.O.
Rzepin
Słubice
Wolfsburg
Genthin
E30
Königs Wusterhsn.
Cybinka
257
Haldensleben
219
Burg
Beeskow
Eisenhüttenstadt
Belzig
Luckenwalde
Treuenbr.
E55
Lübben
W.-Pieck-Stadt Guben
Krosno Odrz.
Gubin
MAGDEBURG
Zerbst
Jüterbog
Lutherstadt Wittenberg
Peitz
Cottbus
E49
Halberstadt
Dessau
Dahme
Luckau
E36
Forst
Żary
Żagań
Bernburg
Quedlinburg
Aschersleb.
Köthen
E51
Bitterfeld
Bad Düben
Herzberg
Finsterwalde
Torgau
Spremberg
Bad Muskau
Elsleben
Nordhausen
HALLE
Eilenburg
Bad Liebenwerda
Hoyerswerda
Sangerhsn.
Wurzen
Oschatz
Grossenhain
Niesky
Merseburg
LEIPZIG
Görlitz
Sondershsn.
Weissenfels
Grimma
Meissen
Bautzen
Löbau
Lubań
Straussfurt
Naumbg.
Zeitz
Borna
Nossen
E40
DRESDEN
Rumburk
Zittau
ERFURT
Weimar
Altenburg
Freiberg
Pirna
LIBERE

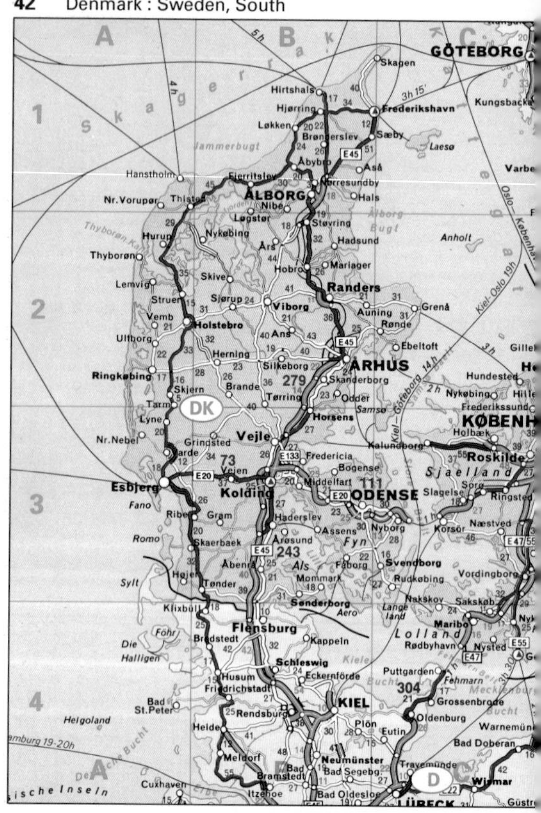
Skagerrak
Skagen
Hirtshals
Hjørring
Frederikshavn
Løkken
Brønderslev
Sæby
Læsø
Jammerbugt
Åbybro
Ålborg
Hanstholm
Fjerritslev
Nørresundby
Hals
Nr.Vorupør
Thisted
Nibe
Løgstør
Støvring
Ålborg Bugt
Nykøbing
Hurup
Thyborøn Kanal
Thyborøn
Års
Hadsund
Hobro
Mariager
Skive
Lemvig
Randers
Struer
Sjørup
Viborg
Grenå
Vemb
Holstebro
Auning
Rønde
Ulfborg
Ans
Ebeltoft
Herning
Århus
Ringkøbing
Silkeborg
Skjern
Brande
Skanderborg
Tarm
DK
Tørring
Odder
Samsø
Horsens
Lyne
Nr.Nebel
Grindsted
Vejle
Kalundborg
Varde
Fredericia
Bogense
Esbjerg
Vejen
Middelfart
Kolding
Odense
Fano
Ribe
Gram
Haderslev
Assens
Nyborg
Romo
Skaerbaek
Årøsund
Fyn
Åbenrå
Als
Fåborg
Svendborg
Sylt
Højer
Tønder
Mommark
Rudkøbing
Sønderborg
Aero
Klixbüll
Langeland
Föhr
Flensburg
Bredstedt
Kappeln
Die Halligen
Schleswig
Husum
Eckernförde
Friedrichstadt
Kieler Bucht
Bad St.Peter
Rendsburg
Kiel
Helgoland
Heide
Plön
Eutin
Meldorf
Neumünster
Bad Segebg.
Bad Bramstedt
Itzehoe
Bad Oldesloe
Cuxhaven
Travemünde
D
Wismar
Lübeck
Göteborg
Kungsbacka
Varberg
Anholt
Oslo–København
Kiel-Oslo 19h
Kiel–Göteborg 14h
Gilleleje
Hundested
Nykøbing
Frederikssund
København
Holbæk
Roskilde
Sjælland
Slagelse
Sorø
Ringsted
Korsør
Næstved
Vordingborg
Nakskov
Sakskøbing
Maribo
Lolland
Rødbyhavn
Nysted
Puttgarden
Fehmarn
Grossenbrode
Oldenburg
Warnemünde
Bad Doberan
Mecklenburger Bucht
Nordfriesische Inseln
Deutsche Bucht
Hamburg 19-20h
E45
E20
E133
E47
E55

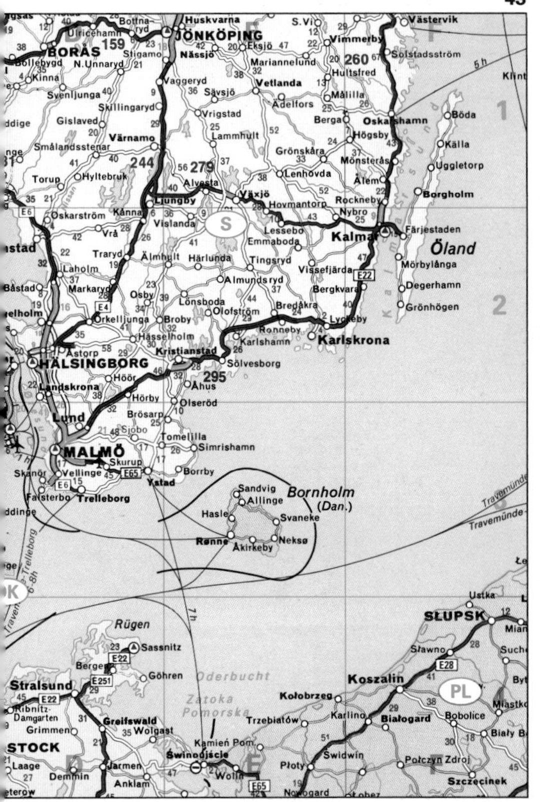
Huskvarna
JÖNKÖPING
Västervik
Ulricehamn
Bottna-ryd
BORÅS
Stigamo
Nässjö
Eksjö
Vimmerby
Solstadsström
Bollebygd
N.Unnaryd
Mariannelund
Hultsfred
Kinna
Vaggeryd
Vetlanda
Klint
Svenljunga
Sävsjö
Ädelfors
Målilla
Skillingaryd
Vrigstad
Gislaved
Lammhult
Berga
Oskarshamn
Böda
Värnamo
Högsby
Smålandsstenar
Grönskåra
Källa
Mönsterås
Uggletorp
Torup
Hyltebruk
Lenhovda
Alvesta
Ålem
Växjö
Borgholm
Ljungby
Rockneby
Hovmantorp
Oskarström
Kånna
Nybro
Vislanda
S
Lessebo
Färjestaden
Vrå
Kalmar
Emmaboda
Öland
Traryd
Älmhult
Härlunda
Tingsryd
Mörbylånga
Laholm
Vissefjärda
Almundsryd
Degerhamn
Båstad
Markaryd
Bergkvara
Osby
Lönsboda
Grönhögen
Olofström
Bredåkra
Örkelljunga
Broby
Lyckeby
Ronneby
Hässelholm
Karlshamn
Karlskrona
Åstorp
Kristianstad
HÄLSINGBORG
Sölvesborg
Höör
Landskrona
Åhus
Hörby
Olseröd
Brösarp
Lund
Sjöbo
Tomelilla
Simrishamn
MALMÖ
Skurup
Skanör
Vellinge
Borrby
Ystad
Sandvig
Allinge
Bornholm
(Dan.)
Falsterbo
Trelleborg
Travemünde
Hasle
Svaneke
Rønne
Åkirkeby
Neksø
Ustka
SŁUPSK
Rügen
Sassnitz
Sławno
Bergen
Göhren
Oderbucht
Koszalin
PL
Stralsund
Zatoka
Pomorska
Kołobrzeg
Ribnitz-Damgarten
Greifswald
Trzebiatów
Karlino
Białogard
Bobolice
Grimmen
Wolgast
Biały Bór
STOCK
Kamień Pom.
Świnoujście
Swidwin
Połczyn Zdrój
Laage
Jarmen
Płoty
Demmin
Anklam
Wolin
Szczecinek
Nowogard
E6
E4
E22
E65
E28
E251
159
244
279
260
295
1
2

OSLO

HAMAR

Gjøvik

Brumunddal
Nedreberg
Elverum
Finnskog
Klarabro
Johannisholm
Leksand
Rättvik
Rånndal
Falun
BORL
Tinajön
Säter
Hedemora
Ludvika
Smedje-
backen

Dalby
Malung
Näs
Rämshyttan
Sunnansjö
Fredriks-
berg

Kongsvinger
Osebøl
Stöllet
Sågen
Ekshärad
Hagfors

Torsby
Lysvik
Långban
Kopparberg
Löa
Karma

Sunne
Munkfors
Hällefors
Filipstad
Molkom
Grythyttan
Lindesbe
Köp
Fellingsbro
Arbo

Arvika
Brunsberg
Fagerås
Forshaga
Storfors
Nora
Karlskoga

Vännacka
Årjäng
Malsjö
KARLSTAD
Kristinehamn
ÖREB

Kumla
Hallsberg
Påls-
boda
Vinc
Hjor

Nysäter
Bengtsfors
Säffle
Åmål
Gullspång
Laxå

Åskersund
Aspa
Medevi
Finspå
Borens

Bäckefors
Kompannebro
Mariestad
Töreboda

Färgelanda
Mellerud
Karlsborg
Sötene
Vadstena
Motala

Lidköping
Skara
Tibro
Skämninge
Mjölby
Boxholm

Uddevalla
Trollhättan
Grästorp
Jung
Skövde
Hjo
Ödeshög
Gränna
Tranås
Österbymo

Vänersborg
Vara
Falköping
Tidaholm

GÖTEBORG
Mölndal
Borås
Ulricehamn
Bottna
JÖNKÖPING
Nässjö
Eksjö
Mariannelu
Vetlanda

Kungsbacka
Kinna
Svenljunga
Skillingaryd
Vaggeryd
Säsjvö
Vrigstad
Lammhult

Varberg
Veddige
Köinge
Gislaved
Värnamo
Smålandsstenar
Torup
Hyltebruk
Grönn

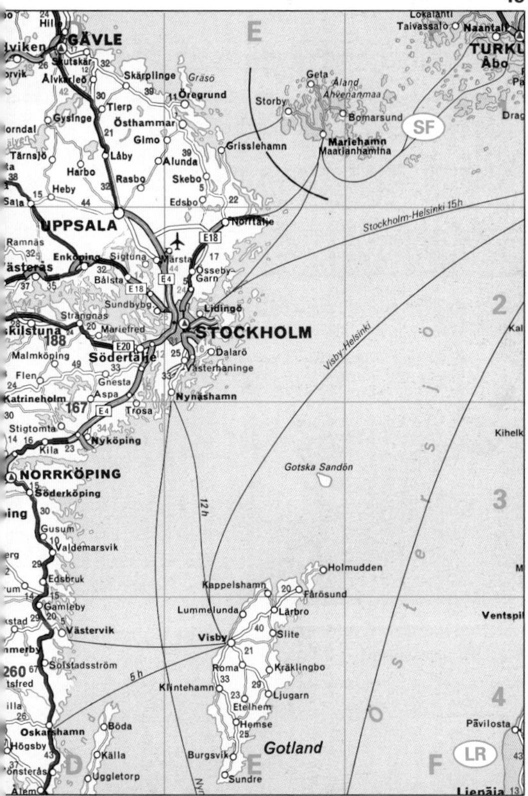
GÄVLE
Skutskär
Älvkarleö
Skärplinge
Gräsö
Öregrund
Tierp
Östhammar
Gysinge
Gimo
Alunda
Låby
Harbo
Rasbo
Skebo
Heby
Edsbo
Sala
UPPSALA
Norrtälje
Enköping
Sigtuna
Märsta
Västerås
Bålsta
Osseby-Garn
Sundbyberg
Lidingö
Strängnäs
Mariefred
STOCKHOLM
Eskilstuna
Malmköping
Södertälje
Dalarö
Västerhaninge
Flen
Gnesta
Aspa
Nynäshamn
Katrineholm
Trosa
Stigtomta
Nyköping
Kila
NORRKÖPING
Söderköping
Gusum
Valdemarsvik
Edsbruk
Gamleby
Västervik
Solstadsström
Oskarshamn
Högsby
Böda
Källa
Uggletorp
Storby
Geta
Åland
Ahvenanmaa
Bomarsund
Grisslehamn
Mariehamn
Maarianhamina
SF
Taivassalo
Naantali
TURKU
Åbo
Stockholm-Helsinki 15h
Visby-Helsinki
Gotska Sandön
12 h
Holmudden
Kappelshamn
Fårösund
Lummelunda
Lärbro
Visby
Slite
Roma
Kräklingbo
Klintehamn
Ljugarn
Etelhem
Hemse
Gotland
Burgsvik
Sundre
5 h
Ventspils
Kihelkonna
Pāvilosta
LR
Liepāja
E
F
D
2
3
4

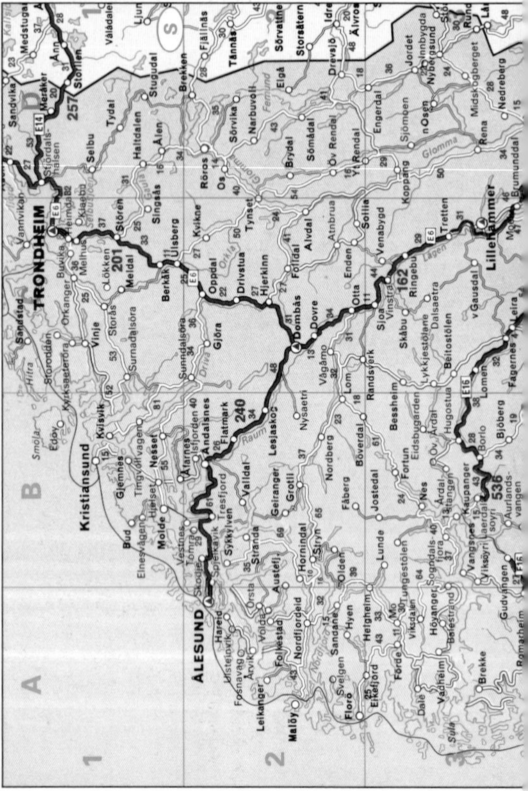

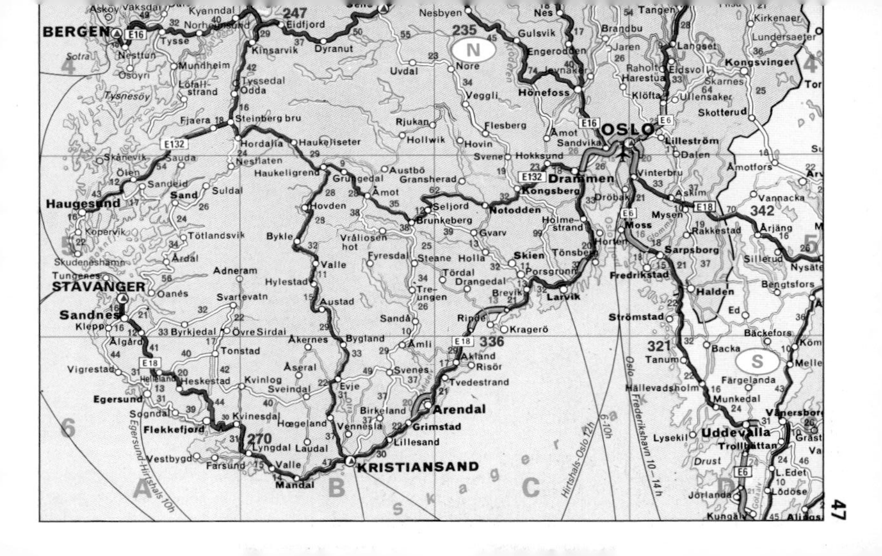
BERGEN
Askøy
Vaksdal
Kyanndal
Norheimsund
Tysse
Sotra
Nesttun
Osöyri
Mundheim
Löfall-
strand
Tysnesöy
247
Eidfjord
Kinsarvik
Dyranut
Tyssedal
Odda
Steinberg bru
Fjaera
Hordalia
Haukeliseter
Nesflaten
Haukeligrend
E132
Skånevik
Sauda
Ölen
Sandeid
Sand
Suldal
Haugesund
Kopervik
Tötlandsvik
Skudeneshamn
Årdal
Tungenes
STAVANGER
Oanés
Adneram
Svartevatn
Sandnes
Klepp
Ålgård
Byrkjedal
Övre Sirdal
Tonstad
Vigrestad
E18
Helleland
Heskestad
Egersund
Sogndal
Flekkefjord
Kvinlog
Sveindal
Kvinesdal
270
Lyngdal
Laudal
Vestbygd
Farsund
Valle
Mandal
Egersund-Hirtshals 10h
Nesbyen
235
N
Uvdal
Nore
Veggli
Rjukan
Hollwik
Flesberg
Hovin
Svene
Austbö
Gransherad
Grungedal
Åmot
Hovden
Bykle
Vrålilosen
hot
Valle
Hylestad
Austad
Fyresdal
Seljord
Brunkeberg
Notodden
Kongsberg
Steane
Holla
Gvarv
Tördal
Drangedal
Tre-
ungen
Sandå
Åkernes
Bygland
Åseral
Evje
Hægeland
Vennesla
Birkeland
Åmli
Svenes
Arendal
Grimstad
Lillesand
KRISTIANSAND
Risör
Akland
Tvedestrand
336
Kragerö
Rinde
Brevik
Porsgrunn
Skien
Larvik
Tönsberg
Holme-
strand
Horten
Drammen
Hokksund
Sandvika
Åmot
Hönefoss
Jevnaker
Engerodden
Gulsvik
Nes
Brandbu
Jaren
Raholt
Harestua
Klöfta
Eidsvoll
Langset
Tangen
OSLO
E16
E6
Lilleström
Dalen
Vinterbru
Dröbak
Moss
Askim
Mysen
Rakkestad
Sarpsborg
Fredrikstad
Halden
Strömstad
Kongsvinger
Kirkenaer
Lundersaeter
Skarnes
Ullensaker
Skotterud
Åmotfors
Vannacka
342
Årjäng
Sillerud
Nysäter
Bengtsfors
Ed
Bäckefors
321
Backa
Tanum
S
Färgelanda
Mellerud
Hällevadsholm
Munkedal
Lysekil
Uddevalla
Vänersborg
Trollhättan
Drust
L.Edet
Lödöse
Jörlanda
Kungälv
Alingsås
Oslo-Frederikshavn 10-14 h
Hirtshals-Oslo 12h
6-10h
Skagerrak
A
B
C
D
4
5
6

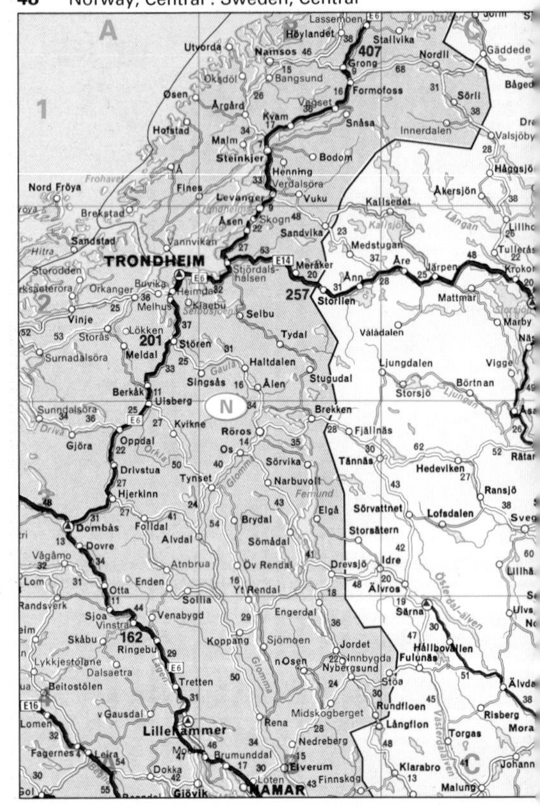
A
B
C
1
2
N
Lassemoen
E6
Höylandet
Stallvika
407
Utvorda
Namsos
Grong
Nordli
Gäddede
Oksdöl
Bangsund
Formofoss
Sörli
Øsen
Årgård
Vegset
Kvam
Snåsa
Innerdalen
Hofstad
Malm
Steinkjer
Bodom
Valsjöby
Henning
Verdalsöra
Vuku
Håggsjö
Nord Fröya
Fines
Levanger
Åkersjön
Kallsedet
Brekstad
Åsen
Skogn
Sandvika
Kallsjön
Sandstad
Vannvikan
Medstugan
Hitra
TRONDHEIM
E14
Meråker
Åre
Järpen
Storodden
Stjördalshalsen
Ånn
Orkanger
Buvika
Heimdal
257
Storlien
Mattmar
Melhus
Klaebu
Vinje
Selbu
Marby
Lökken
201
Storås
Stören
Tydal
Våladalen
Surnadalsöra
Meldal
Haltdalen
Ljungdalen
Vigge
Singsås
Ålen
Stugudal
Börtnan
Berkåk
Storsjö
Ulsberg
Sunndalsöra
Brekken
Kvikne
Röros
Fjällnäs
Gjöra
Oppdal
Os
Tännäs
Hedeviken
Rätan
Sörvika
Drivstua
Tynset
Narbuvoll
Ransjö
Hjerkinn
Femund
Sörvattnet
Lofsdalen
Elgå
Dombås
Folldal
Brydal
Storsätern
Alvdal
Dovre
Sömådal
Vågåmo
Öv Rendal
Drevsjö
Idre
Atnbrua
Lom
Enden
Yt Rendal
Älvros
Otta
Sollia
Särna
Randsverk
Sjoa
Vinstra
Venabygd
Engerdal
162
Skåbu
Ringebu
Koppang
Sjömoen
Jordet
Hällbovallen
Lykkjestølane
Dalsaetra
Osen
Innbygda
Fulunäs
Nybergsund
Tretten
Stöa
Beitostölen
Älvdalen
E16
Rundfloen
Midskogberget
Gausdal
Risberg
Lomen
Lillehammer
Rena
Långflon
Mora
Torgas
Nedreberg
Fagernes
Leira
Moelv
Brumunddal
Elverum
Klarabro
Dokka
Löten
Finnskog
Gjövik
HAMAR
Malung
Österdal-älven
Västerdalälven
Glomma
Gaula
Lågen

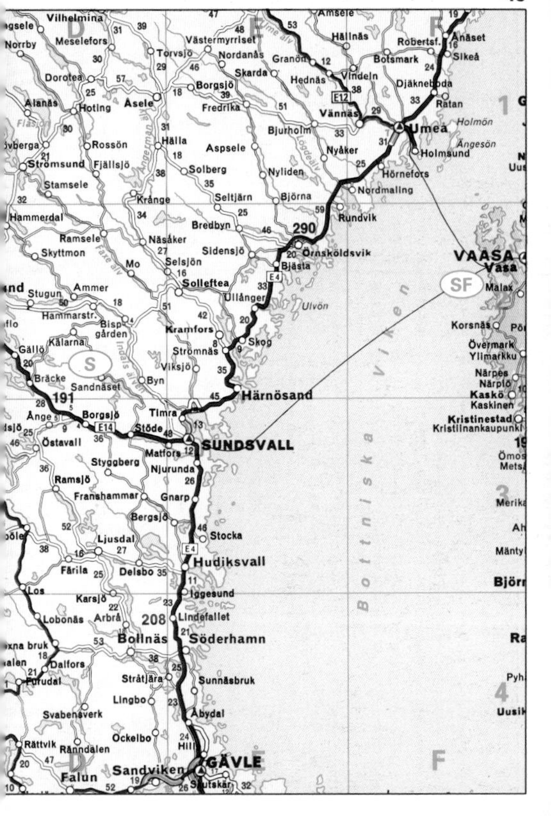
Vilhelmina
Norrby
Meselefors
Dorotea
Alanäs
Hoting
Åsele
Torvsjö
Västermyrriset
Nordanås
Skarda
Borgsjö
Fredrika
Granön
Hednäs
Hällnäs
Vindeln
Vännäs
Robertsf.
Botsmark
Djäknebboda
Ånäset
Sikeå
Ratan
Umeå
Holmön
Ångesön
Holmsund
Bjurholm
Nyåker
Hörnefors
Nordmaling
Rundvik
Rossön
Strömsund
Fjällsjö
Stamsele
Hälla
Aspsele
Solberg
Nyliden
Krånge
Seltjärn
Björna
Hammerdal
Bredbyn
Ramsele
Näsåker
Skyttmon
Sidensjö
Örnsköldsvik
Bjästa
Mo
Selsjön
Sollefteå
Stugun
Ammer
Ullånger
Ulvön
Hammarstr.
Bispgården
Kramfors
Skog
Kälarna
Gällö
Strömnäs
Viksjö
Bräcke
Sandnäset
Byn
Härnösand
Ånge
Borgsjö
Timrå
Stöde
Östavall
SUNDSVALL
Matfors
Styggberg
Njurunda
Ramsjö
Franshammar
Gnarp
Bergsjö
Stocka
Ljusdal
Färila
Delsbo
Hudiksvall
Los
Karsjö
Iggesund
Lobonäs
Arbrå
Lindefallet
Bollnäs
Söderhamn
Dalfors
Furudal
Stråtjära
Sunnäsbruk
Lingbo
Svabensverk
Åbydal
Rättvik
Ockelbo
Ränndalen
Hille
Falun
Sandviken
GÄVLE
Skutskär
VAASA
Vasa
SF
Malax
Korsnäs
Övermark
Ylimarkku
Närpes
Närpiö
Kaskö
Kaskinen
Kristinestad
Kristiinankaupunki
S
Bottniska Viken
E4
E12
E14
290
191
208

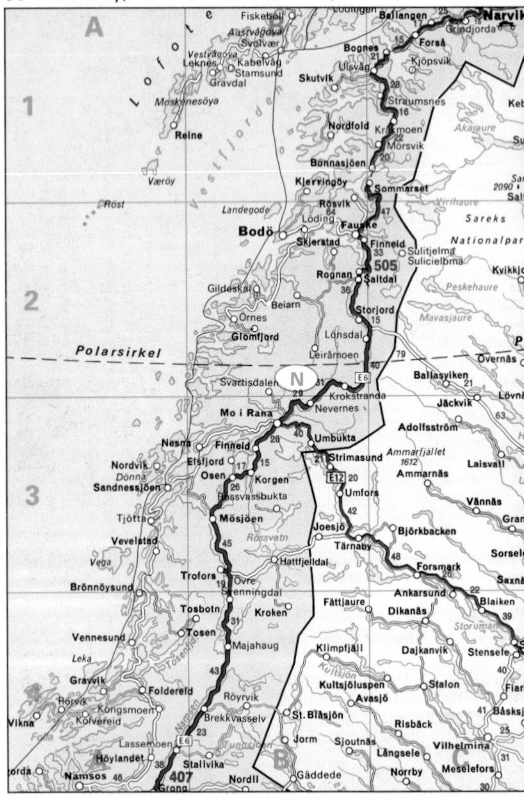

A map page showing the following place names:

Lofoten

Fiskebøl
Austvågøya
Leknes Svolvær
Vestvågøya Kabelvåg
Stamsund
Gravdal

Moskenesøya

Reine

Værøy

Røst

Landegode

Bodø

Gildeskål

Ørnes

Glomfjord

Polarsirkel

Svartisdalen

Mo i Rana

Nesna Finneid
Nordvik Elsfjord Osen
Dønna Korgen
Sandnessjøen Bøssvassbukta
Tjøtta Mosjøen
Vevelstad
Vega

Brønnøysund

Leka Trofors Øvre
Tosbotn Fenningdal
Vennesund Tosen
Grayvik Majahaug
Norvik Folderéid
Vikna Kongsmoen Røyrvik
Kolvereid Brekkvasselv

Lassemoen
Høylandet
Namsos Stallvika Nordli
407 Grong

Fiskebøl Ballangen Narvik
Grindjorda
Bognes Forså
Skutvik Ulvsvåg Kjøpsvik
Straumsnes
Nordfold Kristmoen Morsvik
Bønnasjøen
Kjerringøy Sommarset
Røsvik
Løding Fauske Finneid
Skjerstad Sulitjelma Suliciélma
Rognan Saltdal
Storjord
Beiarn Lønsdal
Leiråmoen
Krokstranda
Nevernes
Umbukta Strimasund
Korgen Umfors
Joesjö
Røssvatn Hattfjelldal Tärnaby
Forsmark
Kroken Ankarsund Blaiken
Fättjaure Dikanäs
Klimpfjäll
Dajkanvik Stalon
Kultsjöluspen Avasjö
St. Blåsjön Risbäck
Jorm Sjoutnäs Långsele Vilhelmina
Gäddede Norrby Meselefors

Akkajure
Keb
Su
Sar
2090
Sal
Virrihaure Sareks
Nationalpark
Peskehaure
Kvikkjo
Mavasjaure
Övernäs
Ballasviken
Löuva
Jäckvik
Adolfsström
Laisvall
Ammarnäs
Ammarfjället
1612
Vännäs
Gran
Björkbacken Sorsele
Saxnä
Stensele
Storuma
Bäsksj
Fásksj
Báskj
25
Narvik

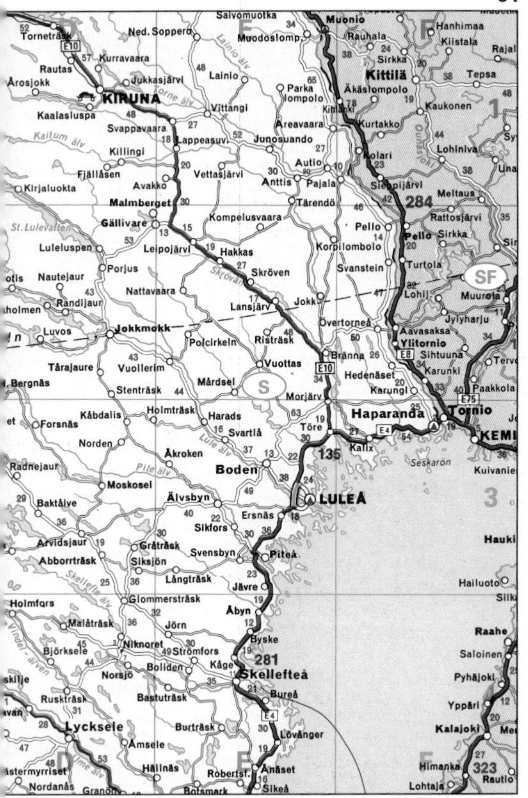
Salvomuotka
Muonio
Hanhimaa
Kiistala
Rajal
Torneträsk
E10
Ned. Soppero
Muodoslomp.
Rauhala
Sirkka
Kittilä
Tepsa
Kurravaara
Rautas
Årosjokk
Jukkasjärvi
Lainio
Lainio älv
Parka lompolo
Äkäslompolo
KIRUNA
Torne älv
Vittangi
Kihlanki
Kaukonen
Kaalasluspa
Svappavaara
Areavaara
Kurtakko
Ounasjoki
Kaitum älv
Lappeasuv.
Junosuando
Lohiniva
Killingi
Kolari
Fjällåsen
Vettasjärvi
Autio
Anttis
Pajala
Una
Kirjaluokta
Avakko
Sieppijärvi
Meltaus
Malmberget
Tärendö
284
Rattosjärvi
St. Lulevatten
Gällivare
Kompelusvaara
Pello
Sirkka
Luleluspen
Leipojärvi
Hakkas
Korpilombolo
Turtola
Porjus
Skröven
Svanstein
SF
Nautejaur
Skrövan
Nattavaara
Lohij.
Muurola
Randijaur
Lansjärv
Jokk
Jylyharju
Jokkmokk
Övertorneå
Aavasaksa
Luvos
Polcirkeln
Risträsk
Ylitornio
Bränna
E8
Sihtuuna
Tårajaure
Vuollerim
Vuottas
Karunki
Hedenäset
E10
Bergnäs
Mårdsel
S
Karungi
Paakkola
Stenträsk
Morjärv
E75
Kåbdalis
Holmträsk
Harads
Haparanda
Tornio
Forsnäs
Töre
E4
KEMI
Norden
Svartlå
Kalix
Lule älv
135
Seskarön
Radnejaur
Åkroken
Kuivanie
Pite älv
Boden
Moskosel
LULEÅ
Baktåive
Älvsbyn
3
Ersnäs
Sikfors
Arvidsjaur
Gråträsk
Hauki
Abborrträsk
Svensbyn
Piteå
Siksjön
Skellefte älv
Långträsk
Hailuoto
Jävre
Glommersträsk
Holmfors
Åbyn
Malåträsk
Jörn
Raahe
Byske
Niknoret
Strömfors
Saloinen
Björksele
281
Vindel-älven
Kåge
Boliden
Pyhäjoki
Norsjö
Skellefteå
Ruskträsk
Bureå
Yppäri
Basturäsk
E4
Lycksele
Burträsk
Kalajoki
Lövånger
Åmsele
Ume älv
Hällnäs
Himanka
323
Robertsf.
Ånäset
Rautio
Nordanås
Sikeå
Lohtaja
Botsmark

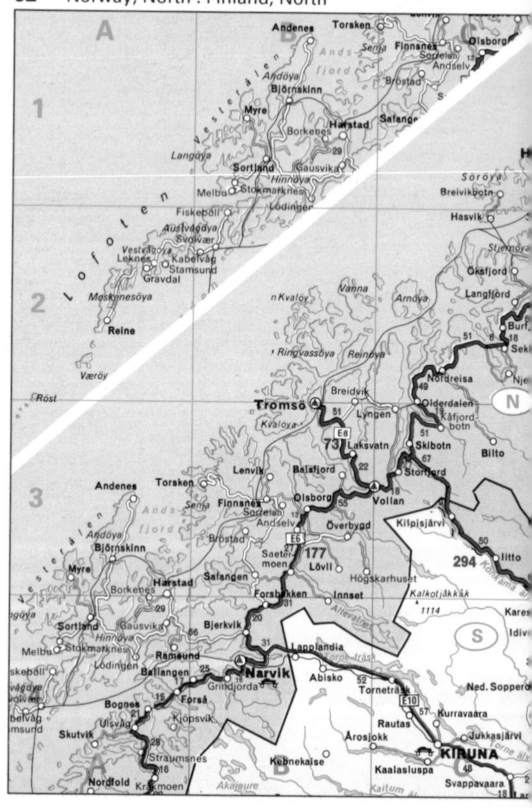

Andenes
Torsken
Senja
Finnsnes
Olsborg
Sorreisa
Andselv
Andöya
Björnskinn
Bröstad
Myre
Harstad
Salangen
Borkenes
Langöya
Sortland
Gausvika
Hinnöya
Melbu
Stokmarknes
Lödingen
Fiskeböll
Austvågöya
Svolvær
Vestvågöya
Leknes
Kabelvåg
Stamsund
Gravdal
Moskenesöya
Reine
Væröy
Röst
Vesterålen
Lofoten
Söröya
Breivikbotn
Hasvik
Stjernöya
Öksfjord
Langfjord
nKvalöy
Vanna
Arnöya
Ringvassöya
Reinöya
Breidvik
Tromsö
Lyngen
Kvaloya
Nordreisa
Olderdalen
Kåfjord-botn
Laksvatn
Skibotn
Bilto
Lenvik
Balsfjord
Storfjord
Vollan
Kilpisjärvi
Överbygd
Saeter-moen
Lövli
Högskarhuset
Iitto
Forsbakken
Innset
Kalkotjåkkåk
Altevatnet
Konkama
Bjerkvik
Lapplandia
Ramsund
Ballangen
Narvik
Grindjorda
Abisko
Torne-träsk
Torneträsk
Ned. Soppero
Bognes
Forså
Kjöpsvik
Ulsvåg
Skutvik
Kurravaara
Rautas
Årosjokk
Jukkasjärvi
Straumsnes
Kebnekaise
KIRUNA
Torne älv
Kaalasluspa
Svappavaara
Nordfold
Kråkmoen
Akajaure
Kaitum
Kares
Idiv
Burf
Sekk
Nje
N
S
A
B
C
1
2
3
H
E6
E8
E10
73
177
294
1114

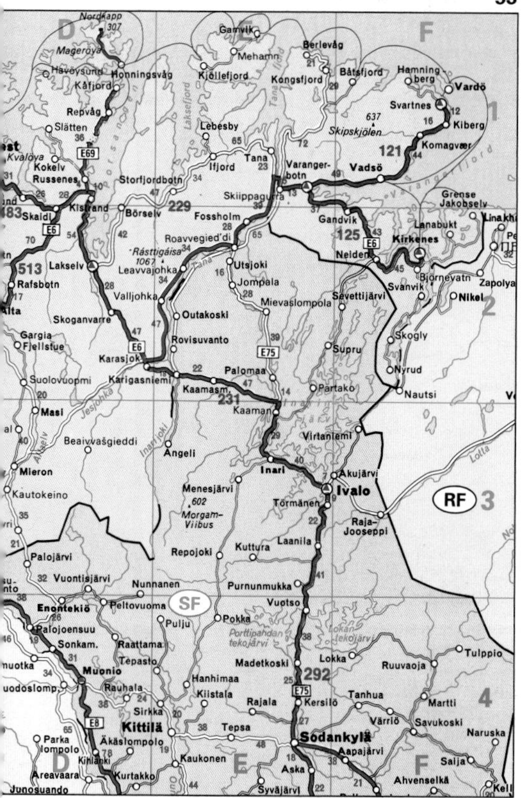
Nordkapp
Magerøya
Havøysund
Honningsvåg
Kåfjord
Repvåg
Slätten
Kvalöya
Kokelv
Russenes
Kistrand
Skaidi
Börselv
Storfjordbotn
Lakselv
Rafsbotn
Alta
Skoganvarre
Valljohka
Gargia
Fjellstue
Karasjok
Suolovuopmi
Masi
Mieron
Kautokeino
Palojärvi
Vuontisjärvi
Enontekiö
Palojoensuu
Sonkam.
Muonio
Parka
lompolo
Kihlanki
Areavaara
Junosuando
Gamvik
Mehamn
Kjöllefjord
Lebesby
Ifjord
Tana
Skiippagurra
Fossholm
Roavvegied'di
Rásttigáisa
1067
Leavvajohka
Utsjoki
Jompala
Outakoski
Rovisuvanto
Karigasniemi
Kaamasm.
Palomaa
Kaaman
Angeli
Beaivvašgieddi
Inari
Menesjärvi
602
Morgam-
Viibus
Repojoki
Kuttura
Laanila
Nunnanen
Peltovuoma
Pulju
Pokka
Purnunmukka
Vuotso
Porttipahdan
tekojärvi
Raattama
Tepasto
Hanhimaa
Kiistala
Rauhala
Sirkka
Kittilä
Äkäslompolo
Kaukonen
Kurtakko
Tepsa
Rajala
Madetkoski
Kersilö
Sodankylä
Aska
Syväjärvi
Berlevåg
Kongsfjord
Båtsfjord
Hamning-
berg
Vardö
Svartnes
Kiberg
637
Skipskjölen
Komagvær
Vadsö
Varanger-
botn
Gandvik
Grense
Jakobselv
Lanabukt
Kirkenes
Neiden
Bjørnevatn
Svanvik
Zapolya
Nikel
Sevettijärvi
Mievaslompola
Supru
Skogly
Nyrud
Partako
Nautsi
Virtaniemi
Akujärvi
Ivalo
Törmänen
Raja-
Jooseppi
Lokan
tekojärvi
Lokka
Tulppio
Ruuvaoja
Tanhua
Martti
Värriö
Savukoski
Naruska
Aapajärvi
Salla
Ahvenselkä
RF
SF
E6
E69
E75
E8
229
231
125
121
292
513
Tana
Laksefjord
Jesjohka
Inarijoki
Lotta
Varangerfjord
D
E
F
1
2
3
4

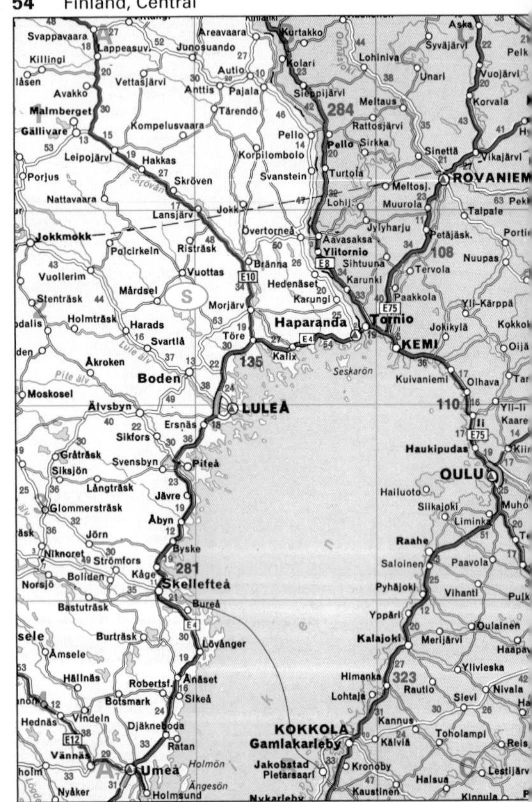
Svappavaara
Lappeasuvi
Areavaara
Kurtakko
Aska
Syväjärvi
Pelk
Killingi
Junosuando
Kolari
Lohiniva
Unari
Vuojärvi
Vettasjärvi
Autio
Pajala
Anttis
Sieppijärvi
Avakko
Meltaus
Korvala
Malmberget
Tärendö
284
Rattosjärvi
Gällivare
Kompelusvaara
Pello
Sirkka
Sinettä
Vikajärvi
Leipojärvi
Hakkas
Korpilombolo
Porjus
Skröven
Svanstein
Turtola
ROVANIEM
Meltosj.
Nattavaara
Lohij.
Muurola
Lansjärv
Jokk
Talpale
Jylyharju
Jokkmokk
Övertorneå
Aavasaksa
Petäjäsk.
Polcirkeln
Risträsk
Ylitornio
Nuupas
Bränna
Sihtuuna
108
Vuollerim
Vuottas
E10
E8
Tervola
Hedenäset
Karunki
Mårdsel
Karungi
Paakkola
Stenträsk
Morjärv
E75
Yli-Kärppä
Holmträsk
Harads
Haparanda
Tornio
Jokikylä
Kokkol
Svartlå
Töre
E4
KEMI
Oijä
Lule älv
Kalix
Åkroken
135
Seskarön
Kuivaniemi
Olhava
Pile älv
Boden
Moskosel
LULEÅ
110
Yli-Ii
Älvsbyn
Ii
Kaare
Ersnäs
Sikfors
Haukipudas
Gråträsk
Svensbyn
Piteå
OULU
Siksjön
Långträsk
Hailuoto
Jävre
Muho
Glommersträsk
Siikajoki
Liminka
Åbyn
Jörn
Raahe
Byske
Niknoret
Strömfors
Saloinen
Paavola
Boliden
Kåge
281
Norsjö
Skellefteå
Pyhäjoki
Vihanti
Pulk
Bastuträsk
Bureå
Yppäri
Oulainen
sele
Burträsk
Lövånger
Kalajoki
Merijärvi
Haapa
Åmsele
Ylivieska
Hällnäs
Robertsf.
Ånäset
Himanka
323
Rautio
Nivala
Botsmark
Sikeå
Lohtaja
Sievi
Hednäs
Vindeln
Djäkneboda
Kannus
Toholampi
E12
KOKKOLA
Ratan
Gamlakarleby
Kälviä
Reis
Vännäs
Holmön
Jakobstad
Pietarsaari
Kronoby
Lestijärv
Umeå
Halsua
Nyåker
Ängesön
Holmsund
Kaustinen
Kinnula
Nykarleby

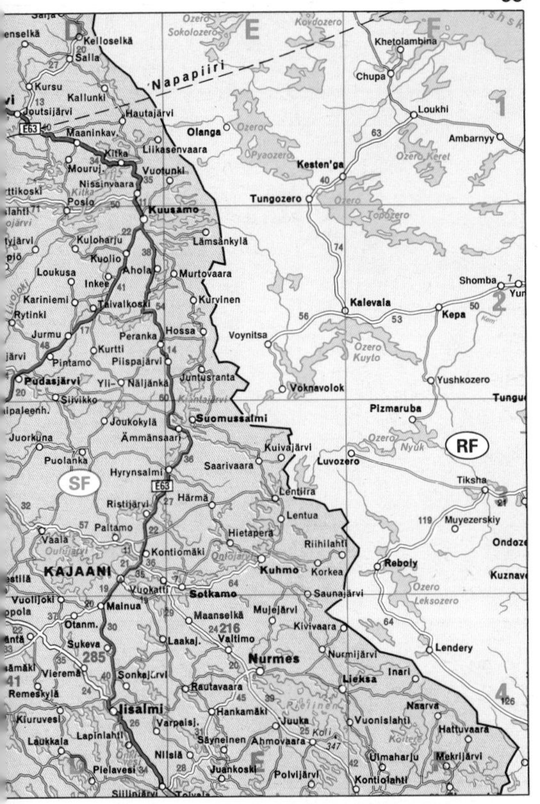
Napapiiri
Kelloselkä
Salla
Kursu
Kallunki
Joutsijärvi
Hautajärvi
Maaninkav.
Kitka
Liikasenvaara
Mouruj.
Vuotunki
Nissinvaara
Posio
Kuusamo
Lämsänkylä
Kuloharju
Kuolio
Loukusa
Inkee
Ahola
Murtovaara
Kariniemi
Taivalkoski
Kuivinen
Rytinki
Jurmu
Peranka
Hossa
Kurtti
Pintamo
Piispajärvi
Pudasjärvi
Näljänkä
Juntusranta
Siivikko
Joukokylä
Suomussalmi
Juorkuna
Ämmänsaari
Puolanka
Hyrynsalmi
SF
Ristijärvi
Härmä
Paltamo
Vaala
Kontiomäki
KAJAANI
Vuokatti
Sotkamo
Vuolijoki
Mainua
Otanm.
Maanselkä
Sukeva
Laakaj.
Valtimo
Vieremä
Sonkajärvi
Nurmes
Remeskylä
Rautavaara
Iisalmi
Hankamäki
Kiuruvesi
Varpaisj.
Säyneinen
Laukkala
Lapinlahti
Nilsiä
Juankoski
Pielavesi
Siilinjärvi
Olanga
Ozero Sokolozero
Kovdozero
Khetolambina
Chupa
Loukhi
Ambarnyy
Pyaozero
Kesten'ga
Tungozero
Topozero
Shomba
Kalevala
Kepa
Voynitsa
Ozero Kuyto
Yushkozero
Voknavolok
Pizmaruba
Ozero Nyuk
RF
Kuivajärvi
Saarivaara
Luvozero
Tiksha
Lentiira
Lentua
Muyezerskiy
Hietaperä
Riihilahti
Ondoz
Kuhmo
Korkea
Reboly
Kuznav
Saunajärvi
Ozero Leksozero
Mujejärvi
Kivivaara
Lendery
Nurmijärvi
Inari
Lieksa
Naarva
Vuonislahti
Hattuvaara
Juuka
Koli
Ahmovaara
Ulmaharju
Mekrijärvi
Polvijärvi
Kontiolahti
E63
216
285

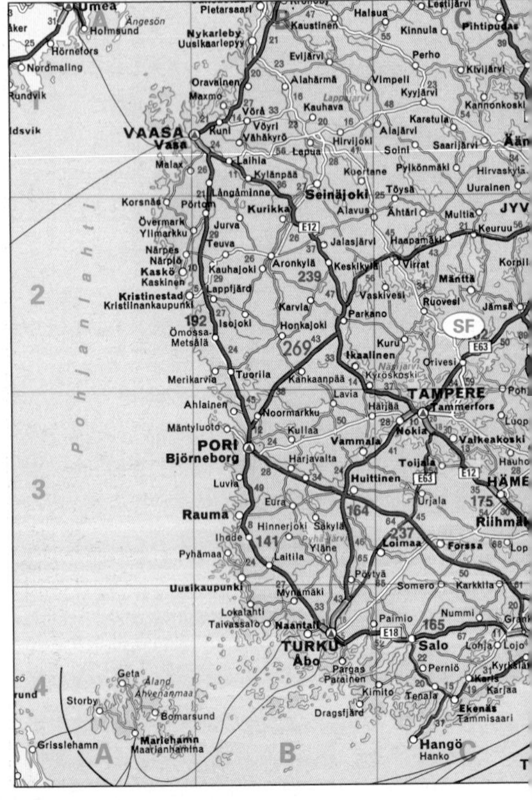

Umeå
Holmsund
Ångesön
Hörnefors
Nordmaling
Rundvik
Pietarsaari
Nykarleby
Uusikaarlepyy
Kaustinen
Halsua
Lestijärvi
Kinnula
Pihtipudas
Perho
Kivijärvi
Evijärvi
Alahärmä
Vimpeli
Kyyjärvi
Kannonkoski
Oravainen
Maxmo
Vörå
Vöyri
Vähäkyrö
Kauhava
Lappajärvi
Karstula
Alajärvi
Hirvijoki
Soini
Saarijärvi
VAASA
Vasa
Runi
Lapua
Laihia
Malax
Kuortane
Pylkönmäki
Hirvaskylä
Kylänpää
Längåminne
Seinäjoki
Töysä
Uurainen
Korsnäs
Pörtom
Kurikka
Alavus
Ähtäri
Multia
JYV
Övermark
Ylimarkku
Jurva
E12
Jalasjärvi
Haapamäki
Keuruu
Närpes
Närpiö
Teuva
Kaskö
Kaskinen
Kauhajoki
Aronkylä
Keskikylä
Virrat
Korpil
Mänttä
Kristinestad
Kristiinankaupunki
Lappfjärd
Vaskivesi
Ruovesi
Jämsä
Karvia
Parkano
Isojoki
Honkajoki
SF
Ömossa-
Metsälä
Kuru
E63
Ikaalinen
Näsijärvi
Orivesi
Merikarvia
Tuorila
Kankaanpää
Kyröskoski
Lavia
TAMPERE
Tammerfors
Ahlainen
Noormarkku
Härjää
Mäntyluoto
Kullaa
Nokia
Valkeakoski
PORI
Björneborg
Vammala
Harjavalta
Toijala
Luvia
Huittinen
HÄME
Eura
Urjala
Rauma
Riihmäki
Hinnerjoki
Säkylä
Ihode
Pyhäjärvi
Loimaa
Forssa
Pyhämaa
Yläne
Laitila
Pöytyä
Uusikaupunki
Mynämäki
Somero
Karkkila
Lokalahti
Nummi
Taivassalo
Naantali
TURKU
Åbo
Paimio
E18
Salo
Lohja
Lojo
Perniö
Pargas
Parainen
Kimito
Tenala
Karis
Karjaa
Dragsfjärd
Ekenäs
Tammisaari
Geta
Åland
Ahvenanmaa
Storby
Bomarsund
Grisslehamn
Mariehamn
Maarianhamina
Hangö
Hanko
Pohjanlahti

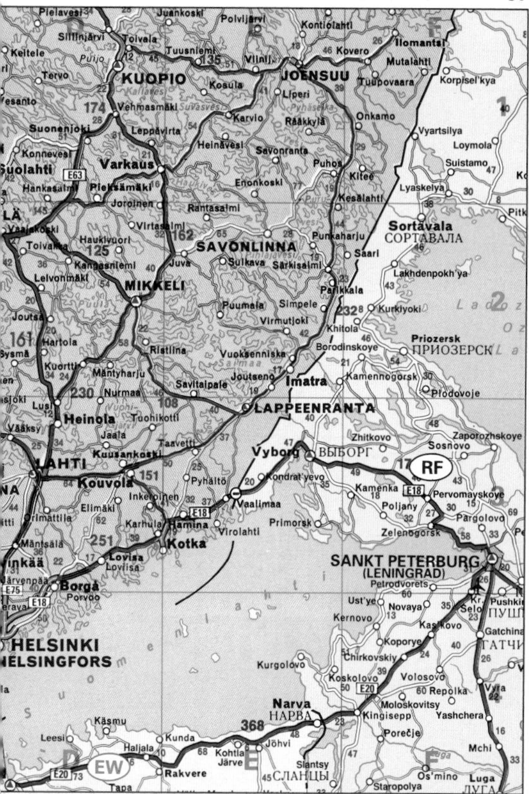

Pielavesi · Juankoski · Polvijärvi · Kontiolahti

Keitele · Siilinjärvi · Toivala · Tuusniemi · Vilnij.. · Kovero · Ilomantsi

Tervo · Pulyo · **KUOPIO** · Kosula · **JOENSUU** · Tuupovaara · Korpisel'kya

Suonenjoki · Vehmasmäki · Liperi · Räakkylä · Onkamo · Vyartsilya

Konnevesi · Leppävirta · Karvio · Savonranta · Puhos · Kitee · Loymola

Varkaus · Heinävesi · Kesälahti · Lyaskelya · Suistamo

Suolahti · Pieksämäki · Enonkoski · Rantasalmi · Kitee · Sortavala · СОРТАВАЛА

LÄ · Joroinen · Virtasalmi · Punkaharju · Saari · Lakhdenpokh'ya

Toivakka · Haukivuori · 162 · **SAVONLINNA** · Pitk

Leivonmäki · Kangasniemi · Juva · Sulkava · Särkisalmi · Parikkala · Kurkijoki

Joutsa · **MIKKELI** · Puumala · Simpele · 232 · Priozersk · ПРИОЗЕРСК

Hartola · Mäntyharju · Vuoksenniska · Borodinskoye · Kamennogorsk

Nurmaa · Ristina · Savitaipale · Joutseno · **Imatra** · Plodovoje

Heinola · Tuohikotti · **LAPPEENRANTA** · Kamennogorsk

Vääksy · Jaala · Kuusankoski · Taavetti · Vyborg · ВЫБОРГ · Zhitkovo · Zapotozhskoye · Sosnovo

LAHTI · **Kouvola** · 151 · Pyhältö · Kondrat'yevo · Kamenka · Pervomayskoye

Inkeroinen · Vaalimaa · Poljany · Pargolovo

Mänтsälä · Elimäki · Karhula · **Hamina** · Primorsk · Zelenogorsk

Borgå · Lovisa · **Kotka** · Virolahti · **SANKT PETERBURG (LENINGRAD)**

Porvoo · Petrodvorets

HELSINKI · **HELSINGFORS** · Ust'ye · Novaya · Selo · Pushki · ПУШ

Kernovo · Kashkovo · Gatchina · ГАТЧИ

Koporye · Chirkovskiy · Volosovo · Repolka · Vyra

Narva · **НАРВА** · Koskolovo · Moloskovitsy · Yashchera

Leesi · Käsmu · Kunda · 368 · Kingisepp · Porečje · Mchi

Haljala · Kohtla · Slantsy · СЛАНЦЫ · Os'mino · Luga · ЛУГА

Rakvere · Järve · Staropolya

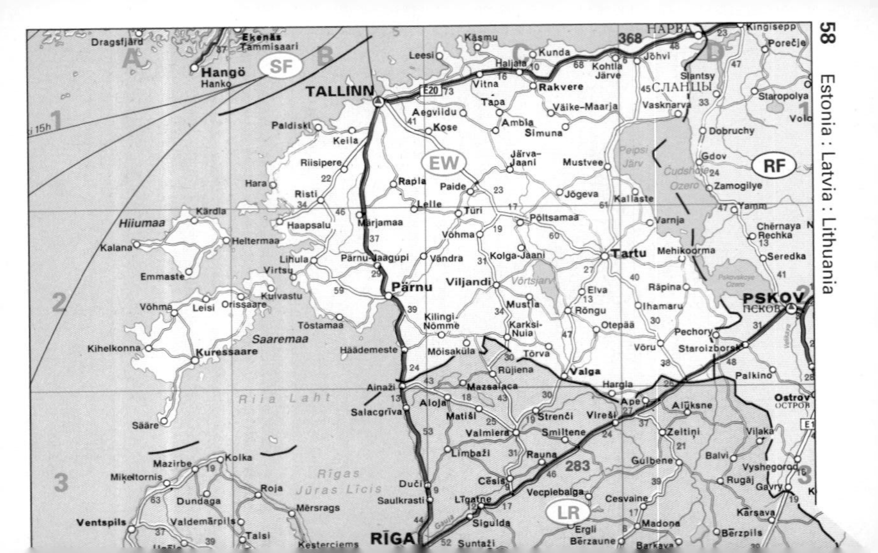
TALLINN
Paldiski
Keila
Leesi
Käsmu
Vitna
Haljala
Kunda
Rakvere
Kohtla Järve
Jõhvi
НАРВА
Slantsy
СЛАНЦЫ
Kingisepp
Tapa
Aegviidu
Kose
Ambla
Simuna
Väike-Maarja
Järva-Jaani
Mustvee
Jõgeva
Kallaste
Varnja
Paide
Türi
Lelle
Rapla
Märjamaa
Pärnu-Jaagupi
Pärnu
Vändra
Võhma
Viljandi
Kolga-Jaani
Põltsamaa
Võrtsjärv
Tartu
Elva
Rõngu
Otepää
Valga
Tõrva
Mustla
Karksi-Nuia
Rūjiena
Mõisaküla
Kilingi-Nõmme
Häädemeste
Tõstamaa
Lihula
Virtsu
Haapsalu
Risti
Riisipere
Hara
Heltermaa
Kärdla
Emmaste
Hiiumaa
Kalana
Kuressaare
Saaremaa
Kihelkonna
Leisi
Orissaare
Kuivastu
Sääre
Võru
Räpina
Ihamaru
Mehikoorma
Pechory
Staroizborsk
PSKOV
ПСКОВ
Palkino
Ostrov
ОСТРОВ
Vyshegorod
Gavry
Kārsava
Rugāj
Balvi
Viļaka
Alūksne
Zeltiņi
Gulbene
Madona
Barkava
Cesvaine
Ērgli
Bērzaune
Vecpiebalga
Smiltene
Strenči
Vireši
Ape
Hargla
Rauna
Valmiera
Cēsis
Sigulda
Līgatne
Limbaži
Matiši
Mazsalaca
Aloja
Salacgrīva
Ainaži
Saulkrasti
Duči
RĪGA
Suntaži
Bērzpils
Rīgas Jūras Līcis
Riia Laht
Mērsrags
Roja
Talsi
Kolka
Dundaga
Valdemārpils
Mazirbe
Miķeltornis
Ventspils
Kesterciems
Hangö
Hanko
Ekenäs
Tammisaari
Dragsfjärd
Gdov
Dobruchy
Zamogilye
Yamm
Chërnaya Rechka
Seredka
Staropolya
Porečje
Vasknarva
Peipsi Järv
Čudskoje Ozero
SF
EW
RF
LR
E20
283
368

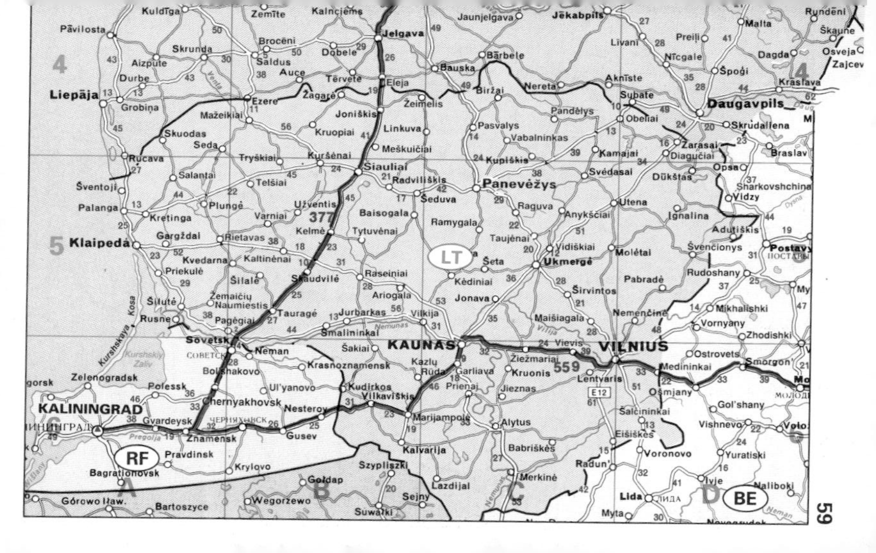
Kuldīga
Zemīte
Kalnciems
Jaunjelgava
Jēkabpils
Malta
Rundēni
Škaune
Osveja
Zajcev
Pāvilosta
Jelgava
Broceni
Skrunda
Saldus
Dobele
Aizpute
Bārbele
Bauska
Līvāni
Preiļi
Nīcgale
Dagda
Durbe
Auce
Tērvete
Eleja
Špoģi
Aknīste
Krāslava
Liepāja
Grobiņa
Ezere
Žagarė
Žeimelis
Biržai
Nereta
Subate
Daugavpils
Mažeikiai
Joniškis
Pandėlys
Obeliai
Skrudallena
Skuodas
Linkuva
Pasvalys
Vabalninkas
Zarasai
Seda
Kruopiai
Meškuičiai
Kupiškis
Kamajai
Diagučiai
Braslav
Rucava
Tryškiai
Kuršėnai
Šiauliai
Svėdasai
Dūkštas
Opsa
Salantai
Telšiai
Radviliškis
Panevėžys
Šventoji
Sharkovshchina
Plungė
Šeduva
Utena
Vidzy
Palanga
Užventis
Raguva
Kretinga
Varniai
Baisogala
Anykščiai
Ignalina
Dysna
377
Ramygala
Gargždai
Kelmė
Tytuvėnai
Adutiškis
Klaipėda
Rietavas
Taujėnai
LT
Vidiškiai
Molėtai
Švenčionys
Postavy
ПОСТАВЫ
Kvedarna
Kaltinėnai
Šeta
Ukmergė
Priekulė
Raseiniai
Rudoshany
Šilalė
Skaudvilė
Kėdiniai
Pabradė
Kosa
Žemaičių Naumiestis
Ariogala
Širvintos
Šilutė
Jonava
Mikhalishki
Rusnė
Tauragė
Jurbarkas
Vilkija
Nemenčinė
Pagėgiai
Maišiagala
Vornyany
Kurshskaya
Nemunas
Neris
Smalininkai
Sovetsk
Šakiai
KAUNAS
Vievis
VILNIUS
Zhodishki
СОВЕТСК
Neman
Žiežmariai
Ostrovets
Kurshskiy Zaliv
Krasnoznamensk
Kazlų Rūda
Garliava
559
Medininkai
Smorgon'
Bolshakovo
Kruonis
Lentvaris
Zelenogradsk
Polessk
Ul'yanovo
Kudirkos
Prienai
Jieznas
E12
Oshmjany
Chernyakhovsk
Vilkaviškis
МОЛОДЕЧНО
KALININGRAD
Nesterov
Šalčininkai
Gol'shany
Gvardeysk
ЧЕРНЯХОВСК
Marijampolė
Alytus
КАЛИНИНГРАД
Pregolja
Znamensk
Gusev
Vishnevo
Eišiškės
RF
Pravdinsk
Kalvarija
Babriškės
Voronovo
Yuratiski
Krylovo
Szypliszki
Radun'
Bagrationovsk
Gołdap
Merkinė
Ivje
Naliboki
Lazdijai
Lida
ЛИДА
BE
Górowo Iław.
Sejny
Bartoszyce
Węgorzewo
Suwałki
Myta
Novogrudok
4
5
A
B
C
D

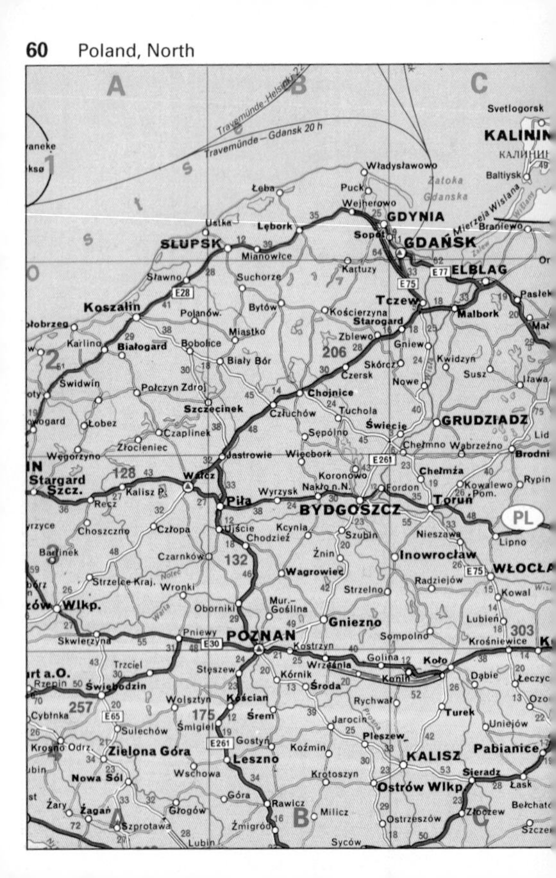
A
B
C
Travemünde–Helsinki 22
Travemünde–Gdansk 20 h
Svetlogorsk
KALININ
КАЛИНИН
Baltiysk
Władysławowo
Zatoka
Gdanska
Mierzeja Wislana
Puck
Łeba
Wejherowo
GDYNIA
Ustka
Lębork
Sopot
SŁUPSK
GDAŃSK
Braniewo
Mianowice
Kartuzy
ELBLAG
E77
Sławno
Suchorze
E75
E28
Tczew
Pasłek
Koszalin
Polanów.
Bytów
Kościerzyna
Malbork
Starogard
Kołobrzeg
Miastko
Zblewo
Karlino
Białogard
Bobolice
206
Gniew
Biały Bór
Skórcz
Kwidzyn
Czersk
Susz
Iława
Świdwin
Połczyn Zdrój
Nowe
Chojnice
Szczecinek
Tuchola
Człuchów
Łobez
Świecie
GRUDZIADZ
Czaplinek
Sępólno
Chełmno
Wąbrzeźno
Złocieniec
Brodnica
Węgorzyno
Jastrowie
Więcbork
E261
Chełmża
Stargard Szcz.
128
Wałcz
Koronowo
Kowalewo Pom.
Rypin
Kalisz P.
Fordon
Recz
Piła
Wyrzysk
Nakło n.N.
Toruń
BYDGOSZCZ
PL
Choszczno
Człopa
Ujście
Kcynia
Szubin
Nieszawa
Chodzież
Lipno
Barlinek
Żnin
Inowrocław
Czarnków
132
E75
WŁOCŁAWEK
Strzelce Kraj.
Wągrowiec
Radziejów
Noteć
Wronki
Strzelno
Kowal
Gorzów Wlkp.
Mur.-Goślina
Obornik
Warta
Lubień
Gniezno
Skwierzyna
Pniewy
POZNAN
Sompolno
303
E30
Krośniewice
Kostrzyn
Trzciel
Frankfurt a.O.
Golina
Koło
Rzepin
Stęszew
Września
Dąbie
Łęczyca
Świebodzin
Kórnik
Konin
Środa
257
Wolsztyn
Kościan
Rychwał
Ozorków
Cybinka
E65
175
Śrem
Turek
Śmigiel
Jarocin
Prosna
Uniejów
Sulechów
Pleszew
E261
Gostyń
Krosno Odrz.
Zielona Góra
Koźmin
KALISZ
Pabianice
Leszno
Wschowa
Krotoszyn
Sieradz
Nowa Sól
Ostrów Wlkp.
Łask
Góra
Żary
Żagań
Rawicz
Głogów
Milicz
Złoczew
Bełchatów
Szprotawa
Ostrzeszów
Szczerców
Żmigród
Lubin
Syców

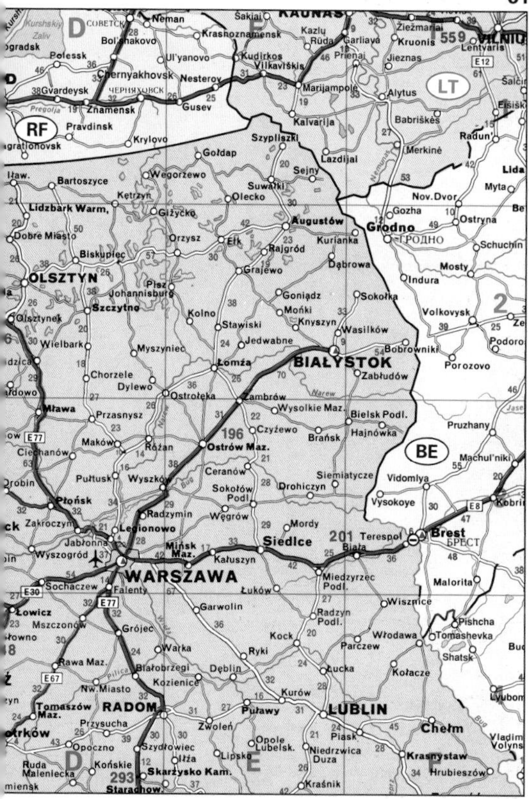
KAUNAS
VILNIUS
Šakiai
Neman
Sovetsk
Kurshskiy Zaliv
Bol'shakovo
Krasnoznamensk
Kazlų Rūda
Garliava
Kruonis
Žiežmariai
Lentvaris
Kudirkos
Vilkaviškis
Prienai
Jieznas
E12
Polessk
Ul'yanovo
Chernyakhovsk
Nesterov
Marijampolė
Alytus
LT
Šalčininkai
38Gvardeysk
Znamensk
Gusev
Pregolja
Eišiškės
RF
Pravdinsk
Kalvarija
Babriškės
Radun'
Krylovo
Szypliszki
Merkinė
Gołdap
Sejny
Lazdijai
Nemunas
Lida
Bartoszyce
Węgorzewo
Suwałki
Myta
Kętrzyn
Olecko
Nov. Dvor
Lidzbark Warm.
Giżycko
Augustów
Gozha
Grodno
Ostryna
ГРОДНО
Dobre Miasto
Orzysz
Ełk
Kurianka
Rajgród
Schuchin
Biskupiec
Dąbrowa
Mosty
OLSZTYN
Grajewo
Indura
Pisz
Johannisburg
Goniądz
Sokółka
Szczytno
Kolno
Mońki
Knyszyn
Volkovysk
Olsztynek
Stawiski
Wasilków
Wielbark
Jedwabne
Bobrowniki
Myszyniec
Łomża
BIAŁYSTOK
Porozovo
Chorzele
Zabłudów
Dylewo
Ostrołęka
Zambrów
Narew
Mława
Przasnysz
Wysokie Maz.
Bielsk Podl.
Pruzhany
196
Czyżewo
Brańsk
Hajnówka
E77
Maków
Różan
Ostrów Maz.
BE
Ciechanów
Machul'niki
Ceranów
Pułtusk
Wyszków
Siemiatycze
Vidomlya
Sokołów Podl.
Drohiczyn
Vysokoye
Płońsk
Radzymin
Węgrów
Mordy
E8
Kobrin
Zakroczym
Legionowo
201
Terespol
Brest
Jabłonna
Siedlce
Wyszogród
Mińsk Maz.
Kałuszyn
Biała
БРЕСТ
WARSZAWA
Miedzyrzec Podl.
E30
Sochaczew
Falenty
Łuków
Malorita
Łowicz
Garwolin
Wisznice
Mszczonów
Radzyn Podl.
Pishcha
Grójec
Kock
Włodawa
Tomashevka
Warka
Ryki
Parczew
Shatsk
Rawa Maz.
Pilica
Białobrzegi
Dęblin
Łucka
Kołacze
E67
Nw. Miasto
Kozienice
Kurów
Lyubom
Tomaszów Maz.
RADOM
Puławy
LUBLIN
Chełm
Przysucha
Zwoleń
Piask
Vladimir Volynskiy
Opoczno
Szydłowiec
Opole Lubelsk.
Niedrzwica Duza
Krasnystaw
Ruda Malenlecka
Końskie
Iłża
Lipsko
Hrubieszów
293
Skarżysko Kam.
Kraśnik
Starachow.
D
E
F

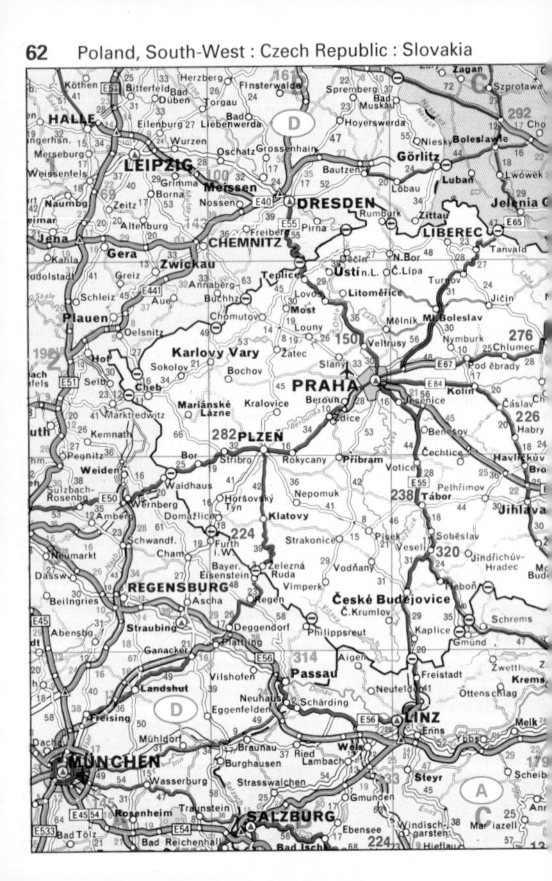
Köthen
Bitterfeld
Herzberg
Finsterwalde
Spremberg
Bad Muskau
Zagan
Szprotawa
Bad Düben
Torgau
Bad Liebenwerda
Hoyerswerda
HALLE
Eilenburg
Wurzen
Niesky
Boleslawiec
Merseburg
Oschatz
Grossenhain
Görlitz
LEIPZIG
Bautzen
Luban
Lwówek
Weissenfels
Grimma
Meissen
Löbau
Borna
Nossen
DRESDEN
Jelenia G
Naumbg.
Zeitz
Rumburk
Zittau
Altenburg
Freiberg
Pirna
LIBEREC
Jena
CHEMNITZ
Tanvald
Gera
Děčín
N.Bor
Kahla
Zwickau
Ústí n.L.
Č.Lípa
Rudolstadt
Greiz
Teplice
Turnov
Annaberg
Lovosice
Litoměřice
Jičín
Schleiz
Aue
Buchhz.
Most
Plauen
Chomutov
Mělník
Ml.Boleslav
Oelsnitz
Louny
Nymburk
Chlumec
Karlovy Vary
Žatec
Veltrusy
Hof
Sokolov
Slaný
Poď ěbrady
Selb
Bochov
PRAHA
Kolín
Cheb
Beroun
Jesenice
Čáslav
Mariánské Lázne
Kralovice
Zdice
Marktredwitz
Benešov
Habry
Kemnath
PLZEŇ
Čechtice
Pegnitz
Bor
Stříbro
Rokycany
Příbram
Havlíčkův Bro
Weiden
Votice
Sulzbach-Rosenbg.
Waldhaus
Nepomuk
Pelhřimov
Wernberg
Horšovský Týn
Tábor
Amberg
Domažlice
Klatovy
Jihlava
Schwandf.
Furth i.W.
Strakonice
Písek
Soběslav
Neumarkt
Cham
Veseli
Jindřichův-Hradec
Dassw.
Bayer. Eisenstein
Železná Ruda
Vodňany
REGENSBURG
Vimperk
Třeboň
Beilngries
Ascha
Regen
České Budějovice
Č.Krumlov
Abensbg.
Straubing
Deggendorf
Philippsreut
Schrems
Kaplice
Gmünd
Plattling
Ganacker
Aigen
Zwettl
Passau
Freistadt
Krems
Vilshofen
Landshut
Neuhaus
Neufelden
Ottenschlag
Schärding
Eggenfelden
Freising
LINZ
Melk
Mühldorf
Enns
Ybbs
Braunau
Ried
Wels
Dachau
MÜNCHEN
Burghausen
Lambach
Scheibb
Wasserburg
Strasswalchen
Steyr
Gmunden
Rosenheim
Traunstein
SALZBURG
Ebensee
Windisch-garsten
Mariazell
Bad Tölz
Bad Reichenhall
Bad Ischl
Hieflau
D
A
C
E51
E40
E55
E65
E441
E67
E84
E50
E45
E56
E54
E533

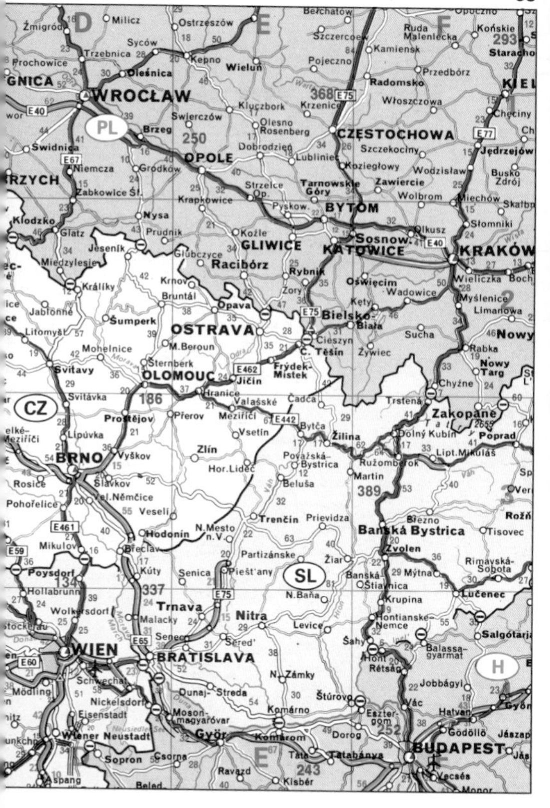
D
E
F
Milicz
Żmigród
Ostrzeszów
Bełchatów
Szczerców
Ruda Malenlecka
Końskie
Syców
Trzebnica
Kępno
Wieluń
Kamiensk
Pojeczno
Prochowice
Oleśnica
Przedbórz
Radomsko
Starachowice
LEGNICA
WROCŁAW
Kluczbork
Krzenice
Włoszczowa
E40
E75
368
293
PL
Brzeg
Świerczów
Olesno Rosenberg
CZĘSTOCHOWA
Chęciny
250
E77
Świdnica
Dobrodzień
Lubliniec
Szczekociny
Jędrzejów
E67
Niemcza
Grodków
OPOLE
Koziegłowy
Wodzisław
Busko Zdrój
WAŁBRZYCH
Ząbkowice Śl.
Strzelce Op.
Tarnowskie Góry
Zawiercie
Krapkowice
Wolbrom
Miechów
Pyskow
BYTOM
Nysa
Słomniki
Kłodzko
Glatz
Prudnik
Koźle
Olkusz
Sosnow.
Jeseník
Głubczyce
GLIWICE
KATOWICE
KRAKÓW
Miedzylesie
Racibórz
Rybnik
Wieliczka
Bochnia
Králíky
Krnov
Oświęcim
Wadowice
Myślenice
Bruntál
Zory
Kety
Limanowa
Jablonné
Opava
Bielsko-Biała
Šumperk
OSTRAVA
Litomyšl
Cieszyn
Sucha
Nowy Sącz
Mohelnice
M.Beroun
Rabka
Česky Těšín
Żywiec
Nowy Targ
Šternberk
Svitavy
OLOMOUC
E462
Frýdek-Místek
Jičin
Chyżne
Hranice
Svitávka
CZ
186
Valašské Meziříčí
Čadca
Trstená
Zakopane
Tatry
Prostějov
Přerov
E442
Bytča
Velké Meziříčí
Lipůvka
Vsetín
Žilina
Dolný Kubín
Poprad
Zlín
Vyškov
BRNO
Považská-Bystrica
Ružomberok
Lipt.Mikuláš
Hor.Lideč
Martin
Rosice
Slavkov
Beluša
389
Pohořelice
Vel.Němčice
Veselí
Trenčín
Prievidza
Brezno
Rožňava
Hodonín
N.Mesto n.V.
Banská Bystrica
Tisovec
E461
Mikulov
Břeclav
Zvolen
E59
Poysdorf
Kúty
Partizánske
Žiar
Rimavská-Sobota
Senica
Piešťany
SL
Banská-Štiavnica
Mýtna
134
337
Hollabrunn
E75
Krupina
Lučenec
Wolkersdorf
Malacky
Trnava
N.Baňa
Nitra
Hontianske-Nemce
Stockerau
Levice
Salgótarján
Senec
Sereď
Šahy
E65
WIEN
BRATISLAVA
Balassa-gyarmat
E60
Hont
Rétság
H
Schwechat
N.Zámky
Mödling
Dunaj-Streda
Jobbágyi
Nickelsdorf
Štúrovo
Vác
Eisenstadt
Moson-magyaróvar
Komárno
Esztergom
Hatvan
Wiener Neustadt
Győr
Komárom
Dorog
252
Gödöllő
Jászapáti
BUDAPEST
Sopron
Csorna
Tata
Tatabánya
243
Aspang
Ravazd
Kisbér
Vecsés
Monor

Ruda
Maleniecka
Przedbórz
Łańskie
Skarżysko Kam.
Starachow.
Ostrowiec
Opatów
Niedrzwica
Duza
Kraśnik
Lipsko
Lubelski
Iłża
Szyzrunow
Opoczno
Lipsko
B
Krasnystaw
Hrubieszów
Zamość
KIELCE
Sandomierz
Szczebrzeszyn
Chęciny
Opatów
Tarnobrzeg
Janów
Lub.
Biłgoraj
Tomaszów
Lub.
Chmielnik
Nisko
Rava-
Russkaya
CHOW
Jędrzejów
Staszów
Baranów
Dęba
Leżajsk
Cieszanów
Nesterov
Yarovov
PL
Busko
Zdrój
Mielec
Sokołów
Sieniawa
Kolbuszowa
339
Jarosław
Gorodok
Miechów
Skalbmierz
Dąbrowa
Tarn
E40
Lańcut
Radymno
Mostiska
Rudki
Koma
Słomniki
TARNÓW
Dębica
RZESZÓW
KRAKÓW
Wieliczka
Brzesko
Bochnia
Pilzno
Strzyżów
Przemyśl
Khyrov
Sambor
Myślenice
Jasło
Domaradz
Sambor
Drogobycz
Limanowa
Gorlice
Krosno
Sanok
Star. Sambor
Sucha
Nowy Sącz
Dukla
Lesko
Ustrzyki
Din.
Borislav
Rabka
Krynica
K
Turka
Skole
Nowy Targ
Stará
L'ubovňa
Bardejov
Svidnik
Cisna
Borinya
220
Zakopane
Kežmarok
Sabinov
Ruske
Dolný Kubín
Poprad
Spišská-N.Ves
Humenné
Vel. Bereznyy
Volovets
Lipt. Mikuláš
Prešov
Vranov
Perechin
Mezhgor'ye
Vernár
Michalovce
Uzhgorod
Kuš
SL
KOŠICE
Sečovce
Chop
Mukachevo
Brezno
Rožňava
Moldava
Trebišov
Beregovo
Halmeu
á Bystrica
Tisovec
Tornaľnémeti
Kisvárda
olen
Rimavská-
Sobota
Šafárikovo
Sátoraljaújhely
Mátészalka
Mýtna
Lučenec
Ózd
Kazincbarcika
Tokaj
Nyírbátor
Carei
Satu Mare
Ardusa
upina
Salgótarján
MISKOLC
Nyíregyháza
B
Benesat
A
Balassa-
gyarmat
Eger
Nyékládháza
Hajdú-
böszörmény
Hajdúhadház
Valea
Tăsnad
Jobbágy
Mezőkövesd
H
Jibou-
Silvaniei
Jászapáti
Füzesabony
Tiszafüred
Hajdúszoboszló
Sácueni
Zalá
BUDAPEST
Gyöngyös
Heves
110
Póctaj
Marghita
C
Vecsés
Jászberény
Kunhegyes
Karcag
Gápölnásny
Sácueni
Monor
Kisújszállás
224
246
Berettyóújfalu
Alesd
DEBRECEN

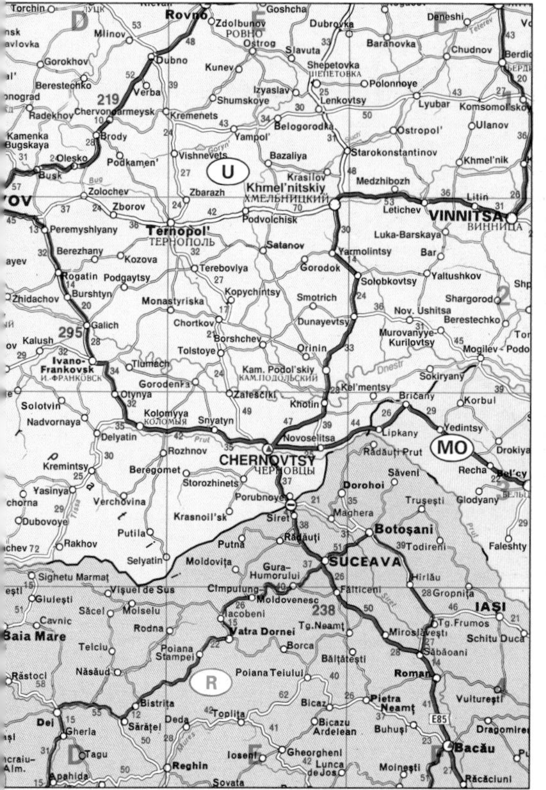
Torchin
Rovno
Goshcha
Deneshi
Zdolbunov
РОВНО
Dubrovka
Mlinov
Ostrog
Slavuta
Baranovka
Chudnov
Berdichev
Dubno
Kunev
Shepetovka
ШЕПЕТОВКА
Gorokhov
Berestechko
Verba
Izyaslav
Polonnoye
219
Shumskoye
Lenkovtsy
Lyubar
Komsomol'skoye
Radekhov
Chervonoarmeysk
Kremenets
Belogorodka
Ulanov
Kamenka Bugskaya
Brody
Yampol'
Ostropol'
Starokonstantinov
Olesko
Podkamen'
Vishnevets
Bazaliya
Khmel'nik
Busk
U
Krasilov
Medzhibozh
Zolochev
Zbarazh
Khmel'nitskiy
ХМЕЛЬНИЦКИЙ
Litin
Zborov
Letichev
VINNITSA
ВИННИЦА
Podvolchisk
Peremyshlyany
Ternopol'
ТЕРНОПОЛЬ
Luka-Barskaya
Berezhany
Kozova
Satanov
Yarmolintsy
Bar
Rogatin
Podgaytsy
Terebovlya
Gorodok
Solobkovtsy
Yaltushkov
Burshtyn
Kopychintsy
Zhidachov
Monastyriska
Smotrich
Shargorod
Galich
Chortkov
Dunayevtsy
Nov. Ushitsa
Berestechko
295
Kalush
Borshchev
Murovanyye-Kurilovtsy
Ivano-Frankovsk
И.-ФРАНКОВСК
Tolstoye
Orinin
Mogilev-Podol'skiy
Tlumach
Kam. Podol'skiy
КАМ.ПОДОЛЬСКИЙ
Dnestr
Gorodenka
Sokiryany
Otynya
Zaleščiki
Kel'mentsy
Solotvin
Kolomyya
КОЛОМЫЯ
Khotin
Bričany
Korbul
Nadvornaya
Snyatyn
Delyatin
Novoselitsa
Lipkany
Yedintsy
Prut
Rozhnov
Rădăuți Prut
MO
Drokiya
Kremintsy
CHERNOVTSY
ЧЕРНОВЦЫ
Beregomet
Săveni
Recha
Bel'cy
Storozhinets
Dorohoi
Yasinya
Porubnoye
Truşeşti
Glodyany
Verchovina
Maghera
Dubovoye
Krasnoil'sk
Siret
Botoşani
Putila
Rădăuți
Rakhov
Todireni
Faleshty
Putna
Selyatin
Moldovița
SUCEAVA
Gura-Humorului
Hîrlău
Sighetu Marmaț
Vişeul de Sus
Cîmpulung Moldovenesc
Fălticeni
Gropnița
Giuleşti
IAŞI
Săcel
Moisei
Iacobeni
238
Cavnic
Rodna
Tg.Neamț
Tg.Frumos
Baia Mare
Vatra Dornei
Miroslăveşti
Schitu Duca
Telciu
Poiana Stampei
Borca
Săbăoani
Năsăud
Băltăteşti
Răstoci
Poiana Teiului
Roman
R
Bistrița
Pietra Neamț
Vultureşti
Dej
Deda
Toplița
Bicaz
Gherla
Sărățel
Bicazu Ardelean
Buhuşi
Dragomireşti
E85
Tagu
Bacău
Reghin
Ioseni
Gheorgheni
Lunca de Jos
Moineşti
Apahida
Sovata
Răcăciuni

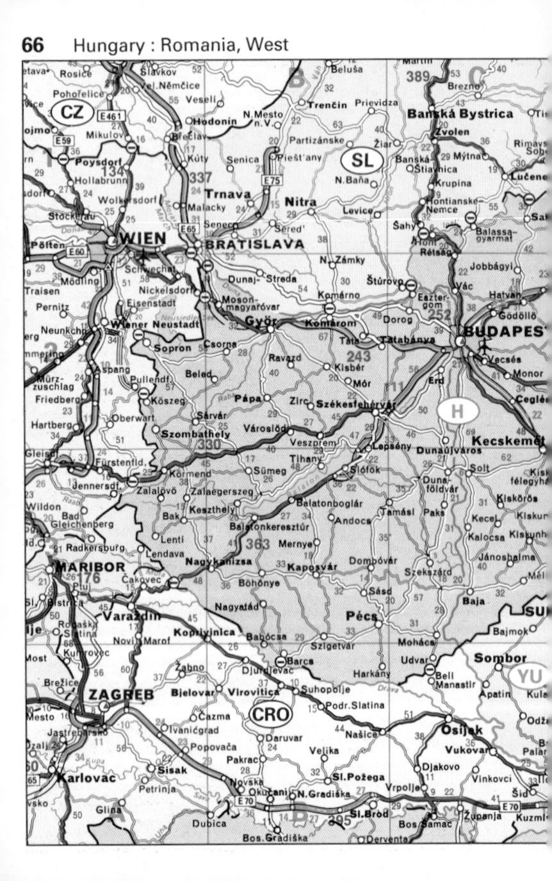
CZ
SL
H
CRO
YU
WIEN
BRATISLAVA
BUDAPEST
ZAGREB
MARIBOR
Banská Bystrica
Zvolen
Trenčin
Prievidza
Hodonín
N.Mesto n.V.
Piešťany
Partizánske
Žiar
Trnava
Nitra
Levice
N.Baňa
Krupina
Šahy
Balassagyarmat
Senica
Malacky
Senec
Sered'
N.Zámky
Dunaj-Streda
Komárno
Štúrovo
Esztergom
Vác
Hatvan
Gödöllő
Jobbágyi
Rétság
Mosonmagyaróvar
Győr
Komárom
Tata
Tatabánya
Dorog
Vecsés
Monor
Cegléd
Érd
Poysdorf
Mikulov
Břeclav
Hollabrunn
Wolkersdorf
Stockerau
Mödling
Schwechat
Nickelsdorf
Eisenstadt
Wiener Neustadt
Neunkirchen
Traisen
Pernitz
Aspang
Mürzzuschlag
Friedberg
Hartberg
Oberwart
Fürstenfld.
Jennersdf.
Wildon
Bad Gleichenberg
Radkersburg
Sopron
Csorna
Pullendf.
Kőszeg
Beled
Ravazd
Kisbér
Mór
Pápa
Zirc
Székesfehérvár
Sárvár
Szombathely
Városiőd
Veszprém
Lepsény
Dunaújváros
Kecskemét
Tihany
Siófok
Solt
Körmend
Sümeg
Zalalövő
Zalaegerszeg
Keszthely
Balatonboglár
Tamási
Paks
Dunaföldvár
Kiskőrös
Kecel
Kalocsa
Bak
Lenti
Balatonkeresztúr
Andocs
Mernye
Lendava
Nagykanizsa
Kaposvár
Dombóvár
Szekszárd
Jánoshalma
Čakovec
Böhönye
Sásd
Baja
Varaždin
Nagyatád
Pécs
Novi Marof
Koprivnica
Babócsa
Szigetvár
Mohács
Bajmok
Sombor
Udvar
Harkány
Barcs
Djurdjevac
Bell Manastir
Apatin
Bjelovar
Virovitica
Suhopolje
Podr.Slatina
Čazma
Ivanićgrad
Daruvar
Našice
Osijek
Popovača
Velika
Vukovar
Pakrac
Djakovo
Vinkovci
Sisak
Karlovac
Petrinja
Novska
Okučani
N.Gradiška
Sl.Požega
Vrpolje
Glina
Dubica
Sl.Brod
Bos.Šamac
Županja
Bos.Gradiška
Derventa
E461
E59
E75
E65
E60
E70

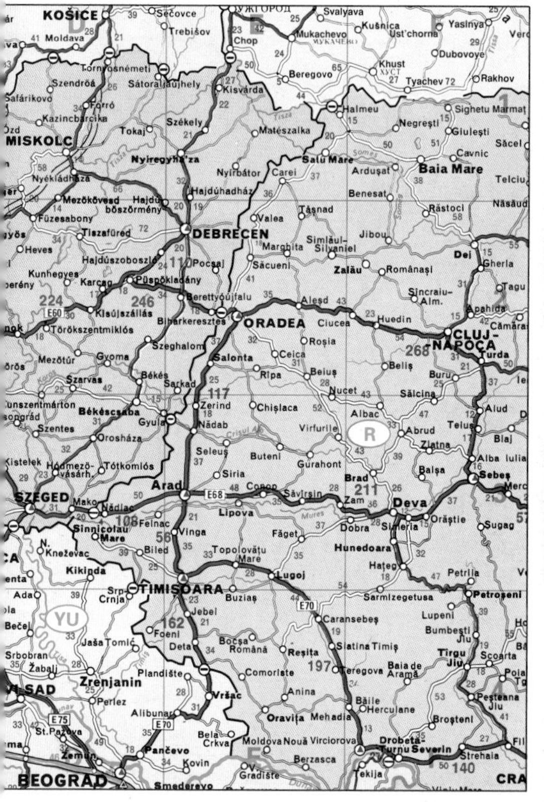
KOŠICE
Sečovce
Trebišov
Moldava
Svalyava
Mukachevo
Chop
Kušnica
Ust'chorna
Yasinya
Dubovoye
Khust
Beregovo
Tyachev
Rakhov
Szendrő
Sátoraljaújhely
Kisvárda
Halmeu
Sighetu Marmaţ
Negreşti
Giuleşti
MISKOLC
Tokaj
Székely
Mátészalka
Cavnic
Săcel
Nyíregyháza
Nyírbátor
Carei
Satu Mare
Arduşat
Baia Mare
Telciu
Hajdúhadház
Benesat
Năsăud
Mezőkövesd
Hajdúböszörmény
Tăşnad
Răstoci
Füzesabony
Valea
Tiszafüred
DEBRECEN
Heves
Marghita
Simlăul-Silvaniei
Jibou
Dej
Hajdúszoboszló
Pocsaj
Săcueni
Zalău
Românaşi
Gherla
Kunhegyes
Karcag
Püspökladány
Berettyóújfalu
Sincraiu-Alm.
Aleşd
Apahida
Kisújszállás
Biharkeresztes
ORADEA
Ciucea
Huedin
CLUJ-NAPOCA
Törökszentmiklós
Szeghalom
Roşia
Mezőtúr
Gyoma
Salonta
Ceica
Turda
Beliş
Szarvas
Békés
Sarkad
Ripa
Beiuş
Buru
Nucet
Sălcina
Békéscsaba
Zerind
Chişlaca
Albac
Alud
Szentes
Gyula
Nădab
Virfurile
Abrud
Teluş
Orosháza
Zlatna
Blaj
Seleuş
Buteni
Gurahont
Alba Iulia
Hódmező-vásárh.
Tótkomlós
Siria
Balşa
Brad
Sebeş
SZEGED
Arad
Conop
Săvîrşin
Zam
Deva
Mako
Nădlac
Lipova
Orăştie
Sugag
Sinnicolau Mare
Felnac
Dobra
Simeria
Făget
Vinga
Hunedoara
N. Kneževac
Biled
Topolovăţu Mare
Haţeg
Kikinda
Lugoj
Petrila
TIMIŞOARA
Buziaş
Sarmizegetusa
Petroşeni
Srp. Crnja
Jebel
Caransebeş
Lupeni
Foeni
Bumbeşti Jiu
Deta
Bocşa Română
Reşita
Slatina Timiş
Jaša Tomić
Tirgu Jiu
Scoarta
Srbobran
Žabalj
Zrenjanin
Plandište
Comorîste
Teregova
Baia de Aramă
SAD
Vršac
Anina
Perlez
Băile Herculane
Peşteana Jiu
Alibunar
Oraviţa
Mehadia
Broşteni
St.Pazova
Bela Crkva
Moldova Nouă
Virciorova
Drobeta-Turnu Severin
Zemun
Pančevo
Kovin
Berzasca
Strehaia
BEOGRAD
V. Gradište
Tekija
Smederevo
E60
E68
E70
E75
YU
R

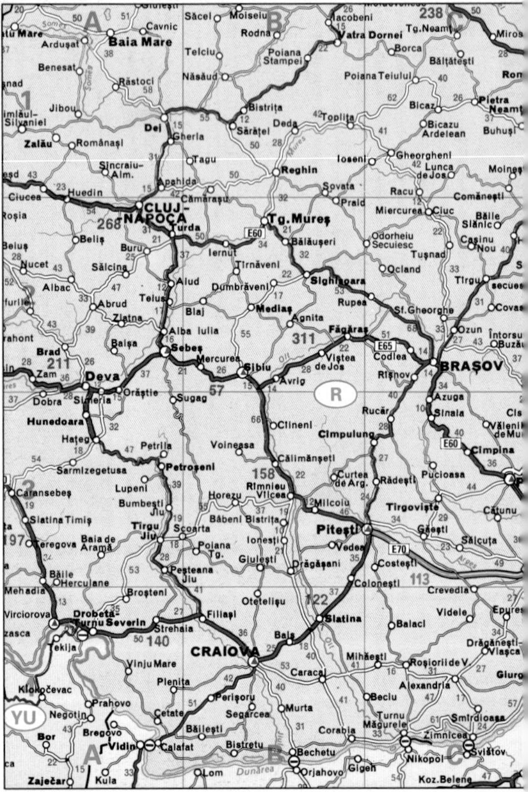

Cavnic • Săcel • Moiseiu • Iacobeni
Baia Mare • Rodna • Vatra Dornei • Tg. Neamț • Miro
Ardusat • Telciu • Poiana Stampei • Borca • Bălțătești • Ron
Benesat • Năsăud • Poiana Teiului • Bicaz • Pietra Neamț
Răstoci • Bistrița • Toplita • Bicazu Ardelean • Buhuși
Jibou • Dej • Gherla • Sărățel • Deda • Ioseni • Lunca de Jos • Moines
Zalău • Românași • Țagu • Reghin • Sovata • Gheorgheni • Racu • Comănești
Sincraiu-Alm. • Apahida • Câmărașu • Praid • Miercurea Ciuc • Băile Slănic
Ciucea • Huedin • CLUJ-NAPOCA • Turda • Ernut • Tg. Mureș • Băluseni • Odorheiu Secuiesc • Tușnad • Casinu Nou
Roșia • Beliș • Buru • Iernut • Tîrnăveni • Sighișoara • Ocland • Tirgu
Belis • Nucet • Sălciua • Aiud • Dumbrăveni • Mediaș • Agnita • Rupea • Sf. Gheorghe • Covas
Albac • Abrud • Zlatna • Teluș • Blaj • Alba Iulia • Ozun • Întorsu Buzău
Brad • Zam • Baița • Sebeș • Mercurea • Sibiu • Avrig • Viștea de Jos • Făgăraș • Codlea • BRAȘOV
Deva • Orăștie • Sugag • Vlcea • Rîșnov • Azuga
Dobra • Simeria • Hunedoara • Voineasa • Clineni • Rucăr • Sinaia • Cîmpina
Hațeg • Petrila • Călimănești • Cîmpulung • Vălenii de Mu
Sarmizegetusa • Petroșeni • Rîmnicu Vîlcea • Curtea de Arg. • Rădești • Pucioasa
Caransebeș • Lupeni • Horezu • Milcoiu • Tirgoviște • Câtunu
Slatina Timiș • Bumbesti Jiu • Scoarta • Pitești • Găești • Salcuta
Teregova • Baia de Aramă • Tirgu Jiu • Poiana Ionești • Vedea • Costesti • Colonesti
Mehadia • Broșteni • Giulești • Drăgășani • Crevedia
Băile Herculane • Pegteana • Otetelișu • Slatina • Balaci • Videle
Vircioarova • Drobeta Turnu Severin • Strehaia • Filiași • Bals • Mihăești • Rosiorile de • Drăgănești-Vlasca • Glur
zasca • Vinju Mare • CRAIOVA • Caracal • Beciu • Alexandria
Kloučevac • Prahovo • Plenița • Perișoru • Segarcea • Murta • Corabia • Turnu Măgurele • Smîrdioasa
YU • Negotin • Cetate • Băilești • Bistretu • Bechetu • Zimnicea
Bor • Brepovo • Vidin • Calafat • Lom • Dunărea • Orjahovo • Gigen • Nikopol • Svištov
Zaječar • Kula • Koz.Belene

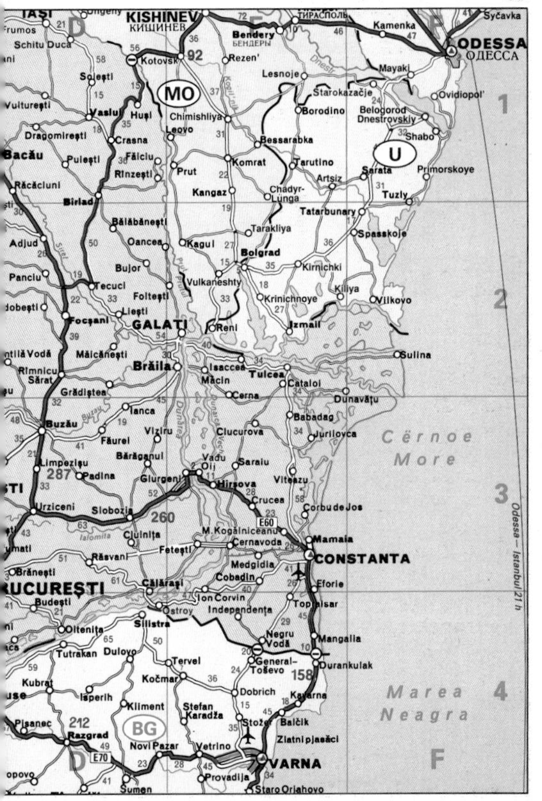

IAȘI
Ungheni KISHINEV
КИШИНЕВ
Frumos 21
Schitu Duca
Sculeni 56 Kotovsk 92
Rezen
Bendery
БЕНДЕРЫ
Kamenka
47
Syčavka
ODESSA
ОДЕССА
Vulturești 58
Vaslui Huși
Chimishliya
Lesnoje
Starokazacie
Mayaki
Borodino
Belogorod
Dnestrovskiy
Ovidiopol'
1
Dragomirești
Crasna
Puiești
Fălciu
Rînzești
Leovo
Prut
Bessarabka
Komrat
Tarutino
Artsiz
Shabo
U
Primorskoye
Bacău
Răcăciuni
Bîrlad
Kangaz
Chădyr-
Lunga
Sarata
31
Tuzly
Bălăbănești
Oances
Kagul
Tatarbunary
Spasskoje
Adjud
Bujor
Tarakliya
Belgrad
36
Panciu
Tecuci
Folteşti
Vulkaneshty
Kirnichki
Kiliya
Vilkovo
2
dobești
Focșani
Liești
GALAȚI
Krinichnoye
Izmail
Reni
Măicănești
Isaccea
Tulcea
Sulina
Rîmnicu
Sărat
Brăila
Măcin
Cataloi
Cerna
Dunavățu
Grădiştea
Babadag
Buzău
Ianca
Viziru
Clucurova
Iurilovca
Cërnoe
More
Făurei
Bărăganul
Vadu
Saraiu
Limpeziu 287
Padina
Giurgeni
Hîrșova
Viteazu
3
Urziceni
Slobozia
Crucea
Corbude Jos
Cuinița
M. Kogălniceanu
Mamaia
Fetești
Cernavoda
CONSTANTA
Răsvani
Medgidia
Călărași
Cobadin
Eforie
Budești
Ostrov
Ion Corvin
Independenta
Topraisar
Oltenita
Silistra
Negru
Vodă
Mangalia
Tutrakan
Duloyo
Tervel
General-
Toševo
Durankulak
Kubrat
Isperih
Kočmar
Dobrich
Kavarna
Marea
Neagra
4
Pisanec 212
Razgrad
Kliment
Stefan
Karadza
Stožer
Balčik
Zlatni piasači
F
Novi Pazar
Vetrino
VARNA
Provadija
Staro Oriahovo
Šumen

Odessa — Istanbul 21 h

Velenje
Sl. Konjice
Varaždin
Nagyatád
Bled
Tržič
SLO
Celje
Rogaška Slatina
Novi Maraf
Koprivnica
Babócsa
Kobarid
Kranj
Zid. Most
Kumrovec
Žabno
Djurdjevac
Tolmin
LJUBLJANA
Zagreb
Bjelovar
Virovitica
Idrija
Kočevje
126
Nove Mesto
ZAGREB
Ivanićgrad
Čazma
Gorizia
Postojna
Polje
Babno
160
Popovača
Daru
TRIESTE
Karlovac
Sisak
Pakrac
Piran
Rupa
Delnice
Vrbovsko
Petrinja
Novska
Buje
Buzet
Ogulin
Glina
Dubica
Bos. Grad
Poreč
Pazin
RIJEKA
Crikvenica
Josipdol
Slunj
Bos. Novi
Prijedor
Laktaš
Rovinj
Rabac
Krk
Senj
Plitvicka
Jitvice
Bos. Krupa
Pula
Cres
403
Otočac
Bihać
Sanski Most
Lošinj
Jablanac
Gospić
Bos. Petrovac
Ključ
Pag
Karlobag
G. Lapac
Drvar
Mrkonjićgrad
Dugi Otok
Zadar
Jasenica
Obrovac
Gračac
Sučević
Crni Lug
Livn
Biograd
Benkovac
Knin
Vrlika
E65
Kornat
Šibenik
Sinj
SPLIT
Žirje
Trogir
Omiš
Senigallia
ANCONA
Brac
Pto. Recanati
Hvar
Macerata
Civitanova Marche
Korčula
Tolentino
Grottammare
Vis
Fermo
S. Benedetto
Ascoli
Porto d'Ascoli
Lastovo
Teramo
Giulianova
Roseto
Gran Sasso d'Italia 2914
E55
PESCARA

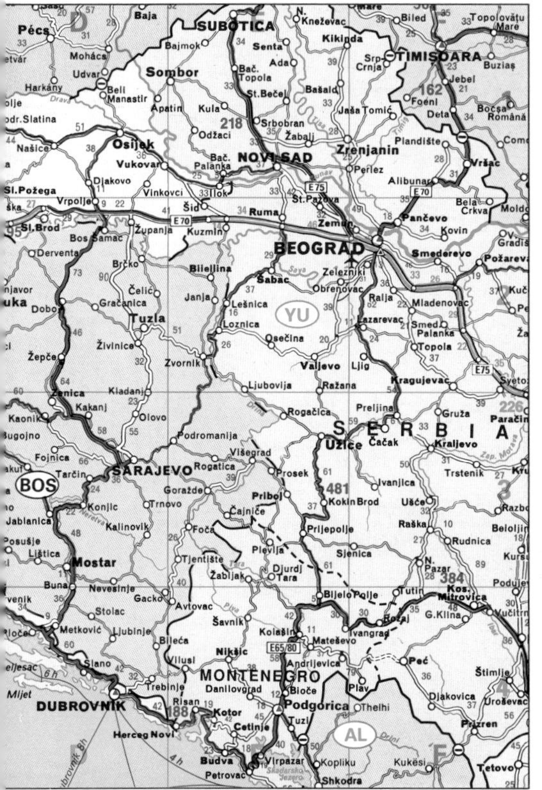

Pécs
Baja
SUBOTICA
N. Kneževac
Biled
Topolovățu Mare
Mohács
Udvar
Bajmok
Senta
Kikinda
Srp. Crnja
TIMIȘOARA
Buziaș
Harkány
Beli Manastir
Sombor
Ada
Bač. Topola
Jebel
Apatin
Kula
St.Bečej
Bašaid
Foeni
Deta
Bocșa Română
Drava
Srbobran
Jaša Tomić
Odžaci
Žabalj
Našice
Osijek
Plandište
Vukovar
Bač. Palanka
NOVI SAD
Zrenjanin
Vršac
Djakovo
Perlez
Alibunar
Sl.Požega
Vinkovci
Ilok
E75
E70
Vrpolje
Šid
St.Pazova
Bela Crkva
Sl.Brod
Ruma
Pančevo
Županja
Kuzmin
Zemun
Bos Šamac
Kovin
Derventa
BEOGRAD
Smederevo
Požarevac
Brčko
Bijeljina
Šabac
Sava
Železnik
Obrenovac
Čelić
Janja
Dobo
Gračanica
Lešnica
YU
Ralja
Mladenovac
Tuzla
Loznica
Lazarevac
Smed. Palanka
Osečina
Živinice
Topola
Žepče
Zvornik
Valjevo
Ljig
Ljubovija
Ražana
Kragujevac
Zenica
Kladanj
Kakanj
Drina
Rogačica
Preljina
Gruža
Paraćin
Kaonik
Olovo
Bugojno
Podromanija
SERBIA
Užice
Čačak
Kraljevo
Fojnica
Višegrad
Zap. Morava
Tarčin
SARAJEVO
Rogatica
BOS
Prosek
Trstenik
Ivanjica
Goražde
Konjic
Trnovo
Priboj
Kokin Brod
Ušće
Jablanica
Čajniče
Kalinovik
Prijepolje
Raška
Foča
Posušje
Rudnica
Lištica
Pljevlja
Sjenica
Mostar
Tjentište
Djurdj Tara
N. Pazar
Žabljak
Buna
Nevesinje
Bijelo Polje
Tutin
Kos. Mitrovica
Gacko
Avtovac
Rožaj
G.Klina
Stolac
Šavnik
Metković
Ljubinje
Kolašin
Ivangrad
Mateševo
Bileća
E65/80
Nikšić
Vilusi
Andrijevica
Peć
Slano
Štimlje
MONTENEGRO
Mljet
Trebinje
Danilovgrad
Plav
Bioče
Djakovica
DUBROVNIK
Risan
Kotor
Podgorica
Thelhi
Uroševac
Prizren
Cetinje
Tuzi
Herceg Novi
AL
Drini
Budva
Virpazar
Kopliku
Kukësi
Tetovo
Petrovac
Skadarsko Jezero
Shkodra

Crkva   Moldova Noua Virciorova   Drobeta-Turnu Severin   Strehaia   Filiasi   Slatina
evo   Kovin
Kovin   Berzasca   Tekija   Vinju Mare   CRAIOVA   Bala
nederevo   Gradiste   Klokocevac   Pleniţa   Caracal   Mihăești
Požarevac   Kučevo   Prahovo   Cetate   Perişoru   Segarcea   Murta   R
adenovac   Petrovac   Negotin   Bregovo   Băileşti   Corabia   Măg
ed   Žagubica   Bor   Vidin   Calafat   Bistreţu   Bechetu   Orjahovo   Plev
lanka
spola   S E R B I A   Resavica   Dunărea   Oljahovo   Kneža   Plev
evac   Svetozarevo   Zaječar   Kula   Olom   Rasovo   Mihajlovo
Gruža   226   Boljevac   Belogradčik   Ružinci   Borovan   Červen Brjag   330
Paraćin   Soko Banja   Dolni Lom   Mihajlovgrad   Teliš   Lukovit
Kraljevo   Knjaževac   Vraca
Trstenik   Kruševac   Kalna   Berkovica   Jablanica
Razbojna   YU   NIŠ   E 80   Bela Palanka   Pirot   Petrohan   Svoge   Botevgrad   B
Belojin   Doljevac   152   Gara Dragoman   Kli
Rudnica   Kuršumlija   Dimitrovgrad   Čurek   Zlatica
N. Pazar   Podujevo   Leskovac   Vlasotince   Trân   SOFIJA   Panagjurišt
384   Lebane   197   Surdulica   Radomir   Pančarevo   Ihtiman
Mitrovica   Tulari   Vranje   Samokov   Kostenec
G.Kilna   Vučitrn   Bosilegrad   Stanke Dimitrov   Jundola
Priština   Gnjilane   Bujanovac   Kjustendil   303   Riiaki manastir   Velingrad
Štimlje   Uroševac   Kr. Palanka   Blagoevgrad   Razlog
Đakovica   Doganović   Stracin   Bansko   Dospe
Prizren   SKOPJE   Kumanovo   Simitli
Tetovo   Probištip   Delčevo   E79   Sandanski   Gpce
hkopija   MAC   Veles   Katlanovo   Kočani   Pehčevo   Delčev
ek   Gostivar   Solunska Gl.   Štip   Petrič   Kulata
Debar   2540   234   Negotino   Strumica   N.Selo   Sidirokastron
Kičevo   Mak.Brod   Stobi   Demir Kapija   Serre
Sopotnica   Prilep   Gevgelija   St.Dojran   Kalokastro
Librazhdi   Struga   Polykastron   Kilkis   Nigrita
AL   -64   Ohrid   Oteševo   Bitola   Oaride   GR   Assiros   Langadas
Pogradeci   Niki   Edessa   E86   Nea Alexandria   THESSALONI

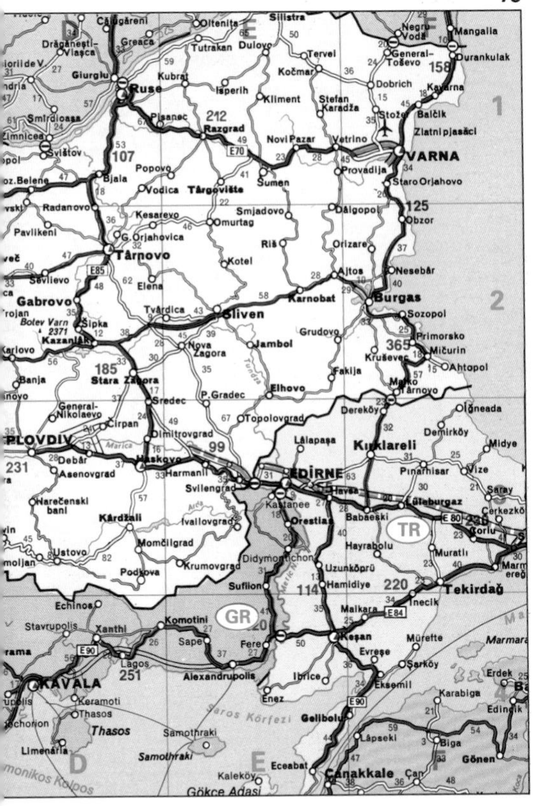
Călugăreni
Oltenita
Silistra
Negru Vodă
Mangalia
Drăgănești-Vlașca
Greaca
Tutrakan
Dulovo
Tervel
General-Toševo
Durankulak
Giurgiu
Kubrat
Kočmar
Ruse
Isperih
Kliment
Stefan Karadža
Dobrich
Kavarna
Smirdioasa
Pisanec
Razgrad
Stožer
Balčik
Zlatni pjasăci
Sviŝtov
Novi Pazar
Vetrino
VARNA
Popovo
Provadija
Bjala
Vodica
Târgovište
Šumen
Staro Orjahovo
Radanovo
Smjadovo
Dâlgopol
Obzor
Pavlikeni
Kesarevo
Omurtag
G. Orjahovica
Riš
Orizare
Târnovo
Kotel
Ajtos
Nesebâr
Sevlievo
Elena
Karnobat
Burgas
Gabrovo
Tvârdica
Sliven
Sozopol
Botev Vary
2371
Šipka
Kazanlâk
Grudovo
Primorsko
Karlovo
Nova Zagora
Jambol
Kruševec
Mičurin
Ahtopol
Banja
Stara Zagora
Fakija
Malko Târnovo
Tundža
Elhovo
General-Nikolaevo
Sredec
P. Gradec
Dereköy
İğneada
Čirpan
Topolovgrad
Demirköy
PLOVDIV
Dimitrovgrad
Lâlapaşa
Kırklareli
Midye
Marica
Debâr
Haskovo
Harmanli
EDİRNE
Pınarhisar
Vize
Asenovgrad
Svilengrad
Havsa
Saray
Narečenski bani
Kastanee
Babaeski
Lüleburgaz
Çerkezköy
Kârdžali
Ivailovgrad
Orestias
Çorlu
TR
Momčilgrad
Hayrabolu
Ustovo
Didymotichon
Muratlı
Krumovgrad
Uzunköprü
Podkova
Sufilon
Hamidiye
Tekirdağ
Echinos
Malkara
İnecik
Stavrupolis
Xanthi
Komotini
GR
Sape
Fere
Keşan
Mürefte
Marmara
Lagos
Evreşe
Şarköy
Alexandrupolis
İbrice
Erdek
KAVALA
Eksemil
Karabiga
Keramoti
Enez
Thasos
Saros Körfezi
Gelibolu
Thasos
Samothraki
Lâpseki
Biga
Limenária
Samothraki
Eceabat
Gönen
Kaleköy
Çanakkale
Çan
Gökçe Adası
E70
E85
E80
E84
E90

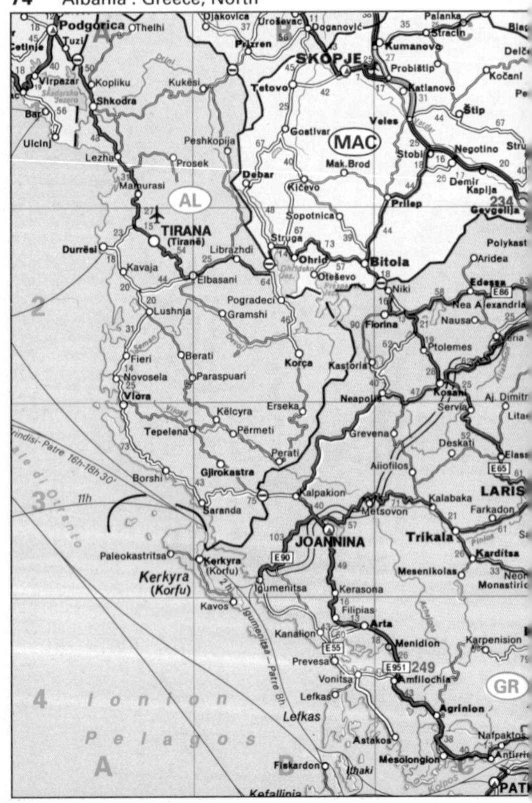
Podgorica
Thelhi
Tuzi
Cetinje
Virpazar
Bar
Ulcinj
Kopliku
Shkodra
Skadarsko Jezero
Kukësi
Drini
Djakovica
Uroševac
Prizren
Doganović
Skopje
Tetovo
Kumanovo
Probištip
Kočani
Delčevo
Katlanovo
Štip
Veles
Gostivar
MAC
Mak.Brod
Stobi
Negotino
Demir Kapija
Gevgelija
Prilep
Debar
Kičevo
Sopotnica
Peshkopija
Prosek
Lezha
Mamurasi
AL
TIRANA
(Tiranë)
Durrësi
Kavaja
Librazhdi
Elbasani
Struga
Ohrid
Ohridsko Jez.
Otoševo
Prespansko Jez.
Bitola
Niki
Polykastro
Aridea
Edessa
E86
Nea Alexandria
Nausa
Veria
Ptolemes
Aliakmon
Florina
Kastoria
Kosani
Servia
Aj. Dimitrios
Neapolis
Grevena
Deskati
Elassona
E65
Aiiofilos
Kalabaka
LARISA
Farkadon
Trikala
Karditsa
Pinios
Metsovon
Kalpakion
Pogradeci
Gramshi
Lushnja
Seman
Devoll
Fieri
Berati
Korça
Novosela
Paraspuari
Vlora
Vjosë
Erseka
Këlcyra
Tepelena
Përmeti
Perati
Gjirokastra
Borshi
Saranda
Brindisi- Patre 16h-18h 30'
11h
Canale di Otranto
Paleokastritsa
Kerkyra
(Korfu)
Kerkyra (Korfu)
JOANNINA
E90
Igumenitsa
Kerasona
Filipias
Arta
Igumenitsa – Patre 8h
Kavos
Kanalion
E55
Preveza
Vonitsa
Menidion
E951
249
Amfilochia
Achelóos
Mesenikolas
Neon Monastirion
Karpenision
Agrinion
GR
Lefkas
Astakos
Nafpaktos
Antirrion
Mesolongion
PATRA
Fiskardon
Ithaki
Kefallinia
Ionion Pelagos
Kolpos

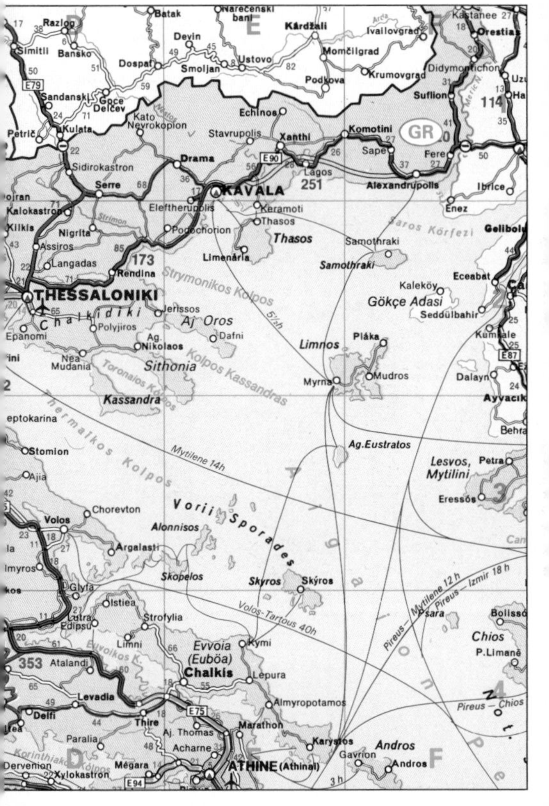
Batak
Narečenski bani
Kărdžali
Razlog
Bansko
Simitli
Devin
Ivailovgrad
Kastanee
Orestias
Dospat
Smoljan
Ustovo
Momčilgrad
Krumovgrad
Didymotichon
Podkova
Uzu
E79
Sandanski
Gotse Delčev
Suflion
Ha
Meriç N.
Nestos
Echinos
Kato Nevrokopion
Petrič
Kulata
Stavrupolis
Xanthi
Komotini
GR
Sape
Fere
Sidirokastron
Drama
E90
Lagos
Alexandrupolis
Ibrice
Serre
KAVALA
Keramoti
Enez
Kalokastron
Eleftherupolis
Thasos
Saros Körfezi
Kilkis
Strimon
Podochorion
Thasos
Samothraki
Gelibolu
Nigrita
Assiros
Limenária
Samothraki
Langadas
Rendina
Strymonikos Kolpos
Eceabat
Kaleköy
THESSALONIKI
Gökçe Adasi
Seddülbahir
Chalkidiki
Jerissos
Polyjiros
Aj Oros
Epanomi
Dafni
Kumkale
Ag. Nikolaos
Pláka
Limnos
E87
Nea Mudania
Sithonia
Toronaios Kolpos
Kolpos Kassandras
Mudros
Myrna
Dalayn
Kassandra
Ayvacık
Leptokarina
Thermaikos Kolpos
Behra
Stomion
Ag.Eustratos
Mytilene 14h
Lesvos, Mytilini
Petra
Ajia
Eressós
Vorii Sporades
Volos
Chorevton
Alonnisos
Argalasti
Almyros
Skopelos
Skyros
Skýros
Glyfa
Mytilene 12 h
Pireus — Izmir 18 h
Pireus
Istiea
Psara
Bolissó
Lutra Edipsu
Strofylia
Volos-Tartous 40h
Chios
Limni
Kymi
P.Limanē
Evvoia (Euböa)
353
Atalandi
Evvoikos K.
Chalkis
Lepura
Levadia
E75
Almyropotamos
Pireus — Chios
Delfi
Thire
Marathon
Aj. Thomas
Paralia
Karystos
Andros
Acharne
Korinthiakos Kolpos
Gavrion
Andros
Dervenion
Mégara
Xylokastron
E94
ATHINE (Athinai)
3 h
D
E
F

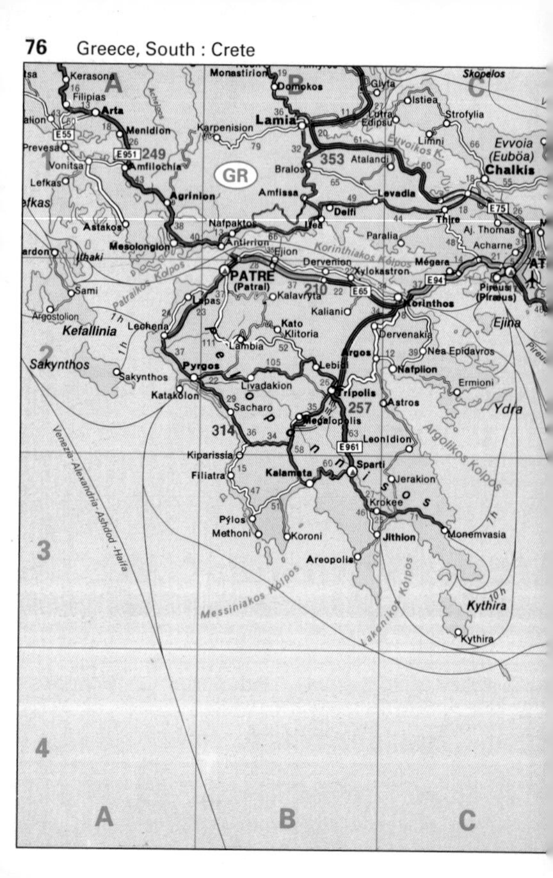

A
B
C
1
2
3
4
GR
Arta
Lamia
Domokos
Monastirion
Kerasona
Filipias
Menidion
Preveza
Vonitsa
Lefkas
Amfilochia
Agrinion
Astakos
Mesolongion
Ithaki
Sami
Argostolion
Kefallinia
Sakynthos
Karpenision
Bralos
Amfissa
Delfi
Levadia
Atalandi
Glyfa
Istiea
Lutra Edipsu
Limni
Strofylia
Evvoia (Euböa)
Chalkis
Skopelos
Evvoikos K.
Thiva
Aj. Thomas
Acharne
Nafpaktos
Antirrion
Ejion
Itea
Paralia
Korinthiakos Kolpos
Patraikos Kolpos
PATRE (Patrai)
Lapas
Lechena
Kalavryta
Kaliani
Kato Klitoria
Dervenion
Xylokastron
Mégara
Korinthos
Pireus (Piraeus)
Ejina
Dervenakia
Nea Epidavros
Nafplion
Argos
Lebidi
Lambia
Pyrgos
Livadakion
Tripolis
Astros
Ermioni
Ydra
Katakolon
Sacharo
Megalopolis
Leonidion
Argolikos Kolpos
Kiparissia
Filiatra
Kalamata
Sparti
Jerakion
Krokee
Monemvasia
Pýlos
Methoni
Koroni
Jithion
Areopolis
Messiniakos Kólpos
Lakonikos Kólpos
Kythira
Peloponnisos
Venezia-Alexandria-Ashdod-Haifa
E55
E951
E75
E94
E65
E961
249
353
210
257
314

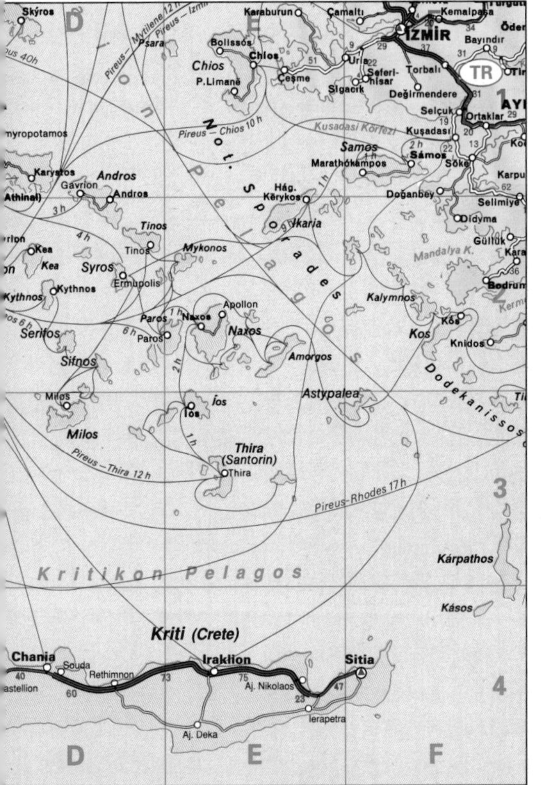
Skýros
Karaburun
Çamaltı
Kemalpaşa
İZMİR
Bayındır
Ödemiş
Psara
Bolissos
Chios
Chios
P.Limanë
Çeşme
Urla
Seferihisar
Sığacık
Torbalı
Değirmendere
TR
Selçuk
Ortaklar
Kuşadası
Kusadasi Körfezi
Pireus – Chios 10 h
Pireus – Mytilene 12 h
Samos
Sámos
Marathókampos
Söke
Karystos
Andros
Gavrion
Andros
Athinai
Hág. Kerykos
Ikaria
Doğanbey
Selimiye
Didyma
Tinos
Tinos
Mykonos
Kea
Kea
Syros
Ermupolis
Kythnos
Kythnos
Mandalya K.
Güllük
Bodrum
Kalymnos
Apollon
Naxos
Naxos
Paros
Paros
Serifos
Sifnos
Amorgos
Kos
Kos
Knidos
Dodekanissos
Milos
Milos
Astypalea
Íos
Íos
Thira
(Santorin)
Thira
Pireus – Thira 12 h
Pireus-Rhodes 17 h
Kárpathos
Kritikon Pelagos
Kásos
Kriti (Crete)
Chania
Souda
Rethimnon
Iraklion
Sitia
Aj. Nikolaos
Ierapetra
Aj. Deka
D
E
F
1
2
3
4

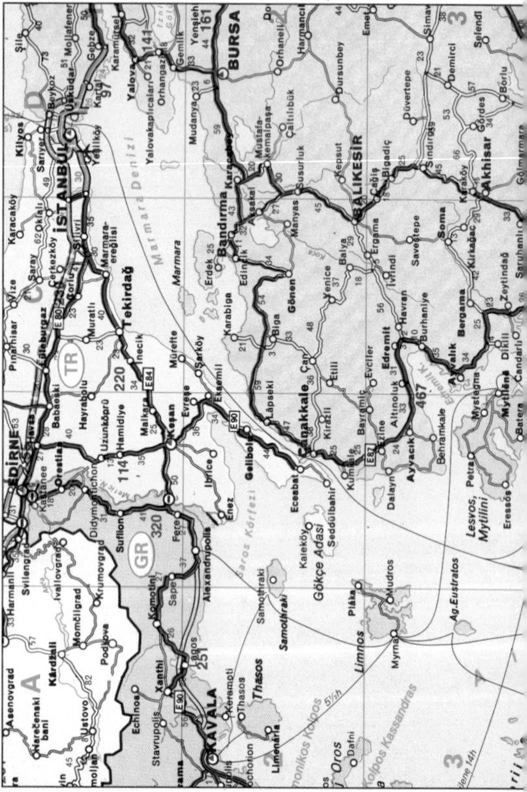

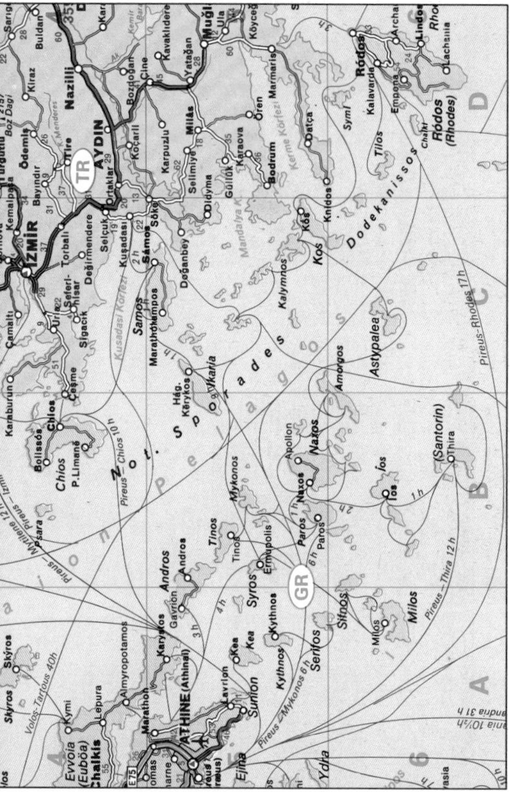

Sarigö

Buldan

Karin

Kiraz

Nazilli

35

60

Muğla

Ula

Köyceğiz

Kavaklıdere

Bozdağ

Archa

Linda

Rho

Lachaila

Turgutlu

Bozdağ 2157

Odemiş

Aydın

TR

Kemalpa

Bayindir

Ortaklar

Tire

28

Köşk

Söke

Bafa

Milas

Karpuzlu

Yatağan

Köyceğiz

Rodos

Kalavarda

Emponas

Rodos (Rhodes)

Symi

Tilos

İZMIR

Çamalti

Seferi-Çinar

Torbali

Dağ-mendere

Selçuk

Kuşadası

Söke

2h

Söke

Didima

Güllük

Bodrum

Datça

Dodekanissos

D

Karaburun

Çeşme

Urla

Kuşadası Körfezi

Samos

Marathókampos

Doğanbey

Kos

Kalymnos

Knidos

Kos

C

Bollseös

Chios

P.Limana

Chios

Pireus-Chios 10h

Z o t.

P i r

Hág. Kýrikos

Ikaría

Leros

Mandalya

Astypalea

Pireus-Rhodos 17h

Chora

Limni 12 h

S p

a d e s

Amorgos

Psara

Mykonos

Apollon

Naxos

Santorin

Pireus-Thira 12h

B

1 h

Skyros

Tinos

Tinos

Paros

Naxos

Ios

Thira

Ios

Skyros

Kými

Andros

Gavrion

Andros

Syros

Ermupolis

Paros

Paros

GR

Sihnos

Pireus-Thira 6h

Pireus-Thira 12h

Lepura

Almyropotamos

Kerykos

Kea

Kea

Kythnos

Serifos

Milos

Yóra

Evvoia (Eubóa)

Chalkis

E75

Athine (Athinai)

Methana

Lavrion

Sunlon

Kythnos

Milos

Milos

A

4 h

Egina

Pireus-Thira 10½ h

Thira 31 h

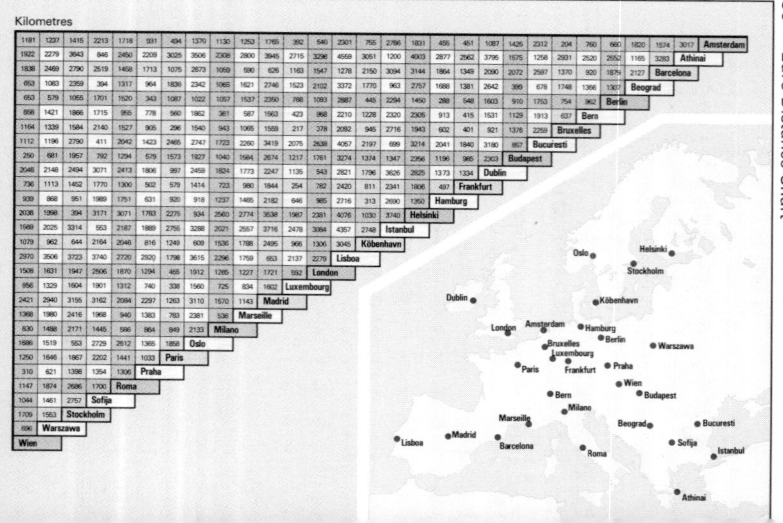

Kilometres

	Wien	Warszawa	Stockholm	Sofija	Roma	Praha	Paris	Oslo	Milano	Marseille	Madrid	Luxembourg	London	Lisboa	København	Istanbul	Helsinki	Hamburg	Frankfurt	Dublin	Budapest	Bucuresti	Bruxelles	Bern	Berlin	Beograd	Barcelona	Athinai
Amsterdam	1181	1237	1415	2213	1718	931	494	1370	1130	1253	1765	392	540	2301	755	2786	1831	456	451	1087	1426	2312	204	760	660	1820	1574	3017
Athinai	1922	2279	3643	846	2450	2209	3026	3506	2308	2800	3945	2715	3298	4559	3051	1200	4003	2877	2562	3795	1575	1258	2931	2520	2552	1165	3283	
Barcelona	1838	2469	2790	2519	1458	1713	1075	2673	1059	590	626	1163	1547	1278	2150	3094	3144	1864	1349	2090	2072	2597	1370	920	1879	2127		
Beograd	653	1083	2359	394	1317	964	1836	2342	1065	1621	2746	1523	2102	3372	1770	963	2757	1688	1381	2642	399	678	1748	1366	1307			
Berlin	653	579	1055	1701	1520	343	1087	1022	1057	1537	2350	768	1093	2887	445	2294	1450	288	548	1603	910	1753	754	962				
Bern	858	1421	1866	1715	956	778	560	1862	361	587	1563	423	968	2210	1228	2320	2305	913	415	1531	1129	1913	637					
Bruxelles	1164	1339	1584	2140	1527	905	296	1540	943	1065	1559	217	378	2092	945	2716	1943	602	401	921	1376	2259						
Bucuresti	1112	1196	2790	411	2042	1423	2465	2747	1723	2260	3419	2075	2638	4057	2197	699	3214	2041	1840	3180	857							
Budapest	250	681	1957	792	1294	579	1573	1927	1040	1564	2674	1217	1761	3274	1374	1347	2356	1196	985	2303								
Dublin	2048	2148	2494	3071	2413	1806	997	2459	1824	1773	2247	1135	543	2821	1796	3626	2825	1373	1334									
Frankfurt	736	1113	1452	1770	1300	502	579	1414	723	980	1844	254	782	2420	811	2341	1806	497										
Hamburg	939	868	951	1989	1751	631	920	918	1237	1465	2182	646	985	2716	313	2690	1350											
Helsinki	2038	1998	394	3171	3071	1783	2275	934	2560	2774	3538	1987	2381	4076	1030	3740												
Istanbul	1569	2025	3314	553	2187	1889	2755	3288	2021	2557	3716	2478	3084	4357	2748													
København	1079	962	644	2164	2046	816	1249	609	1536	1788	2495	966	1306	3045														
Lisboa	2970	3506	3723	3740	2720	2920	1798	3615	2296	1759	653	2137	2279															
London	1508	1631	1947	2506	1870	1294	465	1912	1285	1227	1721	592																
Luxembourg	956	1329	1604	1901	1312	740	338	1560	725	834	1602																	
Madrid	2421	2940	3155	3162	2084	2297	1263	3110	1670	1143																		
Marseille	1368	1980	2416	1968	940	1383	783	2381	536																			
Milano	830	1488	2171	1445	586	864	849	2133																				
Oslo	1686	1519	553	2729	2612	1365	1858																					
Paris	1250	1646	1867	2202	1441	1033																						
Praha	310	621	1398	1354	1306																							
Roma	1147	1874	2686	1700																								
Sofija	1044	1461	2757																									
Stockholm	1709	1553																										
Warszawa	696																											
Wien																												

NEW REPUBLICS
(Formerly USSR in Europe)

KEY TO MAP SYMBOLS

————————	Primary route
‒ ‒ ‒ ‒ ‒ ‒ ‒	Railway
⊕	Airport
————————	International boundary
▲ 4090	Height in metres
Ⓢ	Official National Identification Letters
ⓇⒻ	New Country Abbreviations

Scale 1 : 13 560 000

```
0    50  100          200              300 miles
|----|----|------------|----------------|
0  50 100   200    300    400           km
217 miles to 1 inch   135 km to 1 cm
```

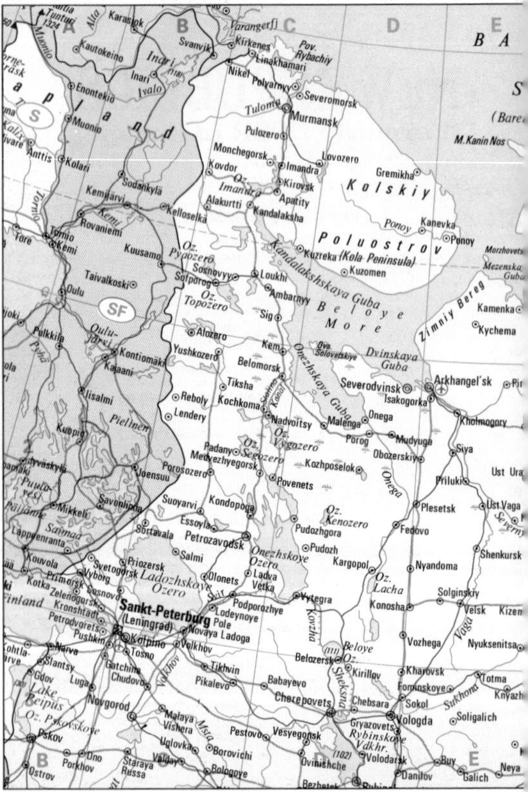

A B C D E

Karasjok · Svanvik · Pov. Rybachiy · B A

Kautokeino · Kirkenes · Polyarnyy · Linakhamari

Enontekiö · Nikel' · Polyarnyy · Severomorsk · Murmansk · M. Kanin Nos

Muonio · Ivalo · Tuloma · (Bare

Kolari · Sodankyla · Monchegorsk · Imandra · Lovozero · Gremikha

Kemijarvi · Kovdor · Oz. Imandra · Kiroysk · Apatity · Kanevka · Kolskiy

Rovaniemi · Kelloselka · Alakurtti · Kandalaksha · Ponoy · Ponoy · Poluostrov

Kuusamo · Pyaozero · Sosnovyy · Kandalakshskaya Guba · Kuzema (Kola Peninsula) · Kuzomen · Mezhenka

Kemijarvi · Oz. Topozero · Salozero · Loukhi · Ambarnyy · Sig · Kem · Kuzomen · Zimniy Bereg · Kychema

Kontiomaki · Yushkozero · Alozero · Beloye More · Solovetskiy · Dvinskaya Guba

Reboly · Belomorsk · Onezhskaya Guba · Severodvinsk · Arkhangel'sk · Pir

Lendery · Tiksha · Kochkoma · Nadvoitsy · Isakogorka · Kholmogory

Padany · Medvezh'yegorsk · Orzega · Malenga · Porog · Mudyuga · Siya · Ust Ura

Joensuu · Porosozero · Oz. Segozero · Kozhposelok · Obozerskiye · Priluki · Ust Vaga

Suoyarvi · Kondopoga · Povenets · Oz. Onega · Plesetsk · Fedovo · Ust Vaga

Essoyla · Oz. Kenozero · Nyandoma · Shenkursk

Sortavala · Petrozavodsk · Pudozh · Pudozhgora · Kargopol' · Oz. Lacha · Solginskiy

Priozersk · Salmi · Olonets · Ladva · Vetka · Konosha · Kizen

Ladozhskoye Ozero · Podporozh'ye · Vytegra · Vozhega · Nyuksenitsa

Sankt-Peterburg (Leningrad) · Lodeynoye Pole · Novaya Ladoga · Koncha · Beloye · Oz. · Solginskiy

Kronshtadt · Tosno · Tikhvin · Belozersk · Oz. · Kirillov · Khatovsk · Fominskoye · Totma

Gatchina · Pikalevo · Babayevo · Cherepovets · Chebsara · Vologda · Soligalich

Novgorod · Malaya Vishera · Pestovo · Vesyegonsk · Pryazovets · Volodark · Danilov · Neya

Staraya Russa · Uglovka · Borovichi · Ovinishche · Rybinskoye Vdkhr. · Buy

Bologoye · Bezhetsk · Rubtsov

SF · Finland

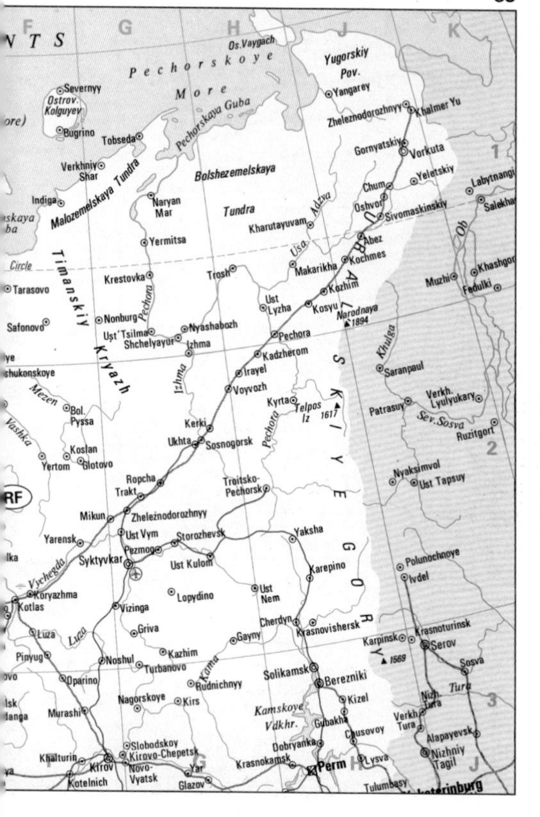

N T S   G   H   J   K

Os Vaygach

Pechorskoye

More

Yugorskiy
Pov.

Severnyy
Ostrov
Kolguyev
(ore)

Yangarey

Bugrino

Tobseda

Zheleznodorozhnyy

Khalmer Yu

Pechorskaya Guba

Gornyatskiy

Vorkuta

Verkhniy
Shar

Bolshezemelskaya

Chum

Yeletskiy

Labytnangi

Salekha

Indiga

Naryan
Mar

Tundra

Malozemelskaya Tundra

Kharutayuvam Usa Olba

Oshvor

Sivomaskinskiy

Ob

Khashgor

Yermitsa

Abez

Kochmes

Tadulki

Circle

Krestovka

Trosh

Makarikha

Muzhi

Tarasovo

Timanskiy Kryazh

Pechora

Ust
Lyzha

Kosyu

Kazhim

Narodnaya
1894

Nonburg

Nyashabozh

Ust Tsilma
Shchelyayur

Izhma

Pechora

Saranpaul

Safonovo

ye

chukonskoye

Irayel

Kadzherom

Kerki

Voyvozh

Kyrta

Telpos
Iz 1617

Verkh.
Lyulyukary

Patrasuy

Sev. Sosva

Ruzitgort

Mezen

Bol.
Pyssa

Ukhta

Sosnogorsk

Pechora

Nyaksimvol

Ust Tapsuy

Vyatka

Koslan

Glotovo

Ropcha
Trakt

Troitsko-
Pechorsk

Yertom

RF

Mikun

Zheleznodorozhnyy

Yaksha

Polunochnoye

Ivdel

Yarensk

Ust Vym

Storozhevsk

Karepino

Vychegda

Koryazhma

Pezmog

Syktyvkar

Ust Kulom

Krasnoturinsk

Kotlas

Vizinga

Lopydino

Ust
Nem

Karpinsk

1569

Serov

Pinyug

Oparino

Noshul

Griva

Kazhim

Cherdyn

Krasnovishersk

Sosva

ovo

Turbanovo

Koma

Nizh.
Tagil

Isk

anga

Nagorskoye

Kirs

Rudnichnyy

Solikamsk

Berezniki

Verkh.
Tura

Alapayevsk

Khalturin

Murashi

Slobodskoy

Kirovo-Chepetsk
Novo-
Vyatsk

Kirs

Kamskoye
Vdkhr.

Kizel

Gubakha

Chusovoy

Nizhniy
Tagil

Kotelnich

Kirov

Glazov

Krasnokamsk

Perm

Dobryanka

Lysva

Yekaterinburg

Tulumbasy

Kotka Imatra Ozo. Kadozhskoye Olonets Oz. Lacha Solginsky
Ozero Vytegra Konosha Vetka Kizer
Finland Kronshtadt Podporozhye Belozersk Vozhega Nyukseritsa
Petrodvorets Lodeynoye Pole Kirillov Kharovsk Totma
Sankt-Peterburg Novaya Ladoga an Beloye Chebsara Sokol Soligalich Knyaz
(Leningrad) Volkhov Cherepovets Gryazovets Vologda
Pushkin Kolpino Tosno Tikhvin Babayevo Vakhr (102) Volodarsk Buy
Gatchina Pikalevo Ovinishche Danilov Galich
Slantsy Chudovo Pestovo Vesyegonsk Rybinsk Kostroma
Luga Novgorod Malaya Vishera Ustyuzhna Bezhetsk Yaroslavl Nerekhta Kineshma
Pskov Uno Staraya Borovichi Bologoye Kashin Rostov Ivanovo Vichuga Gorko Vdkh
Ostrov Porkhov Russa Valday Vyshniy Volochek Kimry Taldom Zagorsk Shuya Vyazniki
Opochka Lokna Kholm Valdayskaya Torzhok Klin Mytishchi Vladimir Kovrov Dzerzhinsk
Velikiye Vozvyshennost Nelidovo Staritsa Tver Moskva Orekhovo-Zuyevo Murom
Nevel Toropets Rzhev Volokolamsk Podolsk Lyubertsy Yegoryevsk Kurlovski Lukoyanov
Vitebsk Velizh Safonovo Vyazma Gagarin Kaluga Serpukhov Kolomna Kasimov
Orsha Smolensk Milyatino Sukhinichi Tula Ryazan Nazarovka Sasovo
Mogilev Rostavl Sredne Belev Novomoskovsk Mikhaylov Ryazhsk Ruza
BE Slavgorod Bryansk Bezhitsa Plavsk Michurinsk Kamenka
Dovsk Unecha Navlya Mtsensk Yefremov Tambov
Chlobin Klintsy Orel Verkhove Yelets RF Rtishchevo
Gomel Dobrush Novgorod Zmiyevka Lipetsk Usman Mordovo Balashov
Inkovichi Severskiy Shostka Russkaya Kursk Voronezh Borisoglebsk Povorino Novoanninskiy
Chernigov Svm Oboyan Staryy Oskol Pavlovsk Mikhaylovka
Kiyev Nezhin Konotop Sumy Korocha Liski Yelatratovsk Frolov
U Priluki Akhtyrka Belgorod Rossosh Kantemirovka Chertkovo Tivlya
Pereyaslav Zolotonosha Kharkov Vozvyshennost Millerovo Volgograd
Cherkassy Merefa Kupyansk Svatovo Chir D
Smela Kremenchugskoye Krasnograd Slavyansk Lischansk Chertkovo Kalach
Kirovograd Poltava Novomoskovsk Artemovsk Stakhanov Lugansk
Dolinskaya Dnepropetrovsk Pavlograd

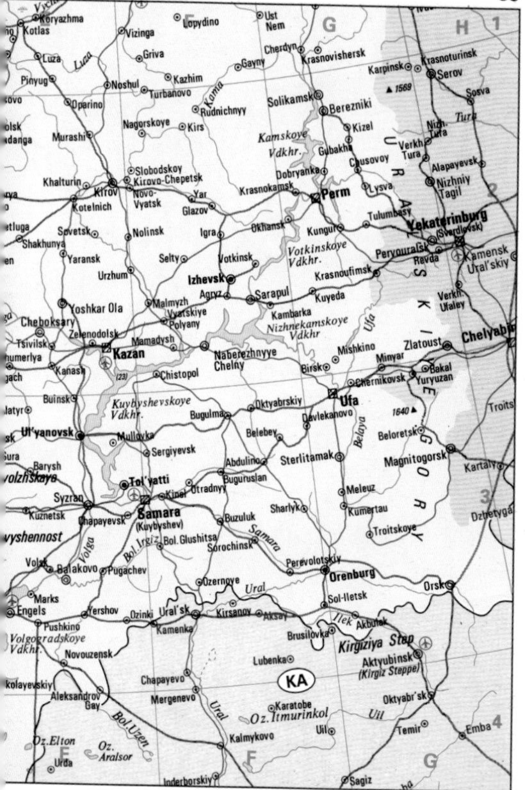
Koryazhma
Kotlas
Lopydino
Ust Nem
G
H
1
Vizinga
Luza
Luza
Griva
Cherdyn
Krasnovishersk
Gayny
Karpinsk
Krasnoturinsk
Serov
Pinyug
Noshul
Kazhim
Turbanovo
Kama
1569
Sosva
Oparino
Rudnichnyy
Solikamsk
Berezniki
Tura
Nagorskoye
Kirs
Kizel
Murashi
Kamskoye Vdkhr.
Gubakha
Nizh. Tura
Verkh. Tura
Chusovoy
Alapayevsk
Slobodskoy
Kirovo-Chepetsk
Dobryanka
Nizhniy Tagil
Khalturin
Kirov
Novo-Vyatsk
Yar
Krasnokamsk
Perm
Lysva
2
Kotelnich
Glazov
Tulumbasy
Yekaterinburg (Sverdlovsk)
Sovetsk
Nolinsk
Igra
Okhansk
Kungur
Shakhunya
Votkinskoye Vdkhr.
Pervouralsk
Revda
Kamensk Ural'skiy
Yaransk
Selty
Votkinsk
Urzhum
Izhevsk
Krasnoufimsk
URAL'SKIYE GORY
Agryz
Sarapul
Kuyeda
Verkh. Ufaley
Yoshkar Ola
Malmyzh
Vyatskiye Polyany
Kambarka
Cheboksary
Nizhnekamskoye Vdkhr
Ufa
Zelenodolsk
Mamadysh
Chelyabinsk
Tsivilsk
Kazan
Naberezhnyye Chelny
Mishkino
Zlatoust
Minyar
Bakal
Kanash
Birsk
Yuryuzan
Chistopol
Chernikovsk
Buinsk
Oktyabrskiy
Ufa
Troitsk
Kuybyshevskoye Vdkhr.
Bugulma
Davlekanovo
1640
Belaya
Ul'yanovsk
Belebey
Beloretsk
Mullovka
Sergiyevsk
Magnitogorsk
Abdulino
Sterlitamak
Kartaly
Barysh
Buguruslan
Tol'yatti
Otradnyy
Meleuz
3
Syzran
Kinel
Sharlyk
Kumertau
Kuznetsk
Chapayevsk
Samara (Kuybyshev)
Buzuluk
Dzhetygara
Samara
Troitskoye
Bol. Irgiz
Bol. Glushitsa
Sorochinsk
Volga
Volsk
Balakovo
Pugachev
Perevolotskiy
Orenburg
Ozernoye
Ural
Orsk
Marks
Sol-Iletsk
Engels
Yershov
Ozinki
Ural'sk
Kirsanov
Aksay
Ilek
Akbulak
Pushkino
Kamenka
Brusilovka
Volgogradskoye Vdkhr.
Kirgiziya Step
Novouzensk
Lubenka
Aktyubinsk
(Kirgiz Steppe)
Chapayevo
KA
Aleksandrov Gay
Mergenevo
Oktyabr'sk
Karatobe
Bol.Uzen
Ural
Oz. Itmurinkol
Uil
Temir
Emba
4
Uil
Oz.Elton
Kalmykovo
Oz. Aralsor
E
F
G
Urda
Inderborskiy
Sagiz

Muksinskaya · Kivyachevo · Kineshma · Vichuga · Sasovo · Tambov

Ucha · KRolovo · Shokhonki · Dolgalich · Kovda · Vyazniki · Murom · Michurinsk · Rasskaz

Vytegra · Kirillov · Danilov · Gryazovets · Ivanovo · Vladimir · Gus-Khrustalnyy · Kurlovsky · Kasimov · Lipetsk

Sokol · Chebsara · Volgda · Yaroslavl · Rostov · Gorelovo · Shuya · Vyaźma · Ryazhsk

RF

Cherepovets · Gryazino · Rybinsk · Nerekhta · Teykovo · Kineshma · Zagorsk · Mikhaylov · Yefremov · Yelets

Beloćr · Petrovsk · Danilovka · Rostov · Tutayev · Kimry · Klin · Tula · Yasnaya Polyana

Babayevo · Pestovo · Borisoglebsk · Kashin · Kimry · **Mosкva** · Serpukhov · Aleksin · Orël · Mtsensk

Pikalevo · Tikhvin · Matva · Bezhetsk · Kalyazin · Volokolamsk · Kaluga · Plavsk · Sukhinichi

Valdayskaya · Bologoye · Volochek · Gzhatsk · Gagarin · Mozhaysk · Kirov · Bryansk

Tikhvin · Vishera · Borovichi · **Vozvyshennost** · Torzhok · Vyazma · Smolensk · Yartsevo · Desna

Volkhov · Malaya Vishera · Valday · Staritsa · Salomno · Dorogobuzh

Sankt-Peterburg (Leningrad) · Novgorod · Kholm · Velikiye Luki · Orsha · Mogilëv · Gomel

Tosno · Chudovo · Staraya Russa · Nevel · Vitebsk · Dobrush

Pushkin · Gatchina · Luga · Porkhov · Velizh · Lepel · **Minsk** · Babruysk · **BE**

Krasnoye Selo · Slantsy · Pskov · Ostrov · Ostrovskaya · Polotsk · Barysaw · Slutsk

Kingisepp · **O.: Peipus** · Opochka · Sebezh · Daugavpils · Pastavy · Slonim · **Polesye**

EW · Narva · Tartu · Valga · Rēzekne · Dzyarzhynsk

Gulf of Finland · Tallinn · Pärnu · **LR** · Daugava · Salihorsk · Pinsk

SF · Helsinki · Espoo · Paldiski · Viljandi · **Riga** · Jēkabpils · **LT** · **Vilnius** · Maladzyechna · Baranavichy

Hanko · Hiiumaa · Saaremaa · Liepāja · Šiauliai · Kaunas · Alytus · Hrodna · Brest · **PL**

Gulf of Riga · Klaipėda · **RF** · Chernyakhovsk · Białystok

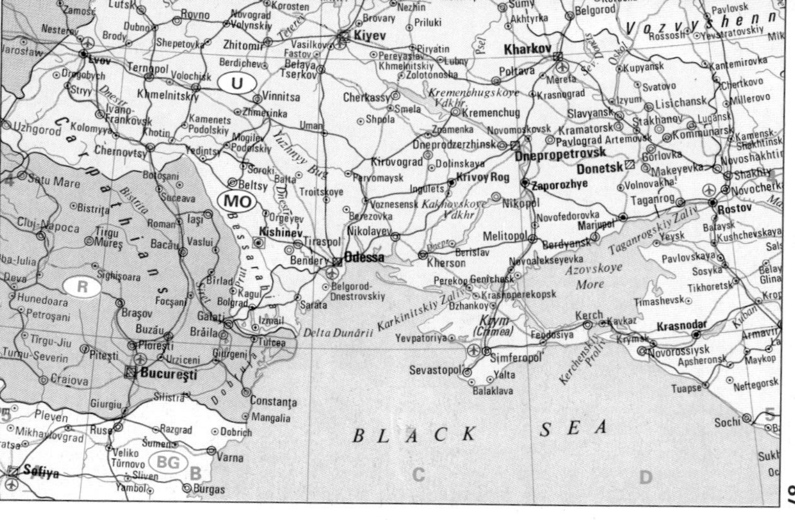
BLACK SEA
B
C
D
4
5
Azovskoye More
Kerchenskiy Proliv
Krym (Crimea)
Carpathians
Bessarabia
Vozvyshenn
U
MO
R
BG
Kiyev
Kharkov
Dnepropetrovsk
Donetsk
Zaporozhye
Krivoy Rog
Odessa
Kishinev
Rostov
Krasnodar
Bucureşti
Sofiya
Lvov
Zhitomir
Vinnitsa
Cherkassy
Kirovograd
Nikolayev
Kherson
Simferopol'
Sevastopol'
Yalta
Balaklava
Feodosiya
Kerch
Kavkaz
Melitopol
Berdyansk
Mariupol
Taganrog
Novorossiysk
Tuapse
Sochi
Maykop
Armavir
Tikhoretsk
Yeysk
Bataysk
Kushchevskaya
Novocherkassk
Shakhty
Lugansk
Kommunarsk
Makeyevka
Gorlovka
Kramatorsk
Slavyansk
Izyum
Kupyansk
Svatovo
Lisichansk
Stakhanov
Poltava
Kremenchug
Sumy
Akhtyrka
Belgorod
Rossosh
Yevstratovskiy
Millerovo
Kantemirovka
Chertkovo
Pavlovsk
Kamensk-Shakhtinskiy
Novoshakhtinsk
Novomoskovsk
Pavlograd
Artemovsk
Dneprodzerzhinsk
Nikopol
Novofedorovka
Volnovakha
Merefa
Krasnograd
Kremenchugskoye Vdkhr.
Kakhovskoye Vdkhr
Zolotonosha
Pereyaslav-Khmelnitskiy
Piryatin
Lubny
Priluki
Nezhin
Brovary
Vasilkov
Fastov
Belaya Tserkov
Uman
Smela
Shpola
Znamenka
Dolinskaya
Ingulets
Voznesensk
Pervomaysk
Berezovka
Troitskoye
Tiraspol
Bendery
Belgorod-Dnestrovskiy
Sarata
Izmail
Tulcea
Constanţa
Mangalia
Delta Dunării
Karkinitskiy Zaliv
Taganrogskiy Zaliv
Yevpatoriya
Dzhankoy
Perekop
Genichesk
Krasnoperekopsk
Novoalekseyevka
Berislav
Balta
Soroki
Beltsy
Orgeyev
Mogilev-Podolskiy
Yedintsy
Zhmerinka
Kamenets-Podolskiy
Khotin
Chernovtsy
Kolomyya
Ivano-Frankovsk
Stryy
Drogobych
Brody
Dubno
Lutsk
Rovno
Novograd-Volynskiy
Korosten
Berdichev
Shepetovka
Volochisk
Khmelnitskiy
Ternopol
Zamość
Nesterov
Jarosław
Uzhgorod
Satu Mare
Cluj-Napoca
Bistriţa
Tîrgu Mureş
Sighişoara
Braşov
Piteşti
Ploieşti
Buzău
Urziceni
Giurgiu
Giurgeni
Brăila
Galaţi
Bîrlad
Vaslui
Iaşi
Roman
Bacău
Focşani
Suceava
Botoşani
Bistrita
Siret
Prut
Bolgrad
Kagul
Craiova
Turnu-Severin
Tîrgu-Jiu
Petroşani
Hunedoara
Deva
Pleven
Mikhaylovgrad
Ruse
Veliko Tŭrnovo
Sliven
Yambol
Burgas
Varna
Dobrich
Razgrad
Šumen
Silistra
Dnestr
Yuzhnyy Bug
Dnepr
Psel
Oskol
Sev. Donets
Kuban
Krymsk
Apsheronsk
Neftegorsk
Pavlovskaya
Sosyka
Timashevsk

Tevstratovsky Kamyshin Nikolayevsky Aleksandrov Mergenevo

Mikhaylovka Frolovo Gay Bol'Uzen

Kupyansk Kantemirovka Don Ilovlya Slov

Lisichansk Chertkovo Dubovka Oz. Elton Oz. Aralsor

U Millerovo Ilovlya Volgograd Volzhsky Urda Inderbors

Stakhanov Lugansk Kamensk-Shakhtinsky Kalach-na-Donu Leninsk Verkh. Baskunchak

Komunarsk Shakhtinsky Tsimlyanskoye Vdkhr. Prikaspiyskaya Nizmennost

Borlovka Novoshakhtinsk Timlyansk Caspian Depression KA

Makeyevka Shakhty Sal Kotelnikovo Oz. Era Sarayc

ovka Novocherkassk Oz. Manych Gudilo Krasnyy Yar

anrog Rostov RF Astrakhan

skiy Zaliv Bataysk Kushchevskaya Yegorlyk Elista Utta

Yeysk Salsk Yashkul

Pavlovskaya Belaya Glina Divnoye

Sosyka Tikhoretsk Ipatovo Svetlograd Azgir Kuma

evsk Kropotkin Stavropol'skaya Budennovsk Kizlyarsky Zaliv

asnodar Armavir Stavropol Nogayskiye CASPIAN

ossiysk Apsheronsk Kuban Vozvyshennost Nevinnomyssk Zelenokumsk Step SEA

apse Neftegorsk Urup Cherkessk Georgievsk Kizlyar Shevch

Maykop K A V K A Z Pyatigorsk K. Lenina

Sochi Bzipi Kislovodsk Mozdok Grozny Khasavyurt

Elbrus 5633 Nalchik Makhachkala

Sukhumi Dykh Tau Vladikavkaz Kazbek Buynaksk

Ochamchire 5203 Tebulos Mta Izberbash

7137 Kutaisi Tskhinvali Telavi 4494 Salak Tsudakhar

Poti Semtredia G Gori Alazani Derbent

Batumi Borzhomi Tbilisi Samur Kuba

Tirebolu Trabzon Akhaltsikhe Rustavi K H R E B E T

Rize Chokhsu Zakatala Kura Sheki

sun Artvin Ardahan Leninakan Kirovakan Gyandzha Sumg

Shimushane 3348 3002 Baku

kanizesi Coruh Nehri Kars Oz. Sevan AZ Alyaty

Daybart Sarikamis Yerevan Stepanakert Mugansiaya Ravnina

liye Pasinler 4090 AR Salyany

incan Erzurum Kagizman 5165 AZ Safarabad

Tunceli Agri (Karakose) Abri Dagi Nakhichevan 8904 Lenkoran

Mazgirt Dogubayazit Khoy Namin

Palu Suphan Dagi Balmas Marand Kühhä-ye Sabalan Ardabil

Ergani Mus 4434 Van Golu Dasycheh-ye Tabriz 4811 IR

Batman Tatvanm Van Oramiyeh Kuh-e Sahand Khalkhal

Diyarbakir Dicle (Tigris) Bitlis Hakkari Orumiyeh 3710 Hasarud Bas

CITY PLANS

KEY TO PLANS
(pages 90 – 136)

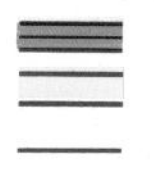

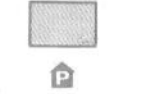

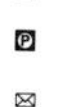

 Motorway

Through route

Railway

- - - o - - - Underground

 Shipping piers/lines

 Public buildings

 Wood

 Park

 Multi-storey car park

P Car park

i Information

Police

Post office

AA ● Automobile club

KEY TO PLANS
(pages 137 – 139)

Primary route

Main road

Other road

Railway with station

  Airport

Woodland, park

City Boundary

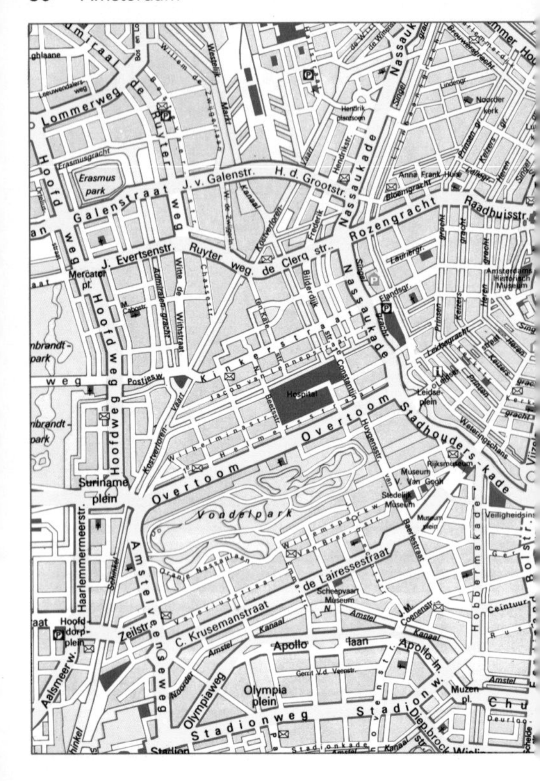
Lommerweg
Erasmus park
Erasmusgracht
Galenstraat
J. v. Galenstr.
H. d. Grootstr.
Nassaukade
Rozengracht
Raadhuisstr.
Anna Frank Huis
Noorder kerk
Bloemgracht
J. Evertsenstr.
Ruyter weg
de Clercq str.
Mercator pl.
Hoofdweg
Admiralen gracht
Witte de Withstraat
Chassestr.
Bilderdijk
Kinkerstraat
Hospital
Constantijn
Jacob van Lennepstraat
Overtoom
Leidse plein
Leidsestr.
Stadhouderskade
Wilhelminastraat
Hemonystraat
Amsterdams Historisch Museum
Rijksmuseum
Museum V. Van Gogh
Stedelijk Museum
Museum plein
Vondelpark
Suriname plein
Amstelveenseweg
de Lairessestraat
C. Krusemanstraat
Scheepvaart Museum
Apollo laan
Olympia plein
Olympiaweg
Stadionweg
Zeilstr.
Haarlemmermeerstr.
Hoofddorp plein
Aalsmeer w.
Hobbemakade
Baerlestraat
Huygensstr.
Weteringschans
Veiligheidsins
Ceintuur
Muzen pl.
Diep.brock str.
Willem de Zwijgerlaan
Westelijk Markt
Hendrik plantsoen
Hendrikstr.
Frederik
Kostverloren vaart
Singel
Prinsen gr.
Keizers gr.
Heren gr.
Lindengr.
Brouwersgracht
Lauriergr.
Elandsgr.
Leidsegracht
Postjesw.
Cabostr.
Vaart
Kanaal
Amstel
Noorder
Oranje Nassaulaan
Valeriusstraat
J. M. Coenenstr.
Apollo ln.
Stadionkade
Station
Gerrit v.d. Veenstr.
Leeuwendalersweg
Bos en Lommerweg
Willem de Zwijgerlaan

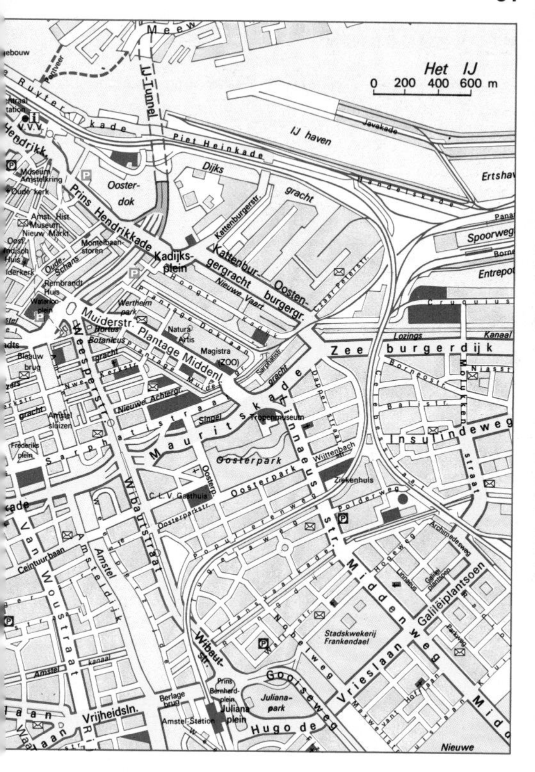

Het IJ
0 200 400 600 m

Het IJ
IJ haven
Javakade
Ertshav
Spoorweg
Entrepo
Panai
Borai

gebouw
e Ruyter kade
Ruyterkade
ahof
hof
VVV
Hendrikk
Oosterdok
Prins Hendrikkade
Amst. Hist.
Museum
Nieuwe Markt
Oude
Oost-
Rembrandt
Huis
Ourkerk
Monteibaan-
storen
Kadijks-plein
Kattenburgerstr.
Kattenburgergracht
Nieuwe Vaart
Kadijk
Katten-
burger
Oosten-
burgergracht
Oosten-
burgerg.
Wertheim
Mudersti
Blauwe
Natura
Artis
Botanicus
Magistra
ZOOL
Plantage Middenl
Zee b u r g e r d i j k
Nieuwe Achter
Stinper
Muderstr
Frankend.
plein
Mauritskade
Oosterpark
Wittenbsh
Oosterpark
Wibaut straat
Wittenbash
Ziekenhuis
Insulindeweg
Oosterspstraat
C.T.V. Gymnas
Oosterspstraat
kade
Amstel
Middenweg
Centuurbaan
Gallieleiplantsoen
Albert Cuyp straat
Wibaut
Wibaut straat
W o u s t r a a t
kanaal
Wibaut
Stadskwekerij
Frankendael
Gooiseweg
Amstel
Berlage
brug
Prins
Bernhard
Juliana-
plein
Juliana-
park
Vrieslaan
Vrijheidsln.
Amstel-Station
Hugo de
aan
Waa
Nieuwe
Midd

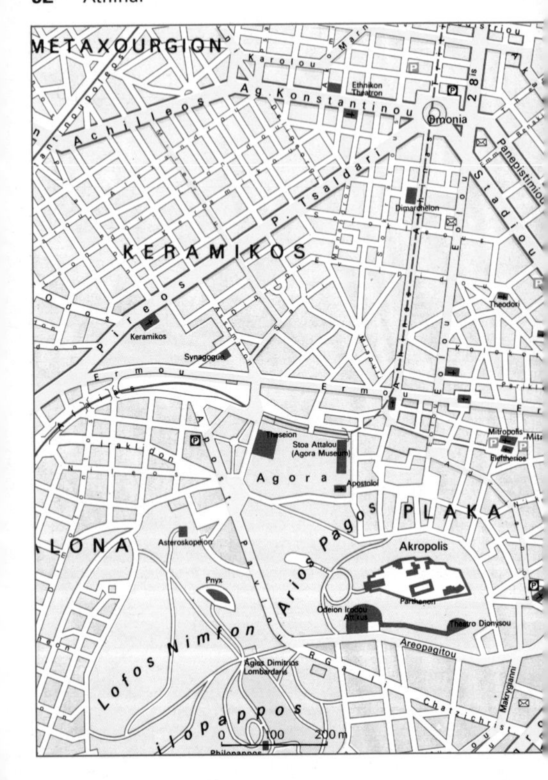
METAXOURGION
Karolou
Ag. Konstantinou
Ethnikon Theatron
Omonia
Achilleos
28is
P. Tsaldari
Panepistimiou
Stadiou
Dimarcheion
KERAMIKOS
Pireos
Keramikos
Synagogue
Ermou
Theodori
Theseion
Stoa Attalou (Agora Museum)
Mitropolis
Eleftherios
Agora
Apostoloi
PLAKA
Akropolis
Parthenon
Asteroskopeion
Pnyx
Arios Pagos
Odeion Irodou Attikus
Theatro Dionysou
Areopagitou
Lofos Nimfon
Agios Dimitrios Lombardaris
Makrygianni
ilopappos
0 100 200 m

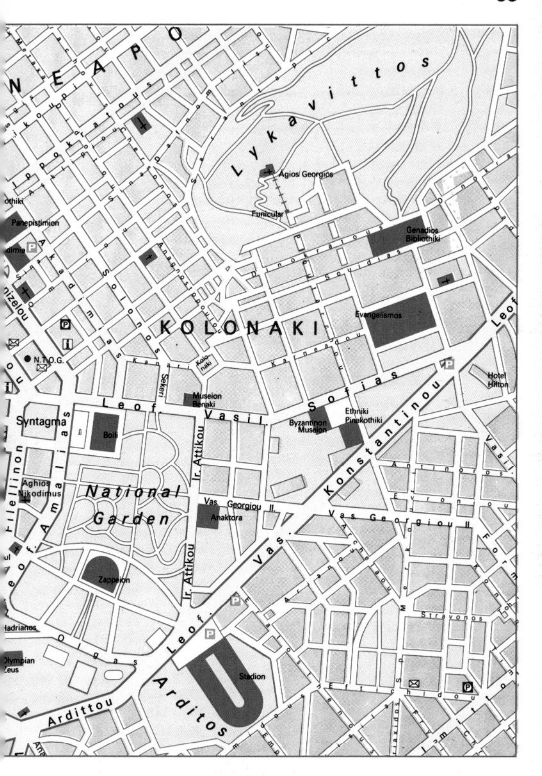

N E A P O

L y k a v i t t o s

Agios Georgios

Funicular

oniki
Panepistimion

ntína

Gennadios
Bibliothiki

N.P.O.G.

K O L O N A K I

Evangelismos

Leof

Hotel
Hilton

Syntagma

Leof

Vasil

Sofias

Museion
Benaki

Bou

Byzantinon
Museum

Etniki
Pinakothiki

lellinon

Ir. Attikou

Konstantinou

National
Garden

Vas. Georgiou II

Anaktora

Vas Georgiou II

Zappion

ladrianos

Silfonos

Olympian
Zeus

Leof

Olgas

Ir. Attikou

Vas.

Leof

Arditou

Arditos

Stadion

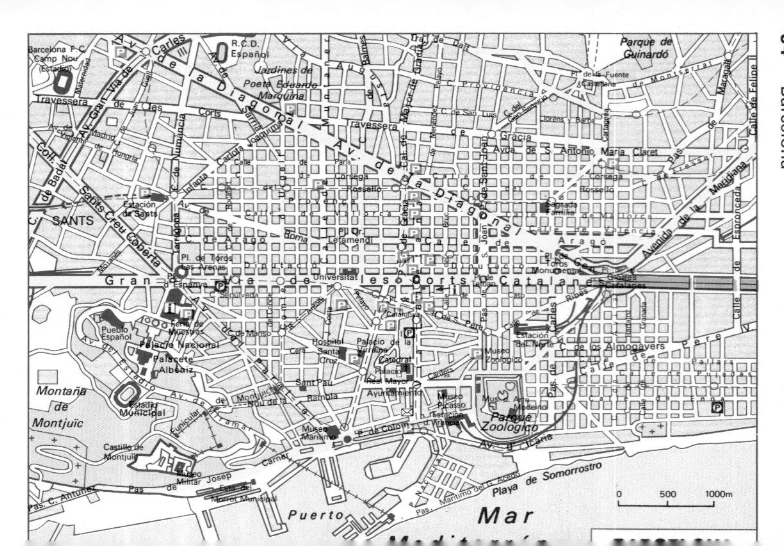
Barcelona F.C. Camp Nou (Estadio)
R.C.D. Español
Jardines de Poeta Eduardo Marquina
Parque de Guinardó
Av. de la Diagonal
Travessera de Corts
Travessera
Gràcia
Avda. de S. Antonio María Claret
SANTS
Estación de Sants
Sants Creu Coberta
Sagrada Familia
Calle de Mallorca
C. de Aragó
Pl. de Toros Las Arenas
Gran Via de les Corts Catalanes
Universitat
Pl. de Toros Monumental
Avenida de la Meridiana
Pueblo Español
Palacio Nacional
Palacete Albéniz
Estación del Norte
C. de los Almogavers
Museo Zoologico
Hospital Santa Cruz
Catedral
Palacio Real Mayor
Ayuntamiento
Museo Picasso
Estación Francia
Parque Zoologico
Montaña de Montjuïc
Estadio Municipal
Funicular
Castillo de Montjuïc
Museo Militar
Museo Marítimo
P. de Colom
Av. d'Icària
Playa de Somorrostro
Puerto
Mar
0
500
1000m

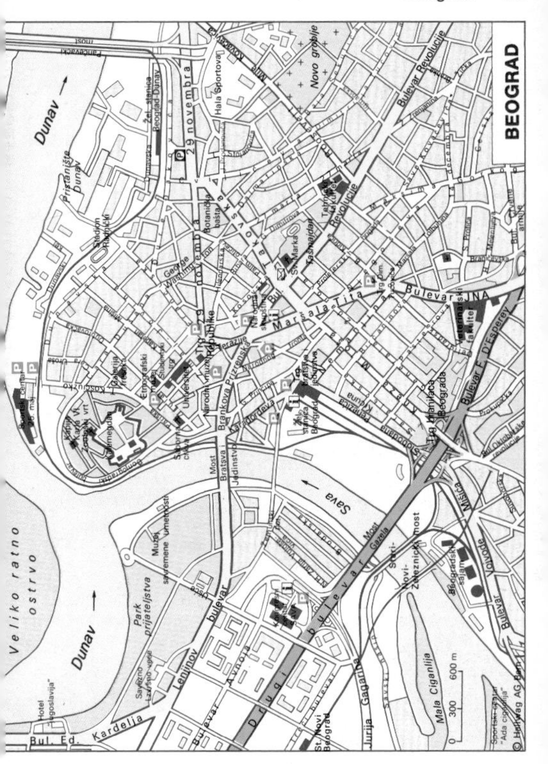
BEOGRAD
Dunav
Sava
Veliko ratno ostrvo
Pančevački most
Žel. stanica Beograd-Dunav
Pristanište Dunav
Stadion Radnički
Hala Sportova
Novo groblje
Botanička bašta
Tašmajdan
Tehnički fakultet
Bulevar Revolucije
Bulevar JNA
Veterinarski fakultet
Bulevar F. D'Esperey
Maršala Tita
Trg Republike
Univerzitet
Narodni muzej
Etnografski muzej
Galerija fresaka
Kalemegdan
Zoološki vrt
Sportski centar 25. maj
Saborna crkva
Most Bratstva i Jedinstva
Žel. stanica Beograd
Most Gazela
Muzej savremene umetnosti
Park prijateljstva
Lenjinov bulevar
Bulevar Avnoja
Drugi bulevar
Bul. Ed. Kardelja
Hotel „Jugoslavija"
Jurija Gagarina
Mala Ciganlija
Beogradski sajam
Bulevar Vojvode Mišića
St. Novi Beograd
Sportski centar „Ada ciganlija"
0 300 600 m
© Hallwag AG Bern

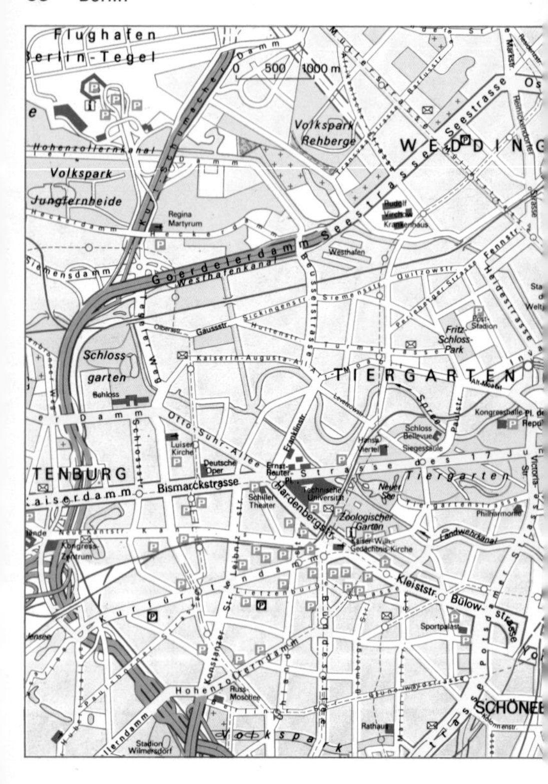
Flughafen
Berlin-Tegel
0 500 1000 m
Volkspark Rehberge
WEDDING
Hohenzollernkanal
Volkspark
Jungfernheide
Regina Martyrum
Rudolf Virchow Krankenhaus
Seestrasse
Goerdelerdamm
Westhafenkanal
Westhafen
Siemensdamm
Beusselstrasse
Fritz-Schloss-Park
Post-Stadion
Schloss-garten
Schloss
TIERGARTEN
Kaiserin-Augusta-Allee
Alt-Moabit
Kongresshalle
Schloss Bellevue
Siegessäule
Hansa-Viertel
Luisen Kirche
Deutsche Oper
Ernst-Reuter-Pl.
Strasse des 17. Juni
Otto-Suhr-Allee
Bismarckstrasse
Kaiserdamm
CHARLOTTENBURG
Schiller Theater
Technische Universität
Hardenbergstr.
Neuer See
Tiergartenstrasse
Philharmonie
Zoologischer Garten
Kaiser-Wilh.-Gedächtnis-Kirche
Landwehrkanal
Kongress-Zentrum
Kantstr.
Kurfürstendamm
Kleiststr.
Bülowstrasse
Sportpalast
Potsdamer Strasse
Konstanzer Str.
Hohenzollerndamm
Russ. Moschee
Bundesallee
Rathaus
SCHÖNEBERG
Volkspark
Stadion Wilmersdorf

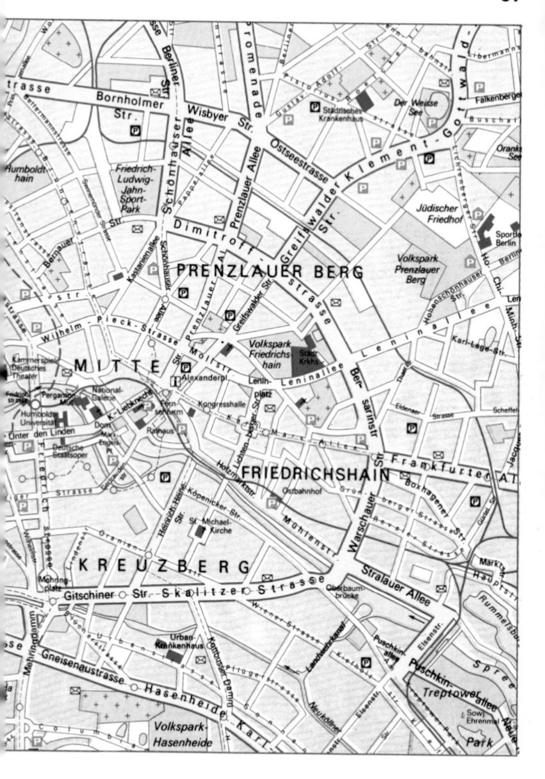
PRENZLAUER BERG
MITTE
FRIEDRICHSHAIN
KREUZBERG
Bornholmer Str.
Wisbyer Str.
Schönhauser Allee
Prenzlauer Allee
Ostseestrasse
Klement-Gottwald-
Greifswalder Str.
Dimitroff-Strasse
Wilhelm-Pieck-Strasse
Leninallee
Frankfurter Allee
Karl-Marx-Allee
Holzmarktstr.
Mühlenstr.
Warschauer Str.
Stralauer Allee
Skalitzer Strasse
Gitschiner Str.
Gneisenaustrasse
Hasenheide
Unter den Linden
Humboldthain
Friedrich-Ludwig-Jahn-Sport-Park
Jüdischer Friedhof
Volkspark Prenzlauer Berg
Volkspark Friedrichshain
Volkspark Hasenheide
Treptower Park
Der Weisse See
Städtisches Krankenhaus
Alexanderpl.
Ostbahnhof
Rathaus
Fernsehturm
Kongresshalle
Urban-Krankenhaus
Oberbaumbrücke
Puschkinallee
Mehringplatz
Mehringdamm
Kottbusser Damm
Landwehrkanal
Spree

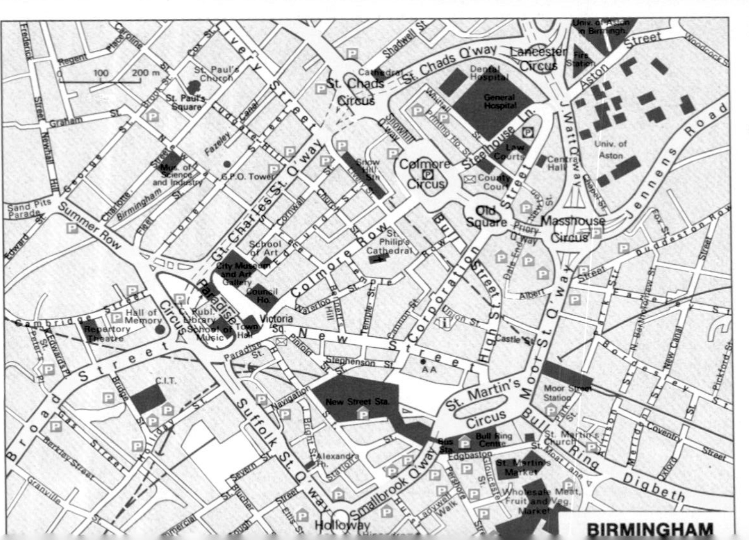
BIRMINGHAM
Frederick St.
Regent Pl.
Caroline St.
Cox St.
Livery Street
St. Paul's Church
St. Paul's Square
Brook St.
0 100 200 m
Graham St.
Newhall Hill
George St.
Sand Pits Parade
Edward St.
Summer Row
Charlotte St.
Birmingham
Fleet St.
Lionel St.
Newhall St.
Mus. of Science and Industry
Fazeley
Ludgate Hill
Canal
G.P.O. Tower
Gt. Charles St. Q'way
Cornwall St.
Church St.
Edmund St.
School of Art
City Museum and Art Gallery
Council Ho.
Paradise Circus
C. Publ. Library
School of Music
Town Hall
Victoria Sq.
Hall of Memory
Repertory Theatre
Cambridge Street
St. Peter's Pl.
Edwards Pl.
Broad Street
Gas Street
Berkley Street
Granville
Bridge St.
Holliday St.
C.I.T.
Suffolk St. Q'way
Severn St.
Blucher St.
Navigation St.
Paradise St.
Pinfold St.
Stephenson St.
New Street
New Street Sta.
Bright St.
Alexandra Th.
Station St.
Smallbrook Q'way
Holloway
Ladywell Walk
Pershore St.
Edgbaston St.
Gloucester St.
Bus Sta.
Bull Ring Centre
St. Martin's Market
Wholesale Meat, Fruit and Veg. Market
St. Martin's Circus
St. Martin's Church
Moat Lane
Bull Ring
Digbeth
Moor St. Q'way
Moor Street Station
Park St.
Coventry Street
Oxford St.
Bordesley St.
New Canal St.
N. Bartholomew St.
Pickford St.
Fox St.
Fazeley St.
Buddeston Row
Jennens Road
Univ. of Aston
Aston Street
Woodcock St.
Univ. of Aston in Birmingh.
Fire Station
Lancester Circus
St. Chads Q'way
Cathedral
St. Chads Circus
Shadwell St.
Dental Hospital
General Hospital
Whittall St.
Printing Ho. St.
Snowhill Q'way
Snow Hill Stn.
Steelhouse Ln.
Law Courts
Central Hall
County Court
J. Watt Q'way
Chapel St.
Colmore Circus
Old Square
Newton St.
Priory Q'way
Masshouse Circus
Dale End
Albert St.
Bull St.
St. Philip's Cathedral
Colmore Row
Temple Row
Temple St.
Waterloo St.
Bennett's Hill
Cannon St.
Corporation Street
Union St.
High St.
Castle St.
AA

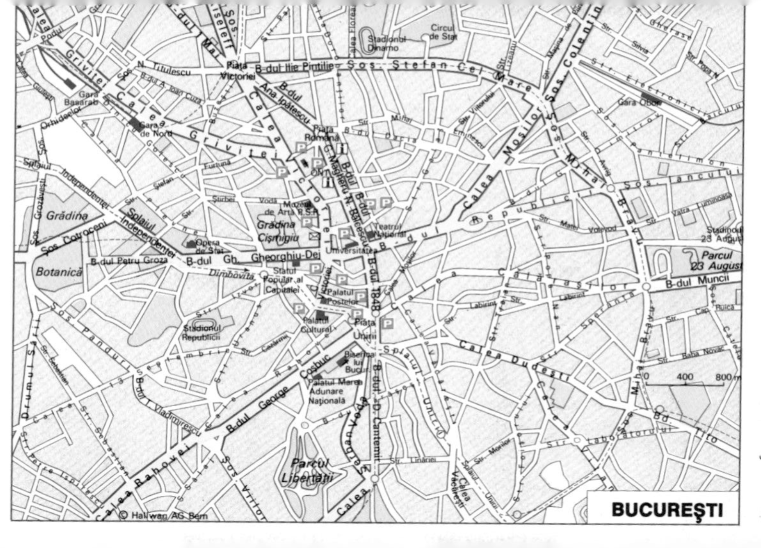
BUCUREȘTI
0
400
800 m
Parcul 23 August
Stadionul 23 August
B-dul Muncii
Calea Moșilor
B-dul 1848
B-dul N. Bălcescu
B-dul G. Magheru
Calea Victoriei
Grădina Cișmigiu
Gara de Nord
Grădina Botanică
Parcul Libertății
Stadionul Republicii
B-dul Gh. Gheorghiu-Dej
Calea Văcărești
B-dul D. Cantemir
Piața Unirii
Piața Romană
Piața Victoriei
B-dul Ana Ipătescu
B-dul Ilie Pintilie
Gara Obor
Gara Basarab
Circul de Stat
Stadionul Dinamo
Opera de Stat
Palatul Culturii
Palatul Postelor
Teatrul Național
Muzeul de Artă R.S.R.
Palatul Marea Adunare Națională
Universitatea
B-dul 1 Mai
Calea Griviței
Calea Dudești
Calea Rahovei
Str. Sebastian
Splaiul Independenței
B-dul Petru Groza
B-dul George Coșbuc
B-dul I. Vladimirescu
Șos. Ștefan cel Mare
Șos. Colentina
Șos. Mihai Bravu
B-dul Republicii
Calea Călărașilor
© Hallwag AG Bern

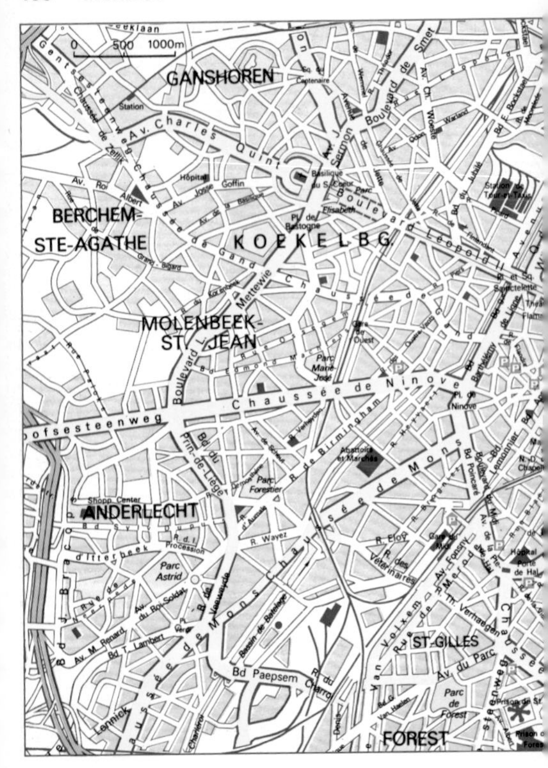
0 500 1000m
GANSHOREN
BERCHEM-
STE-AGATHE
KOEKELBG.
MOLENBEEK-
ST. JEAN
ANDERLECHT
ST-GILLES
FOREST
Av. Charles Quint
Boulevard Léopold II
Chaussée de Gand
Chaussée de Ninove
Chaussée de Mons
Boulevard de Smet de Naeyer
Basilique du S. Coeur
Parc Elisabeth
Pl. de Bastogne
Gare de Ouest
Parc Marie-José
Pl. de Ninove
Abattoirs et Marchés
Parc Forestier
Parc Astrid
Gare du Midi
Station de Tour-et-Taxis
Bd Paepsem
R. de Birmingham
Av. du Parc
Parc de Forest
Prison de St.
Station
Hôpital
Shopp. Center

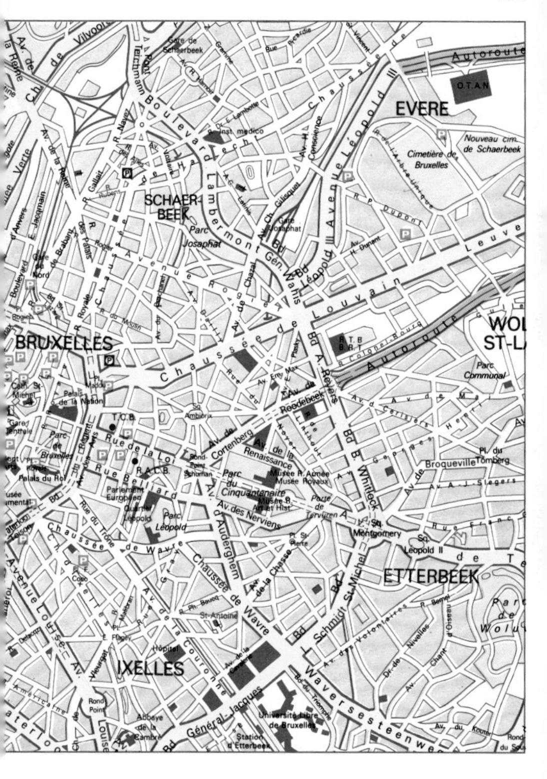
Autoroute
O.T.A.N.
EVERE
Gare de Schaerbeek
Nouveau cim. de Schaerbeek
Cimetière de Bruxelles
SCHAER-BEEK
Parc Josaphat
Gare Josaphat
Boulevard Lambermont
Chaussée de Haecht
Avenue Léopold III
Bd Léopold III
Bd Gén. Wahis
Gare du Nord
Chaussée de Louvain
Avenue Rogier
R. Royale
BRUXELLES
WOL
ST-L
Parc Communal
R.T.B. B.R.T.
Bd A. Reyers
Cath. St-Michel
Palais de la Nation
Gare Centrale
Parc de Bruxelles
Palais du Roi
T.C.B.
Rue de la Loi
R.A.C.B.
Rue Belliard
Parlement Européen
Quartier Léopold
Parc Léopold
Rond-Point Schuman
Parc du Cinquantenaire
Musée R. Armée
Musées Royaux
Musée R. Art et Hist.
Porte de Tervuren
Av. de Cortenberg
Av. de la Renaissance
Av. des Nerviens
Av. d'Auderghem
Sq. Ambiorix
Sq. Montgomery
Sq. Léopold II
Bd B. Whitlock
Av. de Broqueville
Pl. du Tomberg
ETTERBEEK
Parc de Woluwe
Bd St-Michel
Chaussée de Wavre
Chaussée de Wavre
Rue du Trône
Pl. F. Cocq
Avenue Louise
IXELLES
Hôpital
St-Antoine
Bd Général Jacques
Université Libre de Bruxelles
Station d'Etterbeek
Abbaye de la Cambre
Rond Point
Waversesteenweg
Rond Point du Souverain

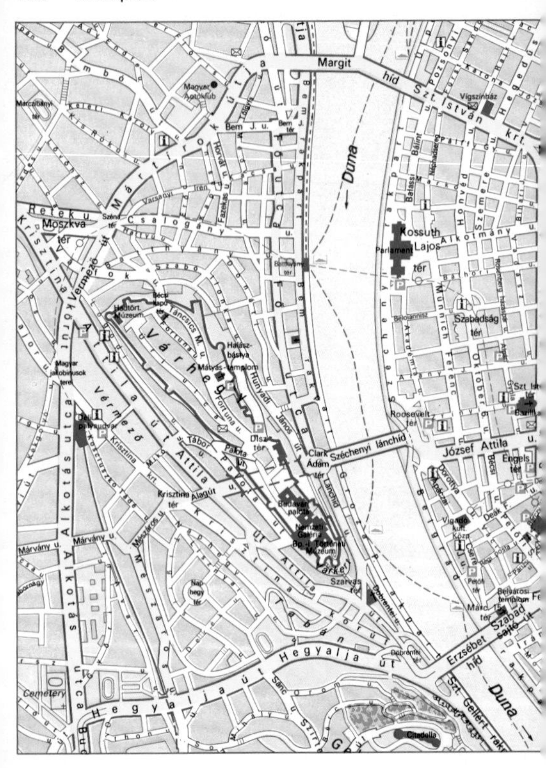
Margit
híd
Szt. István krt.
Duna
Magyar Autóklub
Bem J. u.
Bem tér
Március 15. tér
Moszkva tér
Széna tér
Csalogány u.
Batthyány tér
Kossuth Lajos tér
Parlament
Alkotmány u.
Bécsi kapu tér
Hadtört. Múzeum
Táncsics M. u.
Várhegy
Halász-bástya
Mátyás-templom
Fortuna u.
Hunyadi János út
Szabadság tér
Roosevelt tér
Széchenyi lánchíd
Clark Ádám tér
Lánchíd
József Attila u.
Dísz tér
Déli pályaudvar
Magyar jakobinusok tere
Krisztina krt.
Attila út
Vérmező út
Alagút
Krisztina tér
Budavári palota
Nemzeti Galéria
Bp.-i Történeti Múzeum
Várkert
Szarvas tér
Döbrentei tér
Erzsébet híd
Szt. Gellért rakpart
Hegyalja út
Alkotás utca
Márvány u.
Cemetery
Citadella
Vigadó
Belvárosi templom
Bazilika
Engels tér
Vígszínház

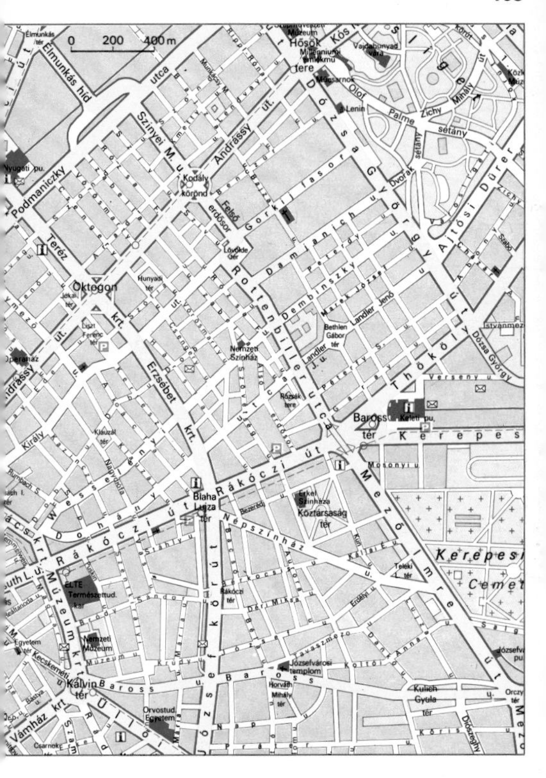

0   200   400 m

Elmunkás tér

Hősök tere

Nyugati pu.

Podmaniczky

Szinei M utca

Andrássy út

Kodály körönd

Teréz krt

Oktogon

Hunyadi tér

Rottenbiller

Ersébet krt

Dembinszky

Bethlen Gábor tér

Nemzeti Színház

Landler

Baross tér Keleti pu.

Kőzsti tér

Király

Kérepes

Mosonyi u.

Izabella

Blaha Lujza tér

Rákóczi út

Népszínház u.

Erkel Színház

Köztársaság tér

Mező

Kérepesi

Temető

ELTE Természettud.

Nemzeti Múzeum

Baross

Kálvin tér

József krt

Üllői út

Józsefvárosi templom

Horváth Mihály tér

Kulich Gyula tér

Orczy

Orvostud. Egyetem

Vámház

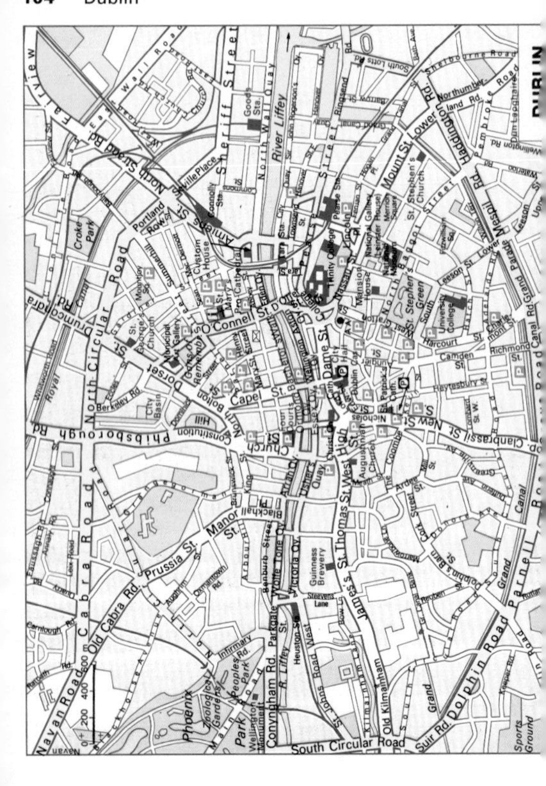
DUBLIN
River Liffey
North Wall Quay
Sheriff Street
Goods Sta.
Connolly Sta.
Amiens St.
Custom House
Portland Row
North Strand Rd.
Croke Park
North Circular Road
Drumcondra Rd.
Royal Canal
Berkeley Rd.
City Basin
Phibsborough Rd.
Constitution Hill
Cabra Road
Old Cabra Rd.
Navan Road
Prussia St.
Manor St.
Blackhall Pl.
Arbour Hill
Benburb Street
Wolfe Tone Qy.
Victoria Qy.
Guinness Brewery
Steevens Lane
Heuston Sta.
Parkgate St.
Conyngham Rd.
R. Liffey
St. Johns Road West
Infirmary Rd.
Peoples Park
Zoological Gardens
Phoenix Park
Wellington Monument
South Circular Road
Old Kilmainham
James's St.
St. Thomas St. West
High St.
Augustinian Church
The Coombe
Christ Ch.
Usher's Quay
Four Courts
Church St.
Capel St.
Dame St.
City Hall
Dublin Cas.
St. Patrick's Cath.
New St. S.
Clanbrassil St.
Harcourt St.
Camden St.
Richmond St.
Charlemont St.
Grand Canal
Dolphin Road
Suir Rd.
Parnell Rd.
Sports Ground
St. Stephen's Green
University College
Leeson St. Lower
Grand Parade
Fitzwilliam Sq.
National Museum
National Gallery
Leinster House
Merrion Square
Mansion House
Trinity College
Nassau St.
Pearse St.
Lincoln Pl.
Westland Row
St. Stephen's Church
Mount St. Lower
Haddington Rd.
Northumberland Rd.
Pembroke Road
Shelbourne Road
Ringsend Rd.
Grand Canal Quay
South Lotts Rd.
O'Connell St.
St. Mary's Pro Cathedral
St. George's Church
Mountjoy Sq.
Municipal Art Gallery
Garden of Remembrance
Dorset St.
Henry St.
Mary St.
Bolton St.
Wellington Quay
Aston Quay
College Green
Grafton St.
0 100 200 300 400 500

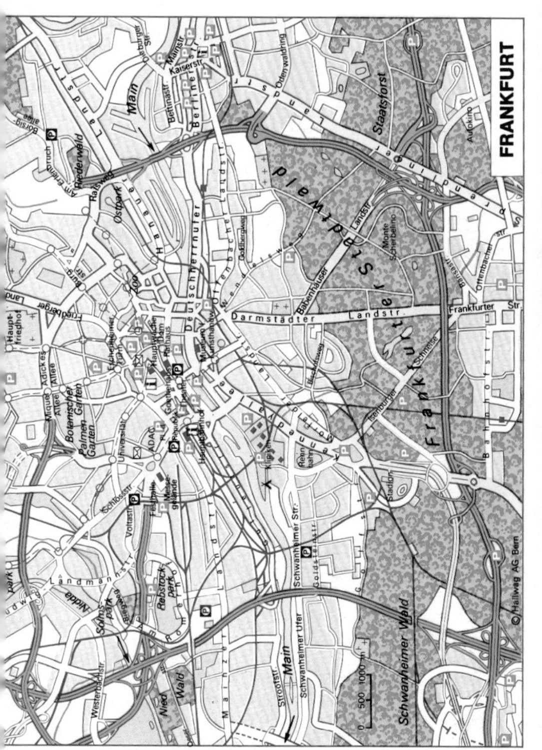
FRANKFURT
Frankfurter Stadtwald
Schwanheimer Wald
Staatsforst
Main
Ostpark
Zoo
Botanischer Garten
Palmen Garten
Rebstock park
Solms-park
Nidda
Nied
Darmstädter Landstr.
Babenhäuser Landstr.
Mainzer Landstr.
Deutschherrnufer
Schwanheimer Ufer
Schwanheimer Str.
Frankfurter Str.
Offenbacher Landstr.
Hanauer Landstr.
Friedberger Landstr.
Hauptbahnhof
Hauptwache
Dom
Römer
Messegelände
Festhalle
Universität
Stadion
Klinikum
Autokino
Monte Scherbelino
Hauptfriedhof
Riederwald
Kaiserstr.
Berliner Str.
Mainstr.
Bettinastr.
Goldsteinstr.
Westerbachstr.
Schlossstr.
Voltastr.
Isenburger Schneise
Bahnhofstr.
0 500 1000 m
©Hallwag AG Bern

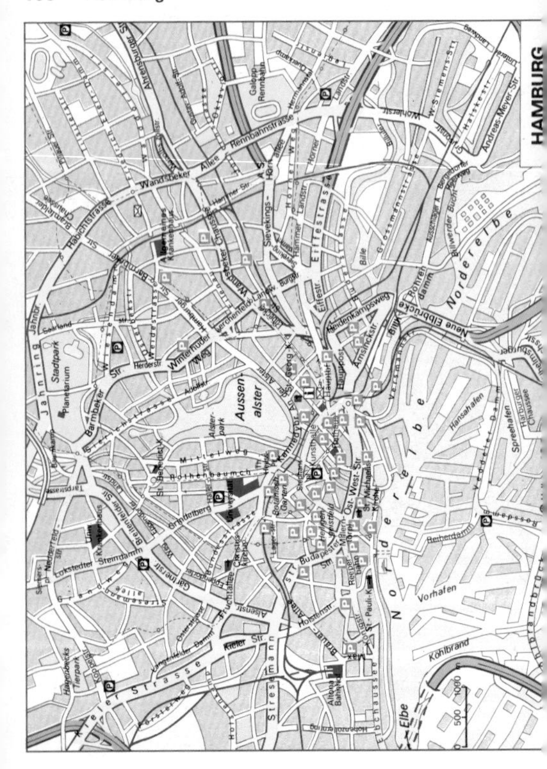
HAMBURG
Aussen-
alster
Stadtpark
Planetarium
Norderelbe
Elbe
Vorhafen
Köhlbrand
Hansahafen
Spreehafen
Reiherdamm
Hauptbf.
Kunsthalle
Universität
Botanischer Garten
Altona Bahnhof
Hagenbecks Tierpark
Galopp-Rennbahn
Rennbahnstrasse
Wandsbeker Allee
Wandsbeker Chaussee
Habichtstrasse
Barmbeker Str.
Jahnring
Winterhuder Weg
Mittelweg
Rothenbaumch.
Grindelberg
Fruchtallee
Kieler Strasse
Stresemann Str.
Holstenstr.
Budapester Str.
Ost-West-Str.
St. Michaelis Kirche
Eiffestrasse
Heidenkampsweg
Amsinckstr.
Neue Elbbrücke
Rohrendamm
Veddeler Damm
Harburger Chaussee
Elbchaussee
Neue Elbbrücke
Sievekingsallee
Hammer Str.
Allgemeines Krankenhaus
Herderstr.
Saarland
Lokstedter Steindamm
Max-Brauer-Allee
Bille
Grossmannstrasse
500
1000 m

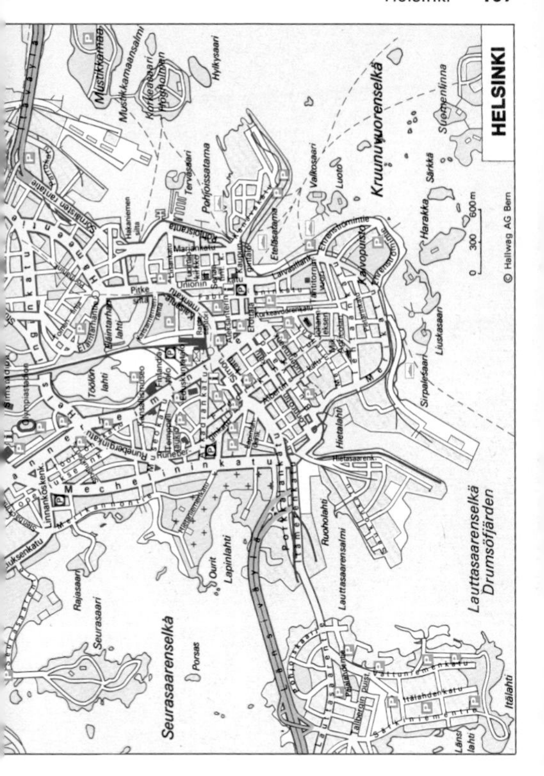
HELSINKI
© Hallwag AG Bern
0 300 600 m
Mustikkamaa
Mustikkamaansalmi
Korkeasaari
Högholmen
Hylkysaari
Tervasaari
Pohjoissatama
Eteläsatama
Valkosaari
Luoto
Kruunuvuorenselkä
Suomenlinna
Särkkä
Harakka
Kaivopuisto
Liuskasaari
Sirpalesaari
Hietalahti
Ruoholahti
Lauttasaarensalmi
Lauttasaarenselkä
Drumsöfjärden
Lapinlahti
Seurasaarenselkä
Seurasaari
Rajasaari
Porsas
Töölönlahti
Eläintarhanlahti
Itälahti
Länsilahti

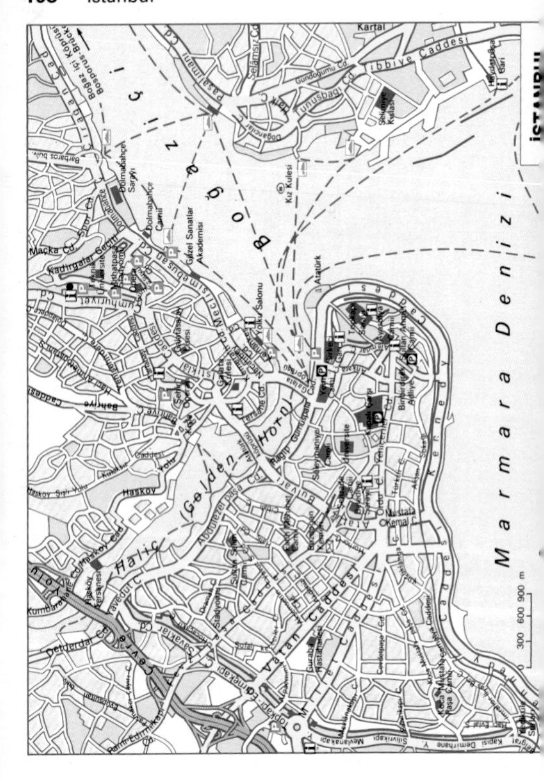
Marmara Denizi
Haliç (Golden Horn)
Boğaziçi
Kartal
Dolmabahçe Sarayı
Dolmabahçe Camii
Güzel Sanatlar Akademisi
Kız Kulesi
Selimiye Kışlası
Haydarpaşa Gari
Atatürk
Topkapı Sarayı
Sultan Ahmet Camii
Kapalı Çarşı
Üniversite
Süleymaniye Camii
Galata Kulesi
Haskoy
Vatan Caddesi
Millet Caddesi
Kennedy Caddesi
Çevre Yolu
Boğaz İçi Köprüsü
Bosporus Bridge
Mustafa Kemal C.
Fatih Camii
Sultan Selim Camii
Guraba Hastahanesi
Stadyomu
Maçka Cd.
Cumhuriyet Cd.
Kadirgalar Geçiti
Teknik Üniversite
Mithatpaşa Stadyomu
Opera
Barbaros bulv.
Yunusbagi Cd.
Tibbiye Caddesi
Yeni Camii
Sirkeci Gari
Ayasofya
Ragıp Gümüşpala Cd.
Tersane Cd.
Halıcıoğlu
Kumbarahane Cd.
Hasköy Cd.
Abdülezel Paşa Cd.
Topkapı-Edirnekapı
Mevlanakapı
Silivrikapı
Koca Mustafa Paşa Camii
300 600 900 m

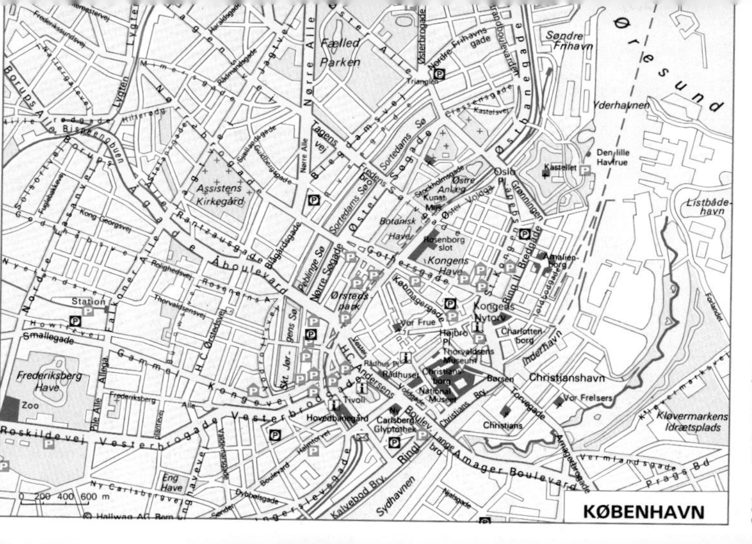
KØBENHAVN
Øresund
Søndre Frihavn
Yderhavnen
Den lille Havfrue
Kastellet
Listbådehavn
Forlandet
Kløvermarkens Idrætsplads
Christianshavn
Inderhavn
Amalienborg
Bredgade
Kongens Nytorv
Charlottenborg
Børsen
Christiansborg
Thorvaldsens Museum
National Museet
Rådhuset
Rådhus Pl.
Vor Frue
Vor Frelsers
Højbro Pl.
Rosenborg slot
Kongens Have
Botanisk Have
Østre Anlæg
Kunst Mus.
Oslo Pl.
Grønningen
Østerbrogade
Nordre Frihavnsgade
Trianglen
Fælled Parken
Tagens vej
Nørre Alle
Sortedams Sø
Peblinge Sø
Nørre Søgade
Sankt Jørgens Sø
Ørsteds park
Købmagergade
Gothersgade
Fredens bro
Blågårdsgade
H.C. Andersens Boulevard
Tivoli
Ny Carlsberg Glyptothek
Hovedbanegård
Vesterbrogade
Torvegade
Amagerbrogade
Amager Boulevard
Langebro
Christians Bry.
Sydhavnen
Kalvebod Bry.
Vermlandsgade
Prags Bd
Assistens Kirkegård
Åboulevard
Ranzausgade
Rosenørns Allé
H.C. Ørstedsvej
Thorvaldsensvej
Gammel Kongevej
Frederiksberg Have
Zoo
Roskildevej
Falkoner Alle
Smallegade
Station
Pile Alle
Allegade
Fredensborg Alle
Eng Have
Dybbølsgade
Halmtorvet
Borups Alle
Bispeengbuen
Lygten
Jagtvej
Kong Georgsvej
Nordre Fasanvej
0 200 400 600 m
© Hallwag AG, Bern

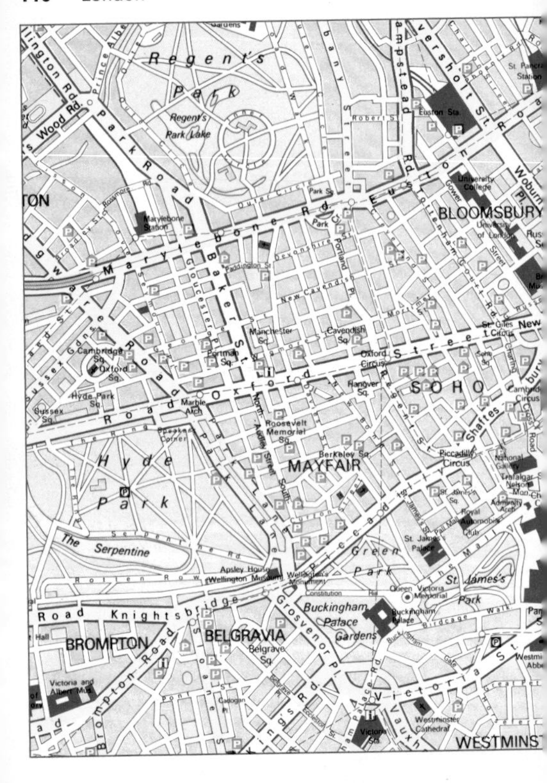
Regent's Park
Regent's Park Lake
Wood Rd.
Park Road
Outer Circle
Park Sq.
Robert St.
Euston Sta.
University College
BLOOMSBURY
University of London
Marylebone Station
Marylebone Rd.
Euston Rd.
Park Cr.
Devonshire Pl.
Portland Pl.
Paddington St.
New Cavendish St.
Mortimer St.
Gloucester Pl.
Baker St.
Manchester Sq.
Cavendish Sq.
Portman Sq.
Oxford Circus
Oxford Street
St. Giles Circus
New
Soho Sq.
Cambridge Sq.
Oxford Sq.
Hyde Park Sq.
Sussex Sq.
Marble Arch
Hanover Sq.
SOHO
Cambridge Circus
Shaftesbury Ave.
Regent St.
Roosevelt Memorial Sq.
Berkeley Sq.
MAYFAIR
Speakers Corner
North Audley Street
South Audley Street
Park Lane
Piccadilly
Piccadilly Circus
National Gallery
Trafalgar Sq.
Nelson Mon.
St. James's Sq.
Admiralty Arch
Royal Automobile Club
Pall Mall
St. James's Palace
The Mall
Hyde Park
The Serpentine
Serpentine Rd.
Rotten Row
Apsley House (Wellington Museum)
Wellington's Monument
Green Park
Constitution Hill
Queen Victoria Memorial
St. James's Park
Buckingham Palace
Buckingham Palace Gardens
Birdcage Walk
Knightsbridge
Grosvenor Pl.
BROMPTON
BELGRAVIA
Belgrave Sq.
Brompton Road
Victoria and Albert Mus.
Victoria St.
Victoria Sta.
Westminster Cathedral
WESTMINSTER
Vauxhall Bridge Rd.
Buckingham Palace Rd.
Cadogan

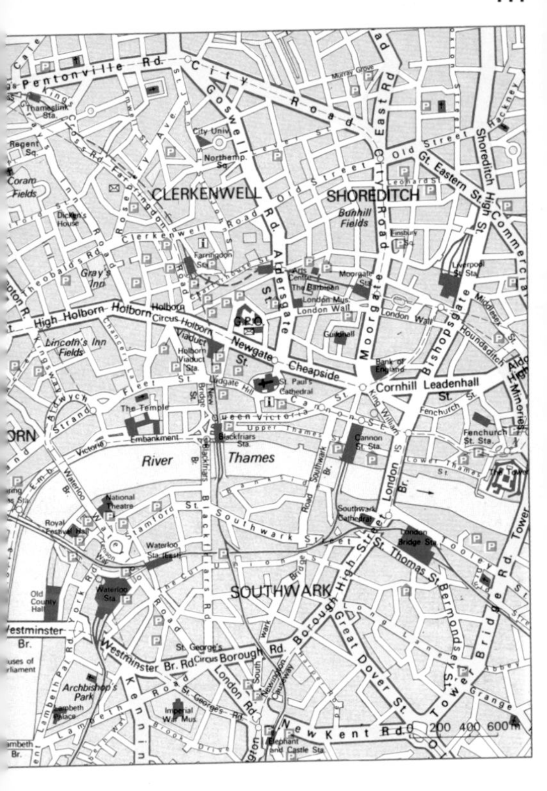
Pentonville Rd.
City Road
Thameslink Sta.
King's Cross Rd.
Regent Sq.
Coram Fields
Farringdon Rd.
City Univ
Northamp. Sq.
Goswell Rd.
Murray Grove
East Rd
Old Street
Gt. Eastern St.
Shoreditch High St.
Hackney
Commercial
Leonard St.
CLERKENWELL
SHOREDITCH
Bunhill Fields
City Road
Dickens House
Clerkenwell Road
Finsbury Sq.
Farringdon Sta.
Aldersgate St.
Arts Centre
The Barbican
Moorgate Sta.
Liverpool St. Sta.
Theobalds Rd
Gray's Inn
London Mus.
London Wall
Moorgate
Bishopsgate
Middlesex
Houndsditch
High Holborn
Holborn
Holborn Circus
Holborn Viaduct
G.P.O.
Guildhall
Lincoln's Inn Fields
Chancery La.
Newgate St.
Holborn Viaduct Sta.
Cheapside
Bank of England
Fleet St.
Ludgate Hill
St. Paul's Cathedral
Cornhill
Leadenhall St.
Aldwych
The Temple
Strand
Cannon St.
King William St.
Fenchurch St.
Minories
Queen Victoria St.
Upper Thames St.
Fenchurch St. Sta.
Embankment
Blackfriars Sta.
Cannon St. Sta.
Victoria
River Thames
Blackfriars Br.
Southwark Br.
London Br.
Lower Thames St.
The Tower
Waterloo Br.
Bankside
National Theatre
Royal Festival Hall
Stamford St.
Southwark Street
Southwark Cathedral
London Bridge Sta.
Tooley St.
Tower
Waterloo Sta. (East)
The Cut
Blackfriars Rd.
St. Thomas St.
Old County Hall
Waterloo Sta.
SOUTHWARK
Borough High St.
Bermondsey St.
Bridge Rd.
Westminster Br.
Great Dover St.
Long Lane
Houses of Parliament
St. George's Circus
Borough Rd.
Westminster Br. Rd.
Kennington
London Rd.
Newington Causeway
Tower Bridge Rd.
Abbey
Archbishop's Park
St. George's Rd.
Grange
Lambeth Palace
Imperial War Mus.
New Kent Rd.
0 200 400 600m
Lambeth Br.
Elephant and Castle Sta.
Brook Drive

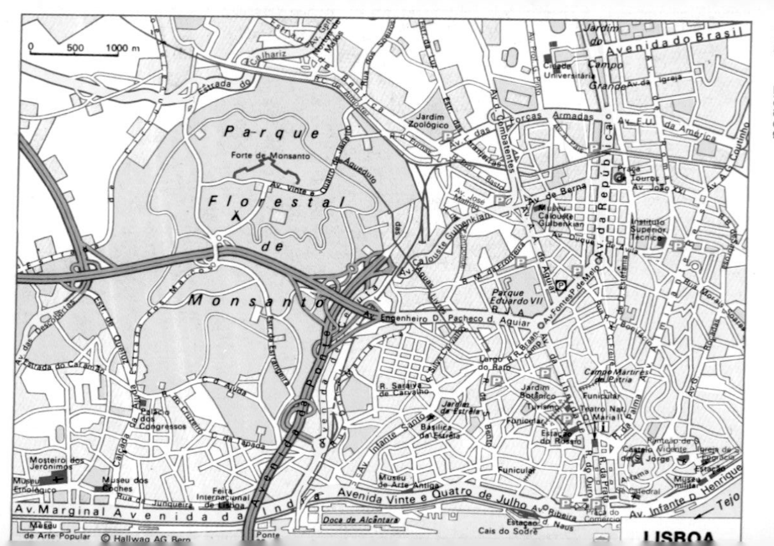
LISBOA
Tejo
Parque Florestal de Monsanto
Forte de Monsanto
Jardim Zoológico
Parque Eduardo VII
Museu Calouste Gulbenkian
Cidade Universitária
Campo Grande
Jardim do Campo Grande
Avenida do Brasil
Av. da República
Av. das Forças Armadas
Av. Prof. G. Pinto
Av. d. Combatentes
Av. de Berna
Av. A. A. de Aguiar
Av. Fontes P. de Melo
Av. da Liberdade
Instituto Superior Técnico
Praça de Touros
Campo Mártires da Pátria
Castelo de S. Jorge
Sé Catedral
Teatro Nal. D. Maria II
Estação do Rossio
R. do Ouro
R. da Prata
Praça do Comércio
Av. Infante D. Henrique
Av. Ribeira d. Naus
Estação
Cais do Sodré
Funicular
Jardim Botânico
Jardim da Estrela
Basílica da Estrela
Largo do Rato
R. Saraiva de Carvalho
Museu de Arte Antiga
Av. Infante Santo
Avenida Vinte e Quatro de Julho
Doca de Alcântara
Av. Engenheiro D. Pacheco
Estr. da Luz
Estr. da Estrangeira
Estr. de Queluz
Estrada do Caramão
Calçada da Ajuda
Palácio dos Congressos
Feira Internacional de Lisboa
Museu dos Coches
Rua da Junqueira
Mosteiro dos Jerónimos
Museu Etnológico
Museu de Arte Popular
Av. Marginal
Avenida da Índia
Avenida da Ponte
Ponte
0 500 1000 m
© Hallwag AG Bern

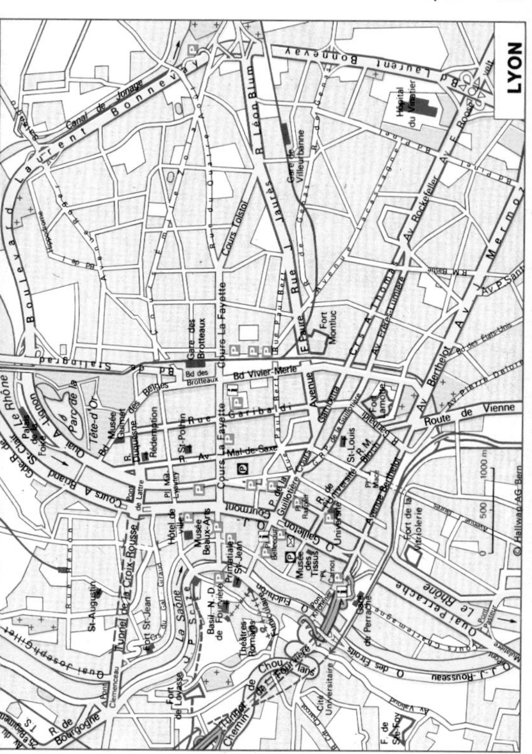
LYON
Bd Laurent Bonnevay
Canal de Jonage
Boulevard Laurent Bonnevay
Hôpital du Vinatier
Av. F. Roosevelt
Gare de Villeurbanne
R. Léon Blum
Rue J. Jaurès
Cours Tolstoï
Cours La Fayette
Gare des Brotteaux
Bd des Brotteaux
Bd Vivier-Merle
Fort Montluc
Av. Rockefeller
Av. J. Mermoz
Crs A. Thomas
Av. Frères-Lumière
Av. Berthelot
Route de Vienne
Bd de Stalingrad
Le Rhône
Palais de la Foire
Parc de la Tête-d'Or
Musée Guimet
Rue Garibaldi
Rédemption
St-Pothin
Av. Mal-de-Saxe
Fort Lamothe
St-Louis
Avenue Gambetta
Cours A. Briand
Pont de Lattre
Pl. Mal Lyautey
Hôtel de ville
Musée Beaux-Arts
Cours de la Liberté
Pl. Bellecour
Musée des Tissus
Pl. Carnot
Université
Avenue Berthelot
Fort de la Vitriolerie
Quai Perrache
Gare de Perrache
Pont Kitchener
Primatiale St-Jean
Basil. N.-D. de Fourvière
Théâtres Romains
Funiculaires
La Saône
Tunnel de la Croix-Rousse
St-Augustin
Fort St-Jean
Quai Joseph Gillet
Pont Clemenceau
Fort de Loyasse
Tunnel de Fourvière
Cité Universitaire
F. de Ste-Foy
R. de Bourgogne
Quai J.-J. Rousseau
Pont Pasteur
Hallwag AG Bern
0 500 1000 m

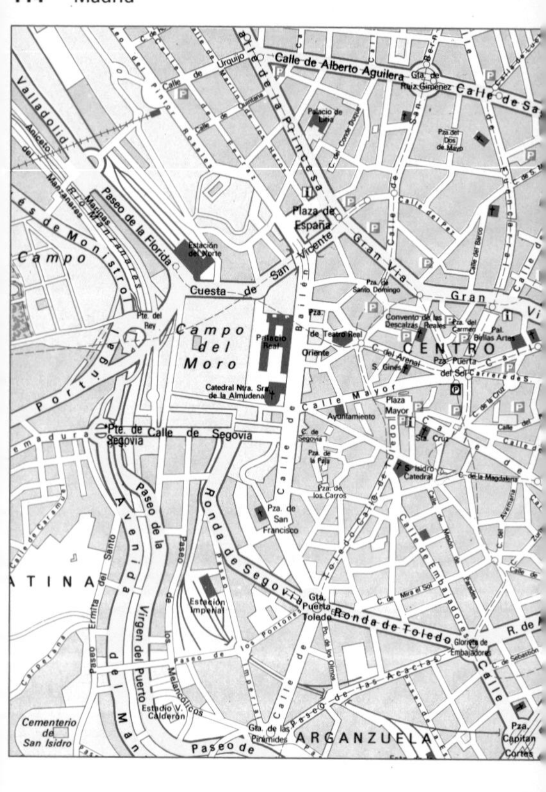
Calle de Alberto Aguilera
Gta. de Ruiz Giménez
Calle de Urquijo
Palacio de Liria
Pza. del Dos de Mayo
Paseo de la Florida
Estación del Norte
Plaza de España
Cuesta de San Vicente
Gran Vía
Pza. de Santo Domingo
Convento de las Descalzas Reales
Pza. del Carmen
Pal. Bellas Artes
CENTRO
Campo del Moro
Palacio Real
Pza. de Oriente
Teatro Real
Calle del Arenal
S. Ginés
Pza. Puerta del Sol
Catedral Ntra. Sra. de la Almudena
Calle Mayor
Plaza Mayor
Ayuntamiento
Sta. Cruz
Pte. del Rey
Pte. de Segovia
Calle de Segovia
Calle de Bailén
Pza. de la Paja
Pza. de los Carros
S. Isidro Catedral
C. de la Magdalena
Pza. de San Francisco
Ronda de Segovia
Gta. Puerta Toledo
Ronda de Toledo
Glorieta de Embajadores
Calle de Toledo
Calle de Embajadores
C. de Mira el Sol
Estación Imperial
Paseo de los Pontones
Paseo de las Acacias
Paseo de los Melancólicos
Estadio V. Calderón
Gta. de las Pirámides
ARGANZUELA
Pza. Capitán Cortés
Cementerio de San Isidro
Virgen del Puerto
Paseo de la Virgen del Puerto
Campo Monistrol
Valladolid
Portugal
Ermita del Santo

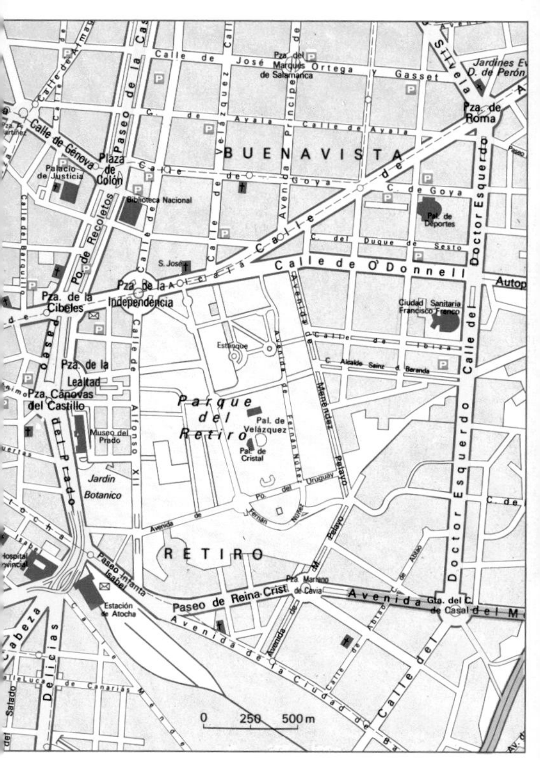
BUENAVISTA
RETIRO
Parque del Retiro
Calle de José Ortega y Gasset
Pza. del Marqués de Salamanca
Calle de Ayala
Calle de Goya
C. de Goya
Calle de Alcalá
Calle de O'Donnell
Calle del Duque de Sesto
Calle de Génova
Plaza de Colón
Paseo de la Castellana
Palacio de Justicia
Biblioteca Nacional
Po. de Recoletos
S. José
Pza. de la Independencia
Pza. de la Cibeles
Pza. de la Lealtad
Pza. Cánovas del Castillo
Museo del Prado
Paseo del Prado
Jardín Botanico
Calle de Alfonso XII
Calle de Velázquez
Avenida Príncipe de Vergara
Calle de Serrano
Pza. de Roma
Jardines Ev. D. de Perón
Pal. de Deportes
Calle del Doctor Esquerdo
Ciudad Sanitaria Francisco Franco
Calle de Ibiza
C. Alcalde Sainz de Baranda
Avenida de Menéndez Pelayo
Estanque
Pal. de Velázquez
Pal. de Cristal
Avenida de Fernán Núñez
Po. del Uruguay
Avenida de Menéndez Pelayo
Paseo de Reina Crist.
Pza. Mariano de Cavia
Avenida del Mediterráneo
Gta. del C. de Casal
Estación de Atocha
Paseo Infanta Isabel
Avenida de la Ciudad de Barcelona
Calle del Doctor Esquerdo
Calle de Abtao
Delicias
Autop
0 250 500 m

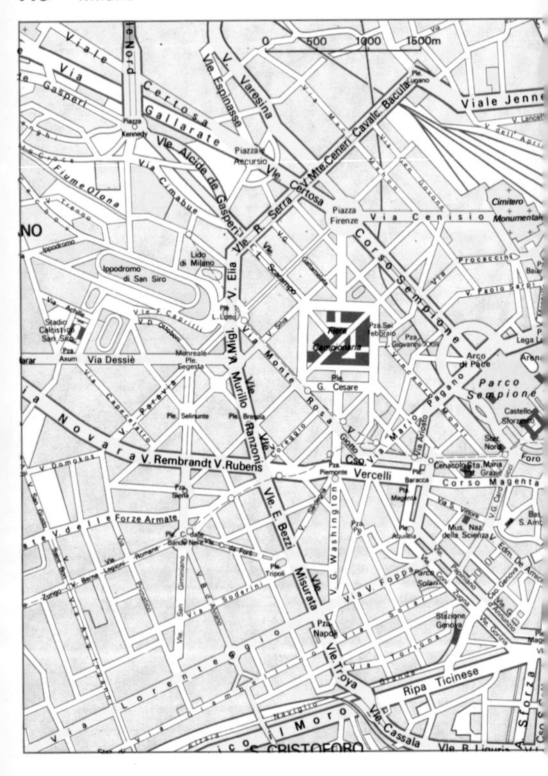
0 500 1000 1500m
Viale
Via Gasperi
Certosa
Gallarate
Piazza Kennedy
Vle. Alcide de Gasperi
Via Cimabue
Fiume Olona
Vle. Espinasse
V. Varesina
Piazzale Accursio
Vle. Certosa
C.so V. Mte.Ceneri Cavalc. Bacula
Ple. Lugano
Viale Jenner
Via Gen. Govone
Cimitero Monumentale
Piazza Firenze
Via Cenisio
Corso Sempione
Ippodromo
Ippodromo di San Siro
Lido di Milano
V. Elia
Vle. R. Serra
Vle. L. Scarampo
Ple. L.Lotto
Via Achille
Stadio Calcistico San Siro
Pza. Axum
Via Dessiè
Monreale
Ple. Segesta
V. Migl.
Via Monte Rosa
V. Silva
Fiera Campionaria
Pza.Sei Febbraio
Pza. Giovanni XXIII
Via Vincenzo Monti
Arco di Pace
Parco Sempione
Castello Sforzesco
Arena
Via Paolo Sarpi
Procaccini
Ple. G. Cesare
Vle. Murillo
Ple. Selinunte
Ple. Brescia
Via Novara
V. Rembrandt
V.Rubens
Vle. Ranzoni
Via Pagano
Via Ariosto
Via Mario
Staz. Nord
Foro
Cso. Vercelli
Pza. Piemonte
Ple. Baracca
Cenacolo
Sta. Maria Grazie
Corso Magenta
Pza. Magenta
Via S. Vittore
Mus. Naz. della Scienza
Bas. S. Amb
Vle. E. Bezzi
V. G. Washington
Pza. Siena
V. delle Forze Armate
Ple. C. dalle Bande Nere
Vle. Legioni Romane
Ple. Tripoli
Vle. Misurata
Pza. Po
Ple. Aquileia
Via V. Foppa
Parco Solari
Vle. Papiniano
Via Zurigo
Via Soderini
Pza. Napoli
Vle. Troya
Via Solari
Via Tortona
Stazione Genova
Via Lorenteggio
Ripa Ticinese
Naviglio Grande
Vle. Cassala
Via Giambellino
Lodovico il Moro
S. CRISTOFORO
Vle. B. Liguria
A. Sforza
Edm. De Amicis
Vle. Gorizia

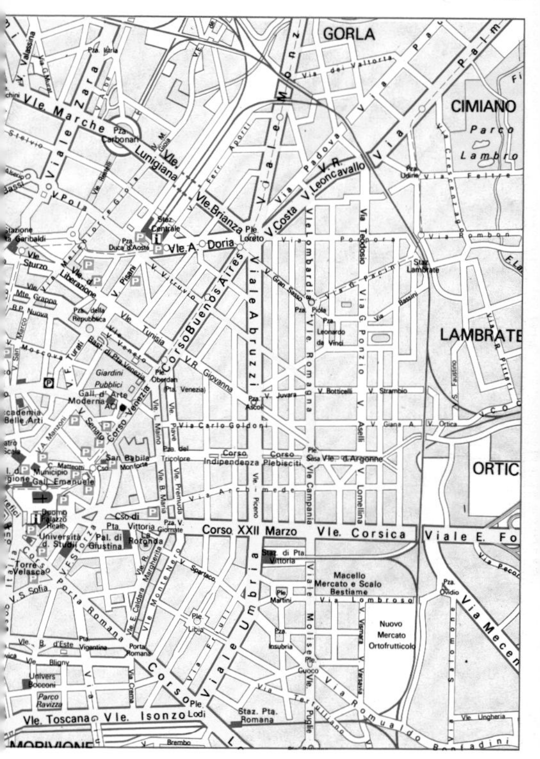
GORLA
CIMIANO
Parco Lambro
LAMBRATE
ORTIC
Stazione Garibaldi
Staz. Centrale
Ple. Loreto
Staz. Lambrate
Giardini Pubblici
Gall. d'Arte Moderna
Accademia Belle Arti
San Babila
Gall. Emanuele
Duomo
Palazzo Reale
Università d. Studi
Pal. di Giustina
La Rotonda
Torre Velasca
Staz. di Pta. Vittoria
Macello Mercato e Scalo Bestiame
Nuovo Mercato Ortofrutticolo
Univers Bocconi
Parco Ravizza
Staz. Pta. Romana
Corso Buenos Aires
Viale Abruzzi
Corso Venezia
Corso XXII Marzo
Vle. Corsica
Viale Umbria
Corso Lodi
Porta Romana
Vle. Toscana
Vle. Isonzo
Vle. Marche
Viale Zara
Vle. Brianza
Vle. A. Doria
V. Costa
V. Leoncavallo
Viale Monza
Via Palmanova
Vle. Lombardia
Vle. Romagna
Vle. Campania
Via Carlo Goldoni
Corso Indipendenza
Corso Plebisciti
Vle. d. Argonne
Viale E. Forlanini
Via Mecenate
Via Romualdo Bonfadini

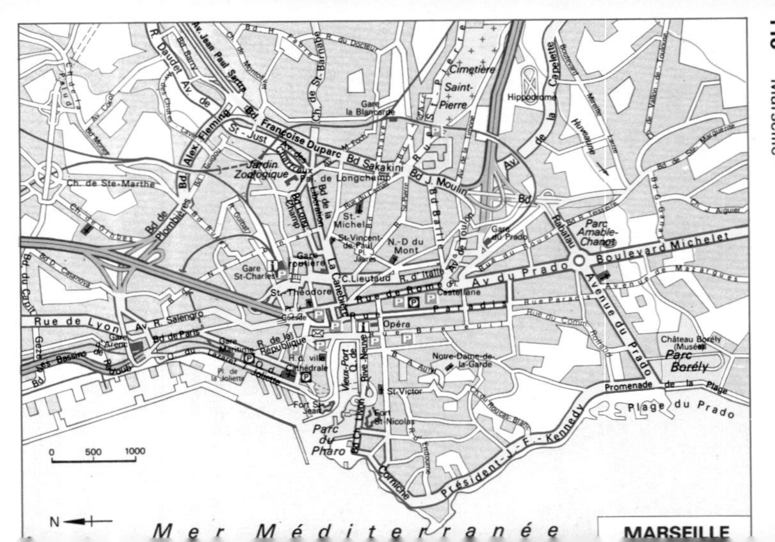
MARSEILLE
Mer Méditerranée
0 500 1000
N
Cimetière Saint-Pierre
Hippodrome
Gare la Blancarde
Av. Jean Paul Sartre
R. Daudet
Bd Barry
Av. de
Alex. Fleming
Bd
St-Just
Bd Françoise Duparc
Bd Sakakini
Bd J. Moulin
Jardin Zoologique
Pal. de Longchamp
Ch. de Ste-Marthe
Ch. de St-Barnabé
Bd de Plombières
Bd Longchamp
Bd de la Libération
St.-Michel
St-Vincent-de-Paul
N.-D du Mont
Gare du Prado
Rabatau
Parc Amable-Chanot
Boulevard Michelet
Av du Prado
Avenue du Prado
Avenue de Mazargues
Gare routière
Gare St-Charles
La Canebière
C. Lieutaud
R. d'Italie
Rue de Rome
Pl. Castellane
Rue Paradis
St.-Théodore
Rue de Lyon
Av. R. Salengro
Bd de Paris
Gare d'Arenc
Gare Maritime
R. de la République
H. d. ville
Cathédrale
Q. de la Joliette
Pl. de la Joliette
Q. du Lazaret
Bd des Bassins de Radoub
Bd du Capit
Opéra
Vieux-Port
Q. de Rive-Neuve
Notre-Dame-de-la-Garde
St-Victor
Fort St-Jean
Fort St-Nicolas
Parc du Pharo
Bd Ch. Livon
Corniche
Président-J.-F.-Kennedy
Endoume
Promenade de la Plage
Plage du Prado
Château Borély (Musée)
Parc Borély
Huveaune
Av. de la Capelette
Bd de Ste. Marguerite
Ch. de Vallon de Toulouse
Bd G. Ganay
Ch. J. Aiguier
Av. de Toulon

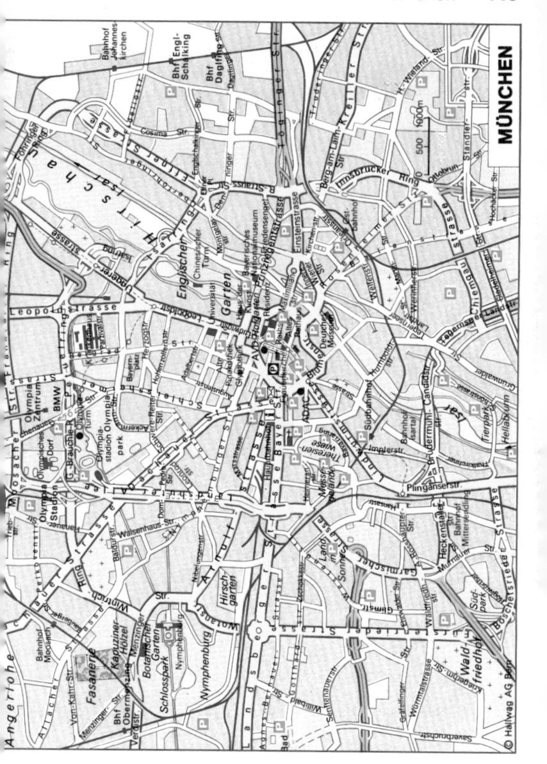
MÜNCHEN
500
1000m
Englischer Garten
Chinesischer Turm
Universität
Residenz
Deutsches Museum
Hauptbahnhof
Theresien-wiese
Messe-gelände
Olympiapark
Olympia-stadion
Olympiaturm
BMW
Hirschgarten
Nymphenburg
Schlosspark
Botanischer Garten
Fasanerie
Waldfriedhof
Südpark
Tierpark
Hellabrunn
Ost-Bahnhof
Südbahnhof
Leopoldstrasse
Ludwigstr.
Lindwurmstr.
Landsberger Str.
Arnulfstr.
Innsbrucker Ring
Isar
© Hallwag AG Bern

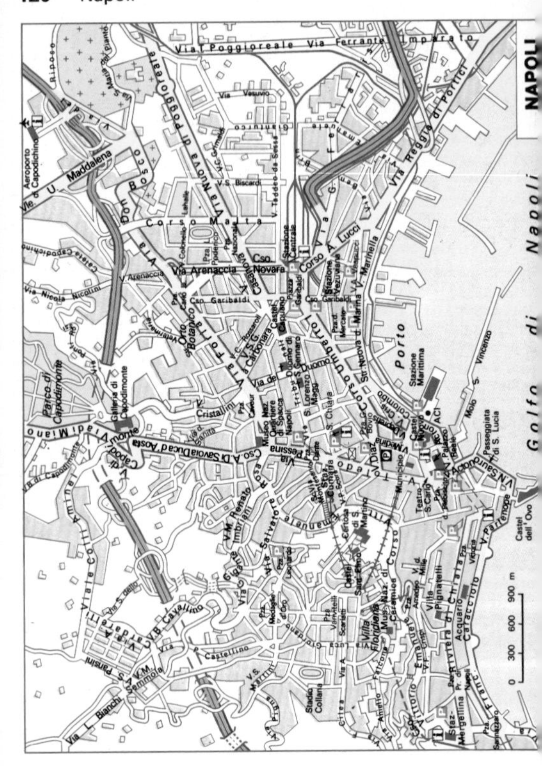
NAPOLI
Golfo di Napoli
Porto
Via Poggioreale
Via Ferrante Imparato
Via Reggia di Portici
Via Nuova di Poggioreale
Corso Malta
Via Arenaccia
Cso. Novara
Corso A. Lucci
Stazione Centrale
Piazza Garibaldi
Cso. Garibaldi
Corso Umberto I
Str. Nuova d. Marina
Stazione Marittima
Orto Botanico
Via Foria
Via Duomo
Museo Naz.
Cso. A. Di Savoia Duca d'Aosta
Parco di Capodimonte
Galleria di Capodimonte
Via Salvatore Rosa
Via Toledo
Castel Nuovo
Palazzo Reale
Teatro S. Carlo
Passeggiata di S. Lucia
Castel dell'Ovo
Certosa di S. Martino
Castel Sant'Elmo
Villa Floridiana
Villa Pignatelli
Acquario
Riviera di Chiaia
Via Caracciolo
Staz. Mergellina
Stadio Collana
Aeroporto di Capodichino
Via Cavallino
Viale Colli Aminei
Via L. Bianchi
0 300 600 900 m

OSLO

Storoveien
Trondheimsveien
Dag Hammarskjölds vei
Store Ringvei
Hjalmar Brantings vei
A. Hedins vei
Torshovparken
Tøyen
Botanisk Hage
Munch-museet
Kjølberggt.
Schweigaards gate
Bispegata
St. Halvards gate
Oslo gt.
Mosseveien
Ekeberg
Bjørvika
Akershus
Akershusstranda
Rådhusgata
Rådhus
Karl Johans gt.
Domkirke
Jernbanetorg
Østbanestasjonen
Vestbanestasjonen
Pipervika
Hovedøya
Slottet
Slottsparken
Oslo Univ.
Riks Hosp.
Gamle Aker kirke
Vestre Aker Kirke
Oslo Universitet
Majorstuen kirke
Vigelandsanlegget
Oslo Bymuseet
Vigelands-museet
Frognerkilen
Frognerstranda
Filipstadveien
Kon-Tiki-museet
Norsk Sjøfartsmuseet
Norsk Folkemuseum
Oscarshall
Ullevålsveien
Kirkeveien
Drammensveien
Bygdøy allé
Sjølystvn.
Messe-hallen
Torgny Segerstedts vei
Store ringvei
Viggo Hansteens vei
Sørkedalsveien
0 500 1000m

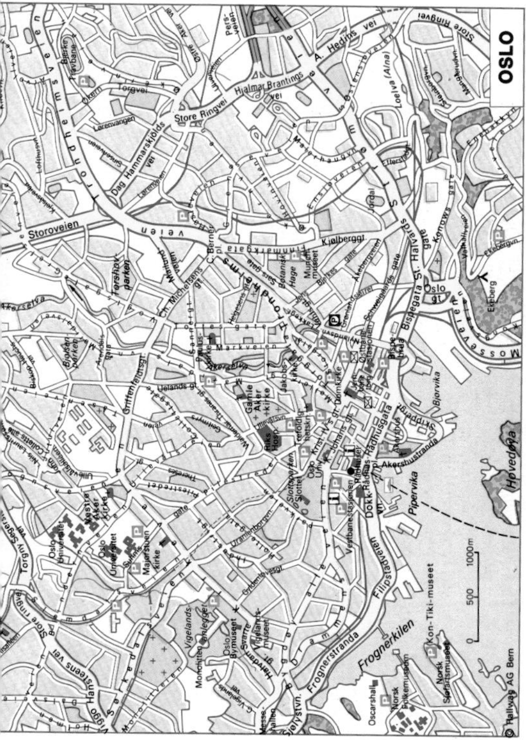

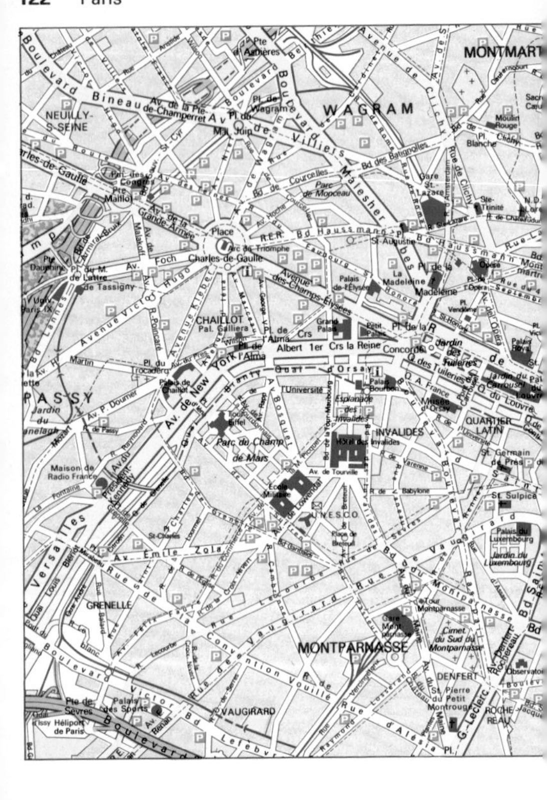
MONTMARTRE
WAGRAM
NEUILLY-S-SEINE
Pte d'Asnières
Pl. de Wagram
Av. de la Pte-de-Champerret
Pl. du Mal. Juin
Bd de Courcelles
Parc de Monceau
Bd des Batignolles
Moulin Rouge
Pl. Blanche
Gare St-Lazare
Ste-Trinité
Pte Maillot
Av. de la Grande-Armée
Place Charles-de-Gaulle
Arc de Triomphe
Av. Foch
Bd Haussmann
St-Augustin
Opéra
La Madeleine
Pl. de la Madeleine
Palais de l'Élysée
Avenue des Champs-Élysées
Pte Dauphine
Pl. du M. de Lattre de Tassigny
Av. Victor Hugo
Av. Kléber
Av. Marceau
Av. George V
CHAILLOT
Pal. Galliera
Pl. de l'Alma
Grand Palais
Petit Palais
Pl. de la Concorde
Jardin des Tuileries
Palais Royal
Pl. du Trocadéro
Palais de Chaillot
Av. de New York
Crs Albert 1er
Crs la Reine
Quai d'Orsay
Palais Bourbon
Musée d'Orsay
Q. des Tuileries
Q. du Louvre
Louvre
PASSY
Jardin du Ranelagh
Av. P. Doumer
L'Université
Esplanade des Invalides
INVALIDES
Hôtel des Invalides
QUARTIER LATIN
St. Germain des Prés
Tour Eiffel
Parc du Champ de Mars
Maison de Radio France
Av. du Président-Kennedy
École Militaire
Av. de Tourville
R. de Varenne
R. de Babylone
St. Sulpice
U.N.E.S.C.O.
Place de Breteuil
Palais du Luxembourg
Jardin du Luxembourg
Bd de Grenelle
Av. Émile Zola
Bd Garibaldi
Bd de Vaugirard
Bd du Montparnasse
Tour Montparnasse
Gare Montparnasse
Cimet. du Sud du Montparnasse
GRENELLE
Rue de la Convention
Rue de Vaugirard
MONTPARNASSE
DENFERT ROCHEREAU
Observatoire
St. Pierre du Petit Montrouge
Pte de Sèvres
Palais des Sports
VAUGIRARD
Héliport de Paris
Bd Lefebvre
R. d'Alésia
Av. G. Leclerc
Bd Victor

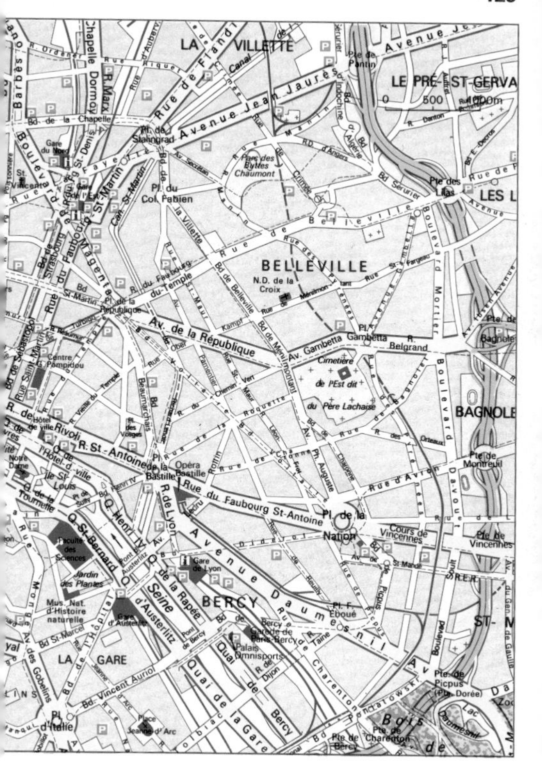
LA VILLETTE
LE PRÉ-ST-GERVA
0 500 1000m
Avenue Jean Jaurès
Rue de Flandre
Canal
Pte de Pantin
Bd de la Chapelle
Pl. de Stalingrad
Gare du Nord
Gare de l'Est
Parc des Buttes Chaumont
Pl. du Col Fabien
Pte des Lilas
LES L
BELLEVILLE
N.D. de la Croix
Rue de Belleville
Bd de Belleville
Rue du Faubourg du Temple
Pl. de la République
Av. de la République
Bd de Ménilmontant
Av. Gambetta
Pl. Gambetta
R. Belgrand
Cimetière de l'Est dit du Père Lachaise
Boulevard Mortier
Boulevard Davout
BAGNOLET
Pte de Bagnolet
Pte de Montreuil
Centre G. Pompidou
Bd de Sébastopol
Bd de Strasbourg
Bd de Magenta
Bd Beaumarchais
Pl. des Vosges
R. de Rivoli
R. St-Antoine
Hôtel de ville
Notre Dame
Ile St-Louis
Pl. de la Bastille
Opéra Bastille
Rue de la Roquette
Rue du Faubourg St-Antoine
Pl. de la Nation
Cours de Vincennes
Pte de Vincennes
R. de Lyon
Gare de Lyon
Avenue Daumesnil
Faculté des Sciences
Jardin des Plantes
Mus. Nat. d'Histoire naturelle
Q. St-Bernard
Q. Henri IV
Pont d'Austerlitz
Gare d'Austerlitz
Seine
BERCY
Gare de Paris-Bercy
Palais Omnisports
Quai de Bercy
Quai de la Gare
Pl. F. Éboué
R. de Charenton
Bd Poniatowski
Pte de Picpus
Pte de Bercy
Pte de Charenton
Bois de
Lac Daumesnil
LA GARE
Bd Vincent Auriol
Av. des Gobelins
Bd St-Marcel
Pl. d'Italie
Place Jeanne-d'Arc
ST-M

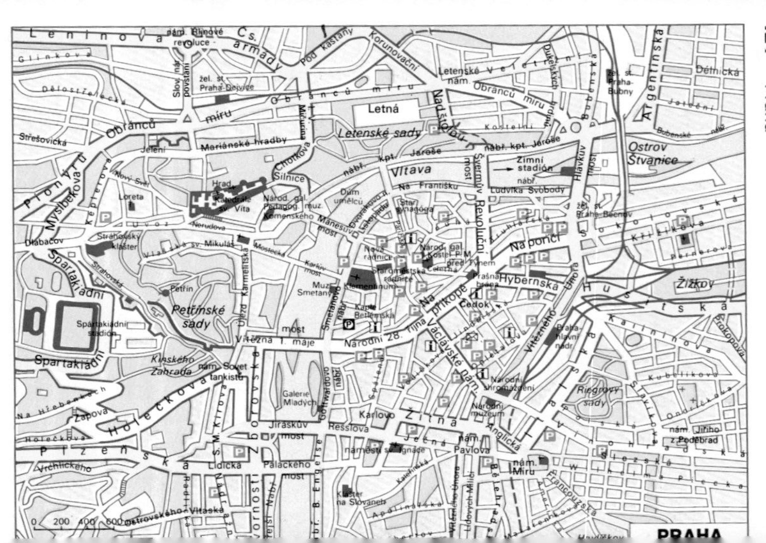
PRAHA
Leninova
Letná
Letenské sady
Vltava
Ostrov Štvanice
Žižkov
Revoluční
Na poříčí
Hybernská
Václavské nám.
Národní muzeum
Na příkopě
Národní 28. října
Karlovo
Žitná
Ječná
Resslova
Petřínské sady
Petřín
Hrad
Katedrála sv. Víta
Loreta
Strahovský klášter
Spartakiádní stadión
Spartakiádní
Vítězná
most 1. máje
Jiráskův most
Palackého most
Mánesův most
Švermův most
Hlávkův most
Riegrovy sady
nám. Míru
nám. Jiřího z Poděbrad
Anglická
Nerudova
Mariánské hradby
Obránců míru
Holečkova
Plzeňská
Kinského Zahrada
Galerie Mladých
Klementinum
Staroměstská radnice
Prašná brána
Čedok
Dlabačov
Střešovická
0 200 400 600

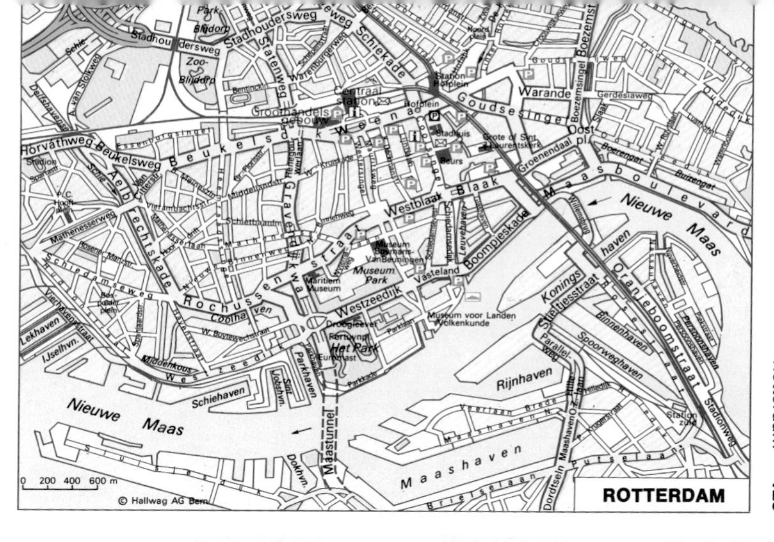
ROTTERDAM
Nieuwe Maas
Maas boulevard
Oranjeboomstraat
Stadionweg
Station Zuid
Persoonshaven
Binnenhaven
Spoorweghaven
Koningshaven
Stieltjesstraat
Parallelweg
Rijnhaven
Maashaven
Maashaven O.Z.
Maastunnel
Parkhaven
Sint Jobshvn.
Dokhvn.
Schiehaven
Westzeedijk
Het Park
Euromast
Parkkade
Museum Park
Museum Boymans-VanBeuningen
Maritiem Museum
Museum voor Landen en Volkenkunde
Boompjeskade
Schiedamsedijk
Leuvehaven
Vasteland
Westblaak
Blaak
Coolsingel
Stadhuis
Beurs
Grote of Sint Laurentskerk
Groenendaal
Oost pl.
Goudsesingel
Warande
Boezemsingel
Gerdesiaweg
Boerengat
Buizengat
Willemsbrug
Schiekade
Station Hofplein
Hofplein
Centraal station
Groothandelsgebouw
Weena
Statenweg
Stadhoudersweg
Blijdorp
Zoo-Blijdorp
Beukelsweg
Beukelsdijk
Horvathweg
Delfshavense Schie
Mathenesserweg
Aelbrechtskade
Middellandstr.
's-Gravendijkwal
Rochussenstraat
Coolhaven
Schiedamseweg
Havenstraat
Westzeedijk
Lekhaven
IJselhvn.
Vierhavenstraat
Dordtselaan
Putselaan
Brielselaan
0 200 400 600 m
© Hallwag AG Bern

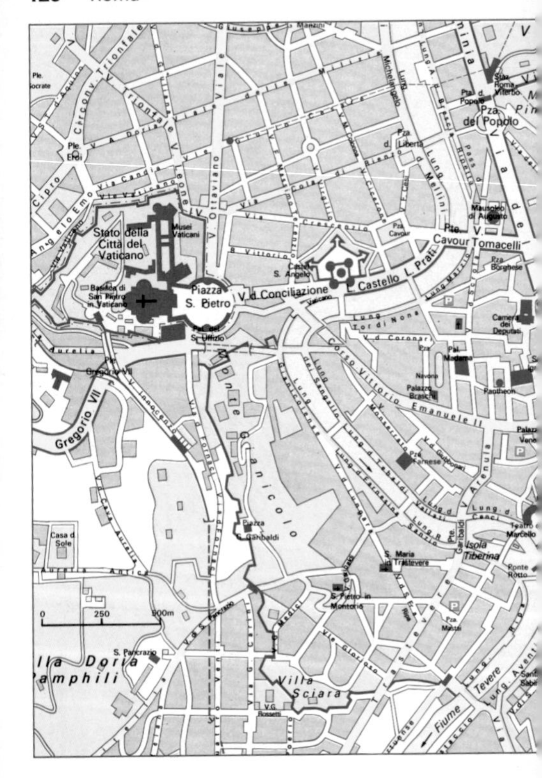
Stato della
Città del
Vaticano
Musei
Vaticani
Basilica di
San Pietro
in Vaticano
Piazza
S. Pietro
V. d. Conciliazione
Castel
S. Angelo
L. Castello
L. Prati
Pza.
del Popolo
Pta. d.
Popolo
Staz.
Roma
Viterbo
Mausoleo
di Augusto
Pte. V.
Cavour
Tomacelli
Pza
Cavour
Pza.
d. Libertà
Camera
dei
Deputati
Pal.
Madama
Navona
Palazzo
Braschi
Pantheon
Corso Vittorio Emanuele II
Pza
Farnese
Gianicolo
Piazza
G. Garibaldi
S. Maria
in Trastevere
Isola
Tiberina
Ponte
Rotto
Teatro
Marcello
S. Pietro in
Montorio
Pza.
Mastai
Villa
Sciara
V.G.
Rossetti
S. Pancrazio
Villa Doria
Pamphili
Casa d.
Sole
Aurelia Antica
Gregorio VII
Ple.
Gregorio VII
Aurelia
Fiume
Tevere
Trastevere
Ple.
Eroi
Ple.
Socrate
Circonv. Trionfale
Trionfale
Viale
Giulio Cesare
Ottaviano
Cola di Rienzo
Crescenzio
Lung. Mellini
Michelangelo
Via Candia
Via Vaticano
Angelo Emo
Cipro
Pal. del
S. Uffizio
Lung. Tor di Nona
V. d. Coronari
Lung. d. Tebaldi
Lung. d. Farnesina
V. d. Lungara
Lung. d. Vallati
Lung. d. Cenci
Lung. Sanzio
Pte. Garibaldi
V. Arenula
Lung. Gianicolense
Lung. dei Sangallo
Lung. Marzio
Via Gloriosa
0
250
500m

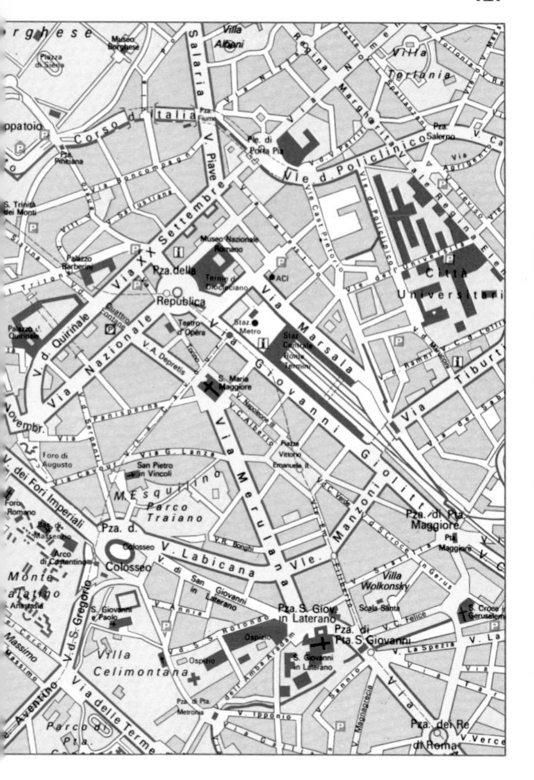
Villa Albani
Museo Borghese
Piazza di Siena
Salaria
Regina Margherita
Villa Torlonia
Corso d'Italia
Pza. Fiume
Ple. di Porta Pia
Pza. Salerno
Pta. Pinciana
V. Piave
Vle d. Policlinico
Via Boncompagni
S. Trinità dei Monti
Via XX Settembre
Museo Nazionale Romano
Palazzo Barberini
Pza. della Repubblica
Terme di Diocleziano
ACI
Città Universitaria
Via Marsala
Palazzo d. Quirinale
V. d. Quirinale
Quattro Fontane
Teatro d'Opera
Staz. Metro
Staz. Centrale Roma Termini
Via Nazionale
V. A. Depretis
S. Maria Maggiore
Via Giovanni Giolitti
Via Tiburtina
V. Panisperna
Foro di Augusto
Via G. Lanza
Via Cavour
San Pietro in Vincoli
Piazza Vittorio Emanuele II
V. dei Fori Imperiali
Foro Romano
M. Esquilino
Parco Traiano
Via Merulana
V. Manzoni
Pza. di Pta. Maggiore
Pta. Maggiore
Pza. d. Colosseo
Colosseo
Arco di Costantino
V. Labicana
V. di San Giovanni in Laterano
Villa Wolkonsky
Monte Palatino
S. Giovanni e Paolo
Pza. S. Giov. in Laterano
Scala Santa
S. Croce in Gerusalemme
Ospizio
Pza. di Pta. S. Giovanni
S. Giovanni in Laterano
Villa Celimontana
V. d. S. Gregorio
Via delle Terme
Aventino
Pza. di Pta. Metronia
V. Ipponio
V. Magnagrecia
Pza. dei Re di Roma
Via Appia Nuova

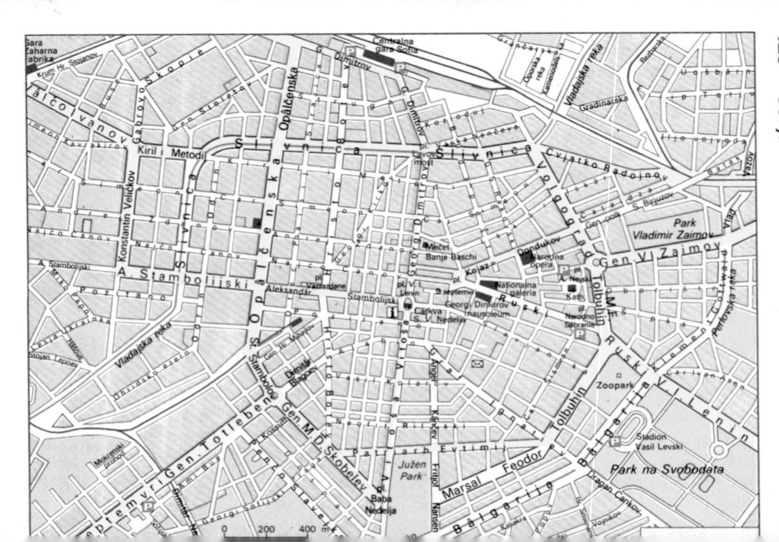
Park Vladimir Zaimov
Stadion Vasil Levski
Park na Svobodata
Zoopark
Tolbuhin
Narodna opera
Nacionalna galerija
Georgi Dimitrov mauzoleum
Banja Baschi
Džamija
Crkva Sv. Nedelja
Južen Park
Centralna gara Sofija
Opalčenska
St. Stambolov
Konstantin Veličkov
Vladajska reka
Perlovska reka
Fritjof Nansen
Kančev
Hristo Botev
Gen. M. D. Skobelev
Dimitar Ne
Sara Zaharna Fabrika
0 200 400 m

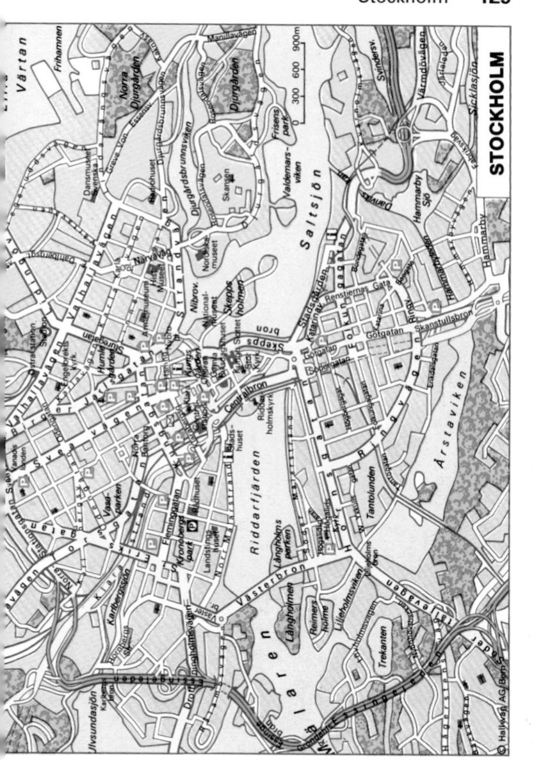
STOCKHOLM
Värtan
Frihamnen
Norra Djurgården
Djurgården
Djurgårdsbrunnsviken
Skansen
Nordiska museet
Frisens park
Valdemarsviken
Saltsjön
Skeppsholmen
Nationalmuseum
Nybroviken
Strandvägen
Narvavägen
Valhallavägen
Östra station
Humlegården
Sveavägen
Vasaparken
Kungsgården
Gamla Stan
Centralbron
Riddarholmskyrkan
Stadshuset
Riddarfjärden
Rådhuset
Kronobergs park
Fleminggatan
Kungsholmen
Västerbron
Långholmen
Reimersholme
Liljeholmsviken
Trekanten
Tantolunden
Ringvägen
Götgatan
Skanstullsbron
Årstaviken
Hammarby Sjö
Hammarby
Sicklasjön
Värmdövägen
Danviksbron
Ulvsundasjön
Karlbergssjön
Essingeleden
Mälaren
Stadsgården
Folkungagatan
Hornsgatan
0 300 600 900m
© Hallwag AG, Bern

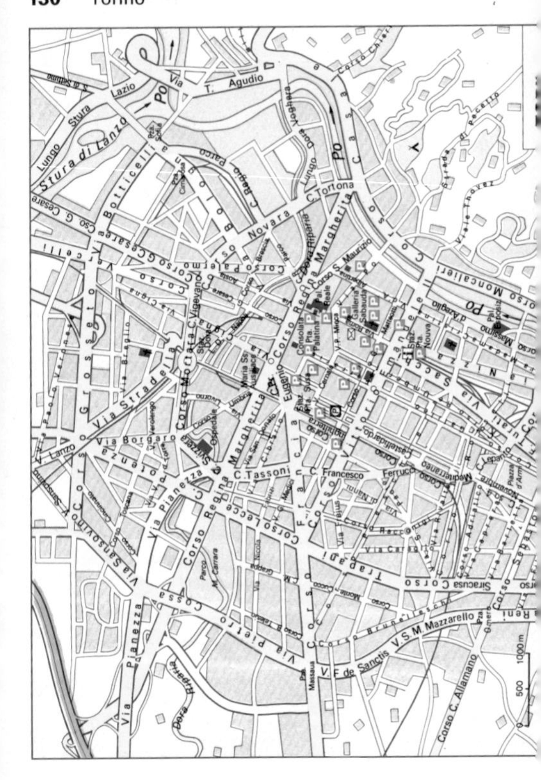
Stura di Lanzo
Lungo Stura Lazio
Po
Via T. Agudio
Corso Botticelli
Corso Novara
C. Tortona
Po
Dora Riparia
Corso Regina Margherita
Corso Palermo
Corso Vigevano
Corso Moncalieri
Via Stradella
Via Borgaro
Corso Grosseto
C. Tassoni
C. Francesco Ferrucci
Corso Lecce
Via Pianezza
Corso Regina Margherita
Via Sansovino
Via Pietro Cossa
Corso Brunelleschi
V. S. M. Mazzarello
V. F. de Sanctis
Corso Francia
Via Frejus
Via Carso
Corso Trapani
Corso Siracusa
Corso Sebastopoli
Corso C. Allamano
Corso Mediterraneo
C. Lepanto
Pal. Reale
Galleria Sabauda
Consolata
Pta. Palatina
Stаz. Dora
Stаz. Pta. Susa
Stаz. Pta. Nuova
Pal. Esposiz.
Ospedale
Parco M. Carrara
Dora
Via Pianezza
Via Nizza
Massimo d'Azeglio
500
1000m

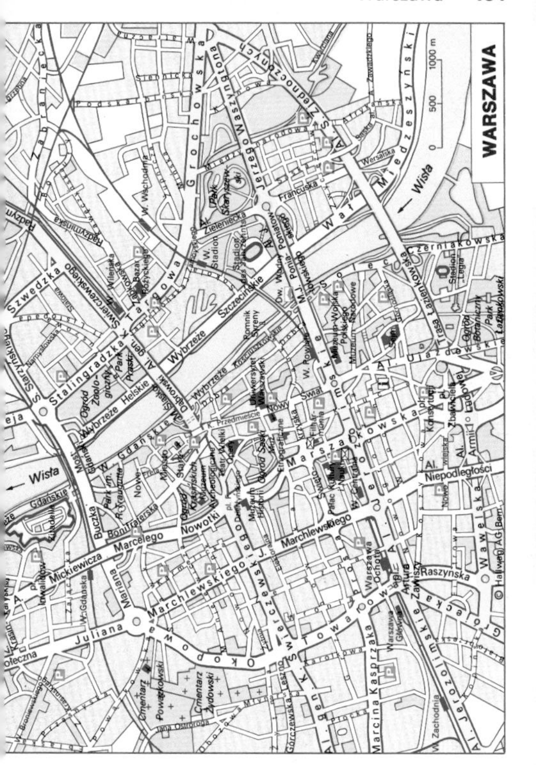
WARSZAWA
0 500 1000 m
Wisła
© Hallwag AG Bern

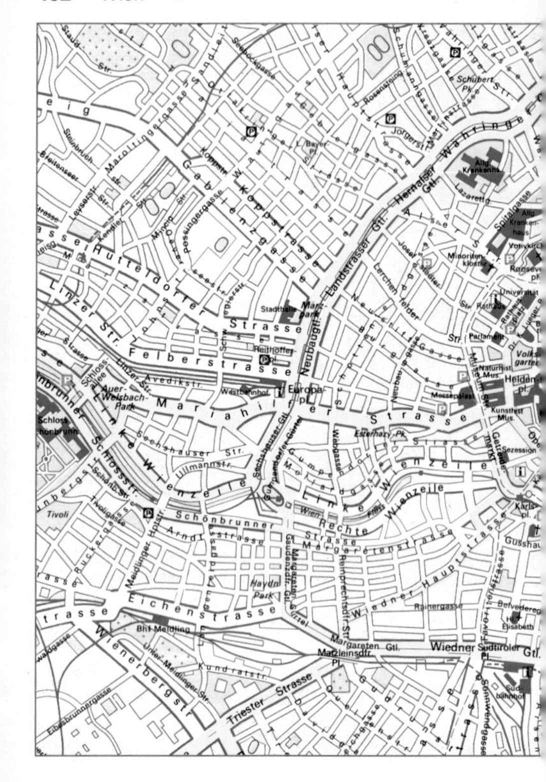
Allg. Krankenhs.
Lazarettg.
Spitalgasse
Allg. Kranken-haus
Votivkirche
Minoriten-kloster
Universität
Rathaus
Parlament
Volksgarten
Naturhist. Mus.
Helden-pl.
Messepalast
Kunsthist. Mus.
Sezession
Karls-pl.
Schubert Pk.
Jorgerstr.
L. Bayer-Pl.
Rosensteing.
Hernalser Gtl.
Währinger Str.
Landstrasser Gtl.
Neubaugtl.
Stadthalle
März-park
Hütteldorfer Strasse
Koppstrasse
Gablenzgasse
Possingergasse
Thaliastr.
Seebockgasse
Maroltingergasse
Steinbruch
Breitenseer
Leyserstr.
Kendlerstr.
Minciostr.
Linzer Str.
Felberstrasse
Reithoffer-Pl.
Westbahnhof
Europa-Pl.
Avedikstr.
Schloss-allee
Auer-Welsbach-Park
Mariahilfer Strasse
Schloss Schönbrunn
Schlossstr.
Sechshauser Str.
Ullmannstr.
Sechshauser Gtl.
Gumpendorfer Gürtel
Gumpendorfer Str.
Esterhazy-Pk.
Webgasse
Linke Wienzeile
Rechte Wienzeile
Wien Fluss
Schönbrunner Strasse
Margaretenstrasse
Arndtstrasse
Tivoli
Tivoligasse
Ruckergasse
Meidlinger Hptstr.
Gaudenzdfr. Gtl.
Margareten Gtl.
Haydn Park
Reinprechtsdfr. Str.
Wiedner Hauptstrasse
Rainergasse
Favoritenstrasse
Belvederegasse
Hl. Elisabeth
Gusshausstr.
Eichenstrasse
Bhf Meidling
Wienerbergstr.
Unter-Meidlinger-Str.
Kundratstr.
Triester Strasse
Matzleinsdfr. Pl.
Margareten Gtl.
Wiedner Gtl.
Südtiroler Pl.
Südbahnhof
Sonnwendgasse
Eibesbrunnergasse
Gudrunstrasse
Quellenstrasse

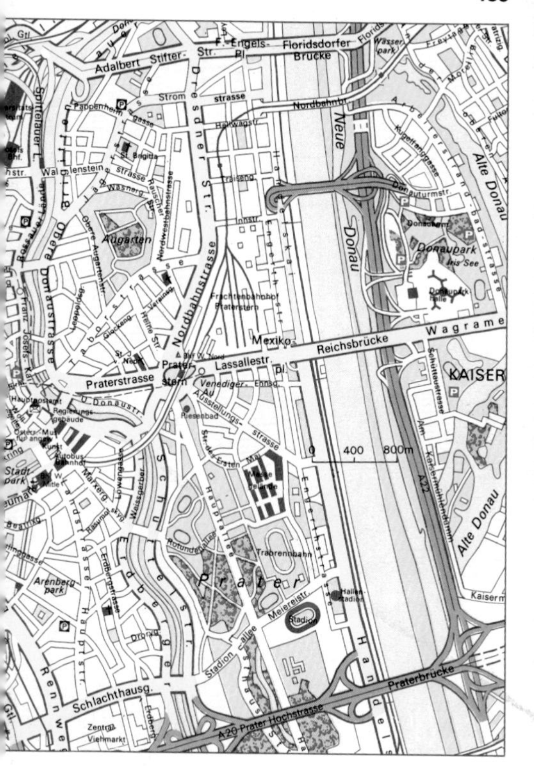

F. Engels-Pl
Floridsdorfer Brücke
Adalbert Stifter-Str.
Spittelauer L.
Pappenheimgasse
Strom strasse
Hallwagstr.
Nordbahnbr.
Neue Donau
Dresdner Str.
Wallensteinstrasse
St. Brigitta
Wasnerg.
Rauscherstr.
Nordwestbahnstrasse
Treiseng.
Donauturmstr.
Arbeiterstrand-bad-strasse
Kugelfanggasse
Alte Donau
Augarten
Obere Augartenstr.
Obere Donaustrasse
Nordbahnstrasse
Frachtenbahnhof Praterstern
Handelskai
Engerthstr.
Donauturm
Donaupark
Iris See
Donaupark-halle
Wagramer
Taborstrasse
Glockeng.
Heinestr.
Mexikopl.
Reichsbrücke
Lassallestr.
Praterstern
Praterstrasse
Venediger-Au
Ennsg.
Ausstellungsstrasse
Riesenbad
Schüttaustrasse
KAISER
Hauptpostamt
Regierungsgebäude
Donaustr.
Autobus-Bahnhof
Stadtpark
Bhf. W. Mitte
Malxerg.
Rasumofskyg.
Weissgerber
Schüttelstr.
Str. des Ersten Mai
Messegelände
Hauptallee
Engerthstrasse
Kaisermühlendamm
A22
Alte Donau
0 400 800m
Rotundenallee
Trabrennbahn
Prater
Meiereistr.
Stadion
Hallenstadion
Kaiserm
Arenbergpark
Erdbergstrasse
Landstrasser Hauptstr.
Erdberger
Rennweg
Stadionallee
Handelskai
Praterbrücke
Schlachthausg.
A20 Prater Hochstrasse
Zentral-Viehmarkt

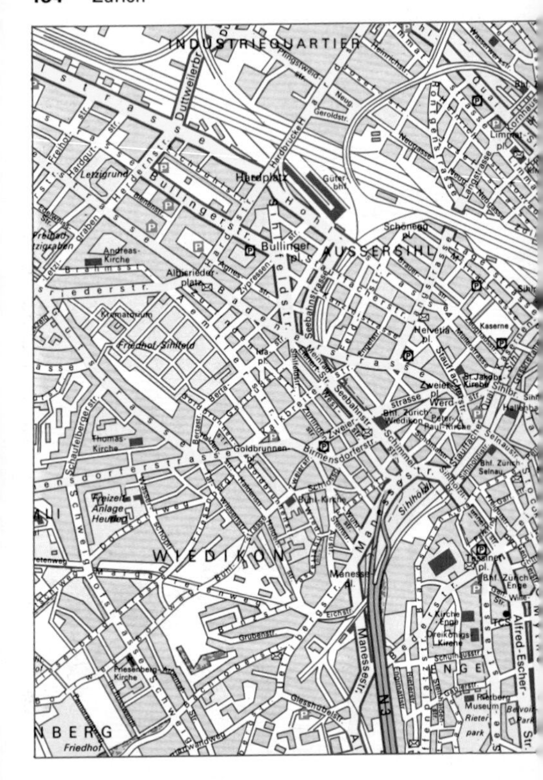
INDUSTRIEQUARTIER
Duttweilerbr.
Pfingstweidstr.
Neug.
Geroldstr.
Heinrichstr.
Hardbrücke
Röntgenstrasse
Neugasse
Limmatpl.
Langstrasse
Güterbhf.
Hardplatz
Bullingerstr.
Letzigrund
Herdernstr.
Hardgutstr.
Freihofstr.
Edelweissstr.
Freibad Letzigraben
Letzigraben
Andreas-Kirche
Bullingerpl.
AUSSERSIHL
Schöneggpl.
Hohlstr.
Sihlfeldstr.
Seebahnstrasse
Albisriederplatz
Badenerstr.
Zypressenstr.
Agnesstr.
Krematorium
Friedhof Sihlfeld
Helvetiapl.
Kaserne
Stauffacherstr.
St. Jakobs-Kirche
Zweierstrasse
Werdstr.
Bhf. Zürich Wiedikon
Peter-Paul-Kirche
Idapl.
Birmensdorferstr.
Goldbrunnenpl.
Zurlindenstr.
Schimmelstr.
Thomas-Kirche
Schaufelbergerstr.
Bertastr.
Gutstr.
Freizeit-Anlage Heuried
Bühl-Kirche
Schlossgasse
Sihlhölzli
Selnaustr.
Bhf. Zürich Selnau
Manessestr.
WIEDIKON
Manessepl.
Tessinerpl.
Bhf. Zürich Enge
Kirche Enge
Dreikönigs-Kirche
TCS
Alfred-Escher-Str.
ENGE
Grubenstr.
Friesenberg-Kirche
Giesshübelstr.
Rietberg Museum
Rieterpark
Belvoir-Park
N3
Friedhof

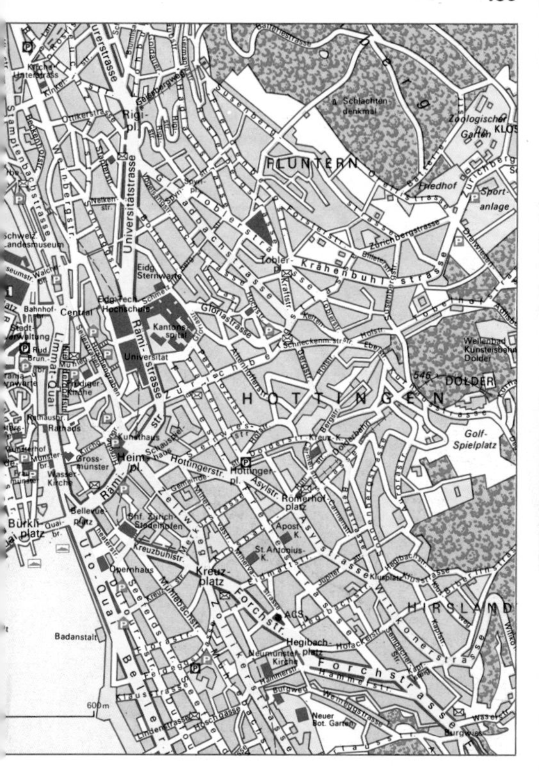

Schlachtendenkmal
Zoologischer Garten
FLUNTERN
Friedhof
Sport-anlage
Zürichbergstrasse
Universitätstrasse
Rigi-pl.
Tobler-pl.
Krähenbühlstrasse
Eidg. Sternwarte
Eidg. Tech. Hochschule
Kantonsspital
Universität
Rämistrasse
Gloriastrasse
Central
Bahnhof-br.
Stadt-verwaltung
Limmat-Quai
Schweiz. Landesmuseum
Wellenbad Kunsteisbahn Dolder
DOLDER
HOTTINGEN
Golf-Spielplatz
Kunsthaus
Heim-pl.
Hottingerstr.
Hottinger-pl.
Asylstr.
Römerhof-platz
Gross-münster
Wasser-Kirche
Rathaus
Prediger-Kirche
Bellevue-Platz
Bhf. Zürich Stadelhofen
Kreuzbühlstr.
Opernhaus
Kreuz-platz
Forchstr.
St. Antonius-K.
Apost. K.
ACS
Hegibach-platz
HIRSLAND
Witikonerstrasse
Neumünster-Kirche
Neuer Bot. Garten
Badanstalt
Utoquai
Seefeldstrasse
Bellerivestrasse
Zollikerstrasse
Bürkli-platz
Quai-br.
600 m

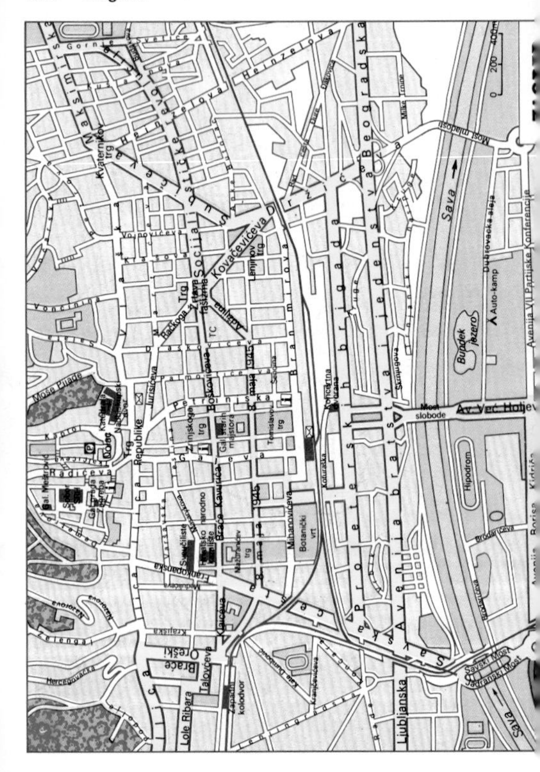
Heinzelova
Maksimirska
Kvaternikov trg
Kovačevićeva
Lenjinov trg
Branimirova
Trg Žrtava fašizma
Račkoga
Vojnovićeva
Draškovićeva
Palmotićeva
Petrinjska
Jurišićeva
Trg Republike
Radićeva
Kaptol
Dolac
Katedrala
Gal. Meštrović
Moše Pijade
Vončinina
Zrinjskoga trg
Gal. starih majstora
Tomislavov trg
Boškovićeva
8 maja 1945
Končertna dvorana
Mihanovićeva
Botanički vrt
Strossmayerov trg
Sveučilište
Frankopanska
Ilica
Nazorova
Zelengaj
Hercegovačka
Krajiška
Braće Oreški
Talovčeva
Lole Ribara
Zapadni kolodvor
Ljubljanska
Savski Most
Jadranski Most
Sava
Beogradska
Most mladosti
Most slobode
Hipodrom
Bundek jezero
Auto-kamp
Dubrovačka aleja
Avenija VII Partijske Konferencije
Brodarićeva
Skrnjugova
0
200
400m

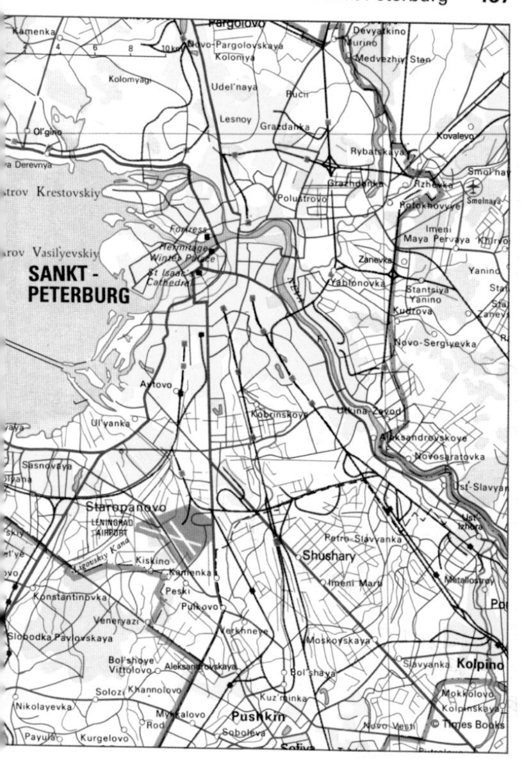
SANKT -
PETERBURG
Pargolovo
Kamenka
10km
Novo-Pargolovskaya
Kolonija
Devyatkino
Murino
Medvezhiy Stan
Kolomyagi
Udel'naya
Ruchi
Lesnoy
Grazdanka
Ol'gino
Kovalevo
Rybatskaya
Derevnya
Smol'naya
Grazhdanka
Rzhevka
Smolnaya
Krestovskiy
Polustrovo
Porokhovyye
Fortress
Imeni
Maya Pervaya
Khirvo
Vasil'yevskiy
Hermitage
Winter Palace
Zanevka
St Isaac's
Cathedral
Yanino
Neva
Yablonovka
Stantsiya
Yanino
Kudrova
Zanevs
Novo-Sergiyevka
Avtovo
Kobrinskoye
Utkina-Zavod
Ul'yanka
Aleksandrovskoye
Novosaratovka
Sasnovaya
Ust'-Slavyanka
Staropanovo
LENINGRAD
AIRPORT
Ust'-
Izhora
Ligovskiy Kanal
Petro-Slavyanka
Kiskino
Shushary
Kamenka
Imeni Marta
Metallostroy
Peski
Konstantinovka
Pulkovo
Veneryazi
Verkhneye
Slobodka Pavlovskaya
Moskovskaya
Bol'shoye
Vittolovo
Aleksandrovskaya
Slavyanka
Kolpino
Bol'shaya
Solozi
Khannolovo
Kuz'minka
Mokkolovo
Nikolayevka
Mykkalovo
Pushkin
Kolpinskaya
Rod
Novo Vesti
Soboleva
Payula
Kurgelovo
Sofiya

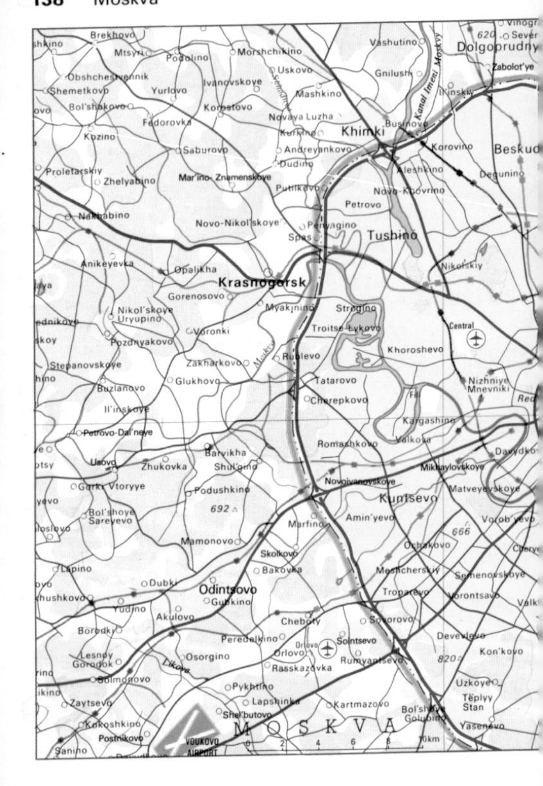
Brekhovo
Mtsyri
Podolino
Morshchikino
Vashutino
620
Sever
Dolgoprudny
Zabolot'ye
Obshchestvennik
Shemetkovo
Yurlovo
Ivanovskoye
Uskovo
Gnilushi
Kanal Imeni Moskvy
Bol'shakovo
Korostovo
Mashkino
Ilinskiy
Fedorovka
Novaya Luzha
Kozino
Kurkino
Khimki
Businovo
Saburovo
Andreyankovo
Korovino
Beskud
Proletarskiy
Dudino
Aleshkino
Zhelyabino
Mar'ino- Znamenskoye
Putilkovo
Degunino
Novo-Khovrino
Petrovo
Nakhabino
Novo-Nikol'skoye
Pervyagino
Spas
Tushino
Anikeyevka
Opalikha
Nikol'skiy
Krasnogorsk
Gorenosovo
Myakinino
Strogino
Nikol'skoye
Uryupino
Troitse-Lykovo
Central
Voronki
Pozdnyakovo
Khoroshevo
Zakharkovo
Moskva
Rublevo
Stepanovskoye
Glukhovo
Tatarovo
Nizhniye Mnevniki
Buzlanovo
Cherepkovo
Fili
Il'inskoye
Kargashino
Petrovo-Dal'neye
Romashkovo
Valkova
Barvikha
Davydkovo
Usovo
Zhukovka
Shulgino
Mikhaylovskoye
Novoivanovskoye
Gorki Vtoryye
Podushkino
Kuntsevo
Matveyevskoye
Bol'shoye Sareyevo
692
Marfino
Amin'yevo
Vorob'yevo
666
Mamonovo
Ochakovo
Lapino
Skolkovo
Bakovka
Meshcherskiy
Semenovskoye
Dubki
Odintsovo
Tropar'evo
Vorontsovo
Gubkino
Yudino
Akulovo
Chebotv
Solovorovo
Borodki
Peredelkino
Solntsevo
Devevlevo
Lesnoy Gorodok
Orlovo
Kon'kovo
Osorgino
Rasskazovka
Rumyantsevo
820
Likova
Solmonovo
Uzkoye
Pykhtino
Zaytsevo
Lapshinka
Kartmazovo
Teplyy Stan
Shel'butovo
Bol'shoye Golubino
Kokoshkino
MOSKVA
Yasenevo
Postnikovo
VNUKOVO AIRPORT
0
2
4
6
8
10km
Sanino

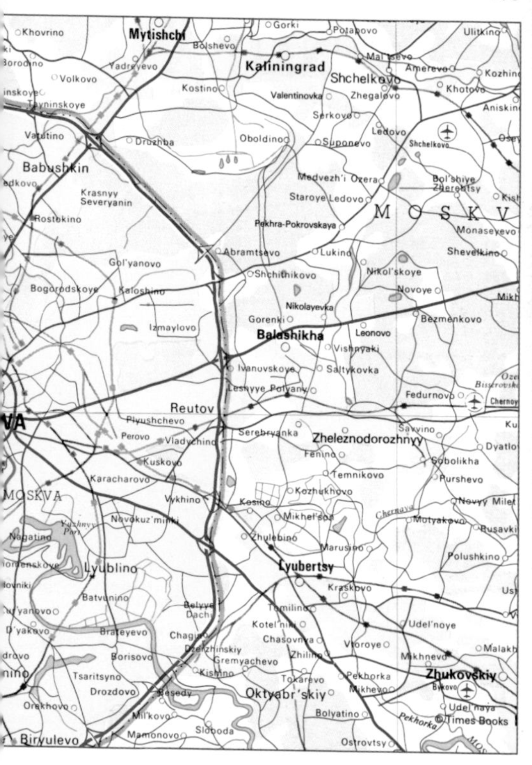
Khovrino
Mytishchi
Gorki
Potapovo
Ulitkino
Bolshevo
Yadreyevo
Kaliningrad
Mal'tsevo
Amerevo
Volkovo
Shchelkovo
Kozhino
Kostino
Valentinovka
Zhegalovo
Khotovo
Tayninskoye
Serkovo
Aniskino
Ledovo
Vatutino
Druzhba
Oboldino
Suponevo
Shchelkovo
Babushkin
Medvezh'i Ozera
Bol'shiye Zherebtsy
Krasnyy Severyanin
Staroye Ledovo
MOSKV
Rostokino
Pekhra-Pokrovskaya
Monaseyevo
Abramtsevo
Lukino
Shevelkino
Gol'yanovo
Nikol'skoye
Shchitnikovo
Bogorodskoye
Kaloshino
Novoye
Nikolayevka
Izmaylovo
Gorenki
Bezmenkovo
Leonovo
Balashikha
Vishnyaki
Ivanovskoye
Saltykovka
Lesnyye Polyany
Fedurnovo
Reutov
Plyushchevo
Serebryanka
Savvino
Perovo
Vladychino
Zheleznodorozhnyy
Dyatlovo
Fenino
Kuskovo
Sobolikha
Temnikovo
Karacharovo
Purshevo
MOSKVA
Kozhukhovo
Vykhino
Kosino
Novyy Milet
Mikhel'son
Novokuz'minki
Motyakovo
Rusavkino
Nagatino
Zhulebino
Marusino
Polushkino
Lyublino
Lyubertsy
Kraskovo
Batyunino
Tomilino
Belyye Dachi
Udel'noye
Kotel'niki
Brateyevo
Chagino
Chasovnya
Vtoroye
Malakhovka
Dzerzhinskiy
Zhilino
Mikhnevo
Borisovo
Gremyachevo
Kishino
Tokarevo
Pekhorka
Zhukovskiy
Tsaritsyno
Drozdovo
Besedy
Oktyabr'skiy
Mikhevo
Bykovo
Orekhovo
Udel'naya
Mil'kovo
Bolyatino
Pekhorka
Mamonovo
Sloboda
Biryulevo
Ostrovtsy

INDEX

In the index, the first number refers to the page, and the following letter and number to the section of the map in which the entry can be found. For example 13A5 Paris means that Paris can be found on page 13 where column A and row 5 meet.

15E4	Alençon
17B5	Alès
67E2	Alesd
34B3	Alessandria
46A2	Ålesund
68C4	Alexandria
75F1	Alexandrupolis
20B3	Alfajarín
25A6	Alfambra
31D1	Alfano
20B2	Alfaro
8C3	Alford
47A5	Ålgård
26A4	Algeciras
29A5	Alghero
27E3	Alhama
26C4	Alhama
30C4	Alia
71F1	Alibunar
27F3	Alicante
24C2	Alijó
44B4	Alingsås
26A1	Aliseda
25A5	Aljezur
25B5	Aljustrel
12C2	Alkmaar
20B4	Allaga
22B2	Allariz
20B4	Allepuz
43E3	Allinge
17D5	Allos
26B2	Almadén
26C2	Almagro
27E2	Almansa
20A3	Almazán
24C2	Almeida
25B4	Almeirim
12D2	Almelo
20A2	Almenar
26A2	Almendralejo
27D4	Almería
43E2	Älmhult
26C2	Almodóvar
25B5	Almodóvar
26A3	Almonte
43E2	Almundsryd
26C4	Almuñecar
26C2	Almuradiel
77D1	Almyropotamos

75D3	Almyros
9D5	Alnwick
58C3	Aloja
75E3	Alonnisos
26B4	Alora
82C2	Alozero
25B4	Alpalhão
42B3	Als (I.)
20A1	Alsasua
38C1	Alsfeld
9C5	Alston
53D2	Alta
33E4	Altamura
34C1	Altdorf
39E1	Altenburg
38B1	Altenkirchen
8C1	Altnaharra
40C2	Altona
58D3	Alūksne
45D1	Alunda
46C2	Alvdal
48C4	Älvdalen
43E1	Alvesta
45D1	Älvkarleö
48C3	Ålvros
51E3	Älvsbyn
88C3	Alyaty
59C6	Alytus
44B2	Åmål
30C1	Amalfi
32C2	Amandola
31D2	Amantea
24B2	Amarante
25B5	Amareleja
82C1	Ambarnyy
39E2	Amberg
16C3	Ambérieu
16B3	Ambert
58C1	Ambia
9C5	Ambleside
18C1	Amboise
12C1	Ameland
40C2	Amelinghausen
12C2	Amersfoort
76A1	Amfilochía
76B1	Amfissa
13A4	Amiens
47B6	Åmli
10C1	Amlwch

19B6 Argelès
18D1 Argent
35E3 Argenta
15E3 Argentan
18C2 Argenton
76B2 Argos
76A2 Argostolion
42B2 Århus
33D4 Ariano
74C2 Aridea
59B5 Ariogala
20A3 Ariza
44B2 Årjang
51D3 Arjeplog
82E2 Arkhangel'sk
7C4 Arklow
17B5 Arles
13C5 Arlon
6C3 Armagh
88B2 Armavir
12A3 Armentieres
30C4 Armerina
16B2 Arnay-le-Duc
20A2 Arnedo
12C2 Arnhem
52C2 Arnöya
39D1 Arnstadt
56B2 Aronkylä
34C1 Arosa
52B4 Årosjokk
42B3 Arøsund
32C2 Arquata
25B4 Arraiolos
9B4 Arran (I.)
13A4 Arras
19B6 Arreau
23D1 Arriondas
15D3 Arromanches
42B2 Års
74B4 Arta
21E4 Artá
87D4 Artemovsk
15F4 Artenay
21D2 Artesa
51D3 Arvidsjaur
46A2 Årvik
44B2 Arvika
84D2 Arzamas
88B1 Arzgir
22B1 Arzúa
42B1 Aså
48C3 Åsarna
39E3 Ascha
38C2 Aschaffenburg
41D4 Aschersleben
32C2 Ascoli
49D1 Åsele
48B2 Åsen
73D3 Asenovgrad
47B6 Åseral
11D2 Ashbourne
10B4 Ashburton
11D2 Ashby
11E4 Ashford
35E2 Asiago
29A4 Asinara, I. (I.)
44C3 Askersund
47D5 Askim
47A4 Asköy
45D2 Aspa
44C3 Aspa
37E2 Aspang
17C4 Aspres-sur-Buëch
49E1 Aspsele
12D1 Assen
42B3 Assens
75D2 Assiros
32B2 Assisi
76A1 Astakos
34B3 Asti
22C2 Astorga
43D2 Åstorp
88C1 Astrakhan
76C2 Astros
77F3 Astypalea (I.)
76C1 Atalandi
7B4 Athenry
Athinai = Athine
76C2 Athine
7B4 Athlone
7C4 Athy
23E3 Atienza
84D3 Atkarsk
46C2 Atnbrua
13B5 Attigny
11F2 Attleborough
45D3 Åtvidaberg
17C6 Aubagne

19B4	Belin
67F2	Beliş
18C3	Bellac
34C2	Bellano
14B4	Belle-Ile (I.)
16C3	Belley
9C5	Bellingham
34C2	Bellinzona
35E2	Belluno
26B2	Belmez
27D1	Belmonte E
24C3	Belmonte P
6A2	Belmullet
72B2	Belogradčik
72A2	Beloljin
82C2	Belomorsk
85G3	Beloretsk
84C2	Belozersk
87B4	Beltsy
63E3	Beluša
31D2	Belvedere Marittima
86B3	Belynichi
41E3	Belzig
22C2	Bembibre
20C2	Benabarre
27D4	Benahadux
20C2	Benasque
22C2	Benavente
87B4	Bendery
67F1	Benesat
62C2	Benešov
33D4	Benevento
44B2	Bengtsfors
20C4	Benicarló
27F2	Benidorm
70B3	Benkovac
38C2	Bensheim
71F2	Beograd
74A2	Berati
35D4	Berceto
39F4	Berchtesgaden
15E2	Berck-Plage
87B4	Berdichev
87D4	Berdyansk
67E2	Berettyóujfalu
86A3	Bereza
85G2	Berezniki
87C4	Berezovka
21D2	Berga E

45D4	Berga S
34C2	Bergamo
40C2	Bergedorf
41E1	Bergen D
40C3	Bergen D
47A4	Bergen N
12C1	Bergen aan Zee
12B3	Bergen op Zoom
38C4	Bergenz
19C4	Bergerac
49E3	Bergsjö
87C4	Berislav
27D4	Berja
46C1	Berkåk
72B2	Berkovica
53E1	Berlevåg
41E1	Berlin
22C3	Bermillo
34B1	Bern
15E3	Bernay
41D4	Bernburg
62B2	Beroun
40B3	Bersenbrück
8D3	Bervie
9C4	Berwick upon Tweed
67E4	Berzasca
58C3	Bērzaune
58D3	Bērzpils
16C2	Besançon
46C3	Bessheim
18C3	Bessines
22B1	Betanzos
20A3	Beteta
13A4	Béthune
8C1	Bettyhill
11E1	Beverley
84C2	Bezhetsk
84B3	Bezhitsa
17A5	Béziers
26C4	Béznar
61F3	Biała
61D4	Białobrzegi
60A2	Białograd
60B2	Biały Bór
61E2	Białystok
19A5	Biarritz
34C2	Biasca
32A1	Bibbiena
38C4	Biberach

60C1	Braniewo
51E2	Bränna
61E3	Brańsk
18C3	Brantôme
68C2	Braşov
63D4	Bratislava
36C2	Braunau
40C3	Braunschweig
7C4	Bray
71D2	Brčko
8C3	Brechin
63D3	Breclav
10C3	Brecon
12C3	Breda
43E2	Bredåkra
49E2	Bredbyn
40C1	Bredstedt
72B1	Bregovo
5E3	Breidhdalsvik
52B2	Breidvik
40C3	Breitenhees
52C1	Breivikbotn
46A3	Brekke
46D2	Brekken
50B4	Brekkvasselv
48A2	Brekstad
40B2	Bremen
40B2	Bremerhaven
40C2	Bremervörde
35D2	Breno
35D3	Brescia
12B3	Breskens
35E1	Bressanone
18B2	Bressuire
14B3	Brest F
86A3	Brest BE
13A4	Breteuil
47C5	Brevik
70B1	Brežice
63F3	Brezno
17D4	Briançon
16A1	Briare
17D4	Brides
10C3	Bridgend
10C3	Bridgwater
9D6	Bridlington
13B6	Brienne
34B2	Brig
11E4	Brighton

59D4	Brigi
17C6	Brignoles
23E4	Brihuega
40B4	Brilon
33F4	Brindisi
10C3	Bristol
19C4	Brive
23E2	Briviesca
63D3	Brno
43D2	Broby
59B4	Broceni
60C2	Brodnica
87B3	Brody
42B1	Brønderslev
50A3	Brönnöysund
8C2	Brora
43E3	Brösarp
52B3	Bröstad
68A4	Broşteni
9C5	Brough
9C6	Broughton
87C3	Brovary
26A1	Brozas
38C3	Bruchsal
36C2	Bruck
37E2	Bruck
12B3	Brugge
46D3	Brumunddal
48C2	Brunflo
35E1	Brunico
47B5	Brunkeberg
44B2	Brunsberg
63D2	Bruntál
12B3	Brussel
	Bruxelles = Brussel
84B3	Bryansk
46D2	Brydal
63D1	Brzeg
64A2	Brzesko
8C2	Buckie
41E3	Bückwitz
68C3	Bucureşti
46B1	Bud
66C2	Budapest
29B4	Buddusó
10B4	Bude
88B2	Budennovsk
69D4	Budeşti
4B2	Búdhardalur

5E2 Budhareyri
5E3 Búdhir
71E4 Budva
71D3 Bugojno
83F1 Bugrino
85F3 Bugulma
85F3 Buguruslan
68C1 Buhuşi
10C2 Builth Wells
85E3 Buinsk
26C3 Bujalance
72A3 Bujanovac
20C3 Bujaraloz
70A2 Buje
69D2 Bujor
34A1 Bulle
68A3 Bumbeşti-Jiu
71D3 Buna
7C4 Bunclody
6C2 Buncrana
51E4 Bureå
52C2 Burfjord
41D3 Burg
73F2 Burgas
39E4 Burghausen
23E2 Burgos
40A3 Burgsteinfurt
45E4 Burgsvik
20B1 Burguete
10C3 Burnham
11D1 Burnley
20C4 Burriana
11D2 Burton
51E4 Burträsk
68A2 Buru
11E3 Bury Saint Edmunds
67E3 Buteni
38A1 Bütgenbach
38C1 Butzbach
48A2 Buvika
11D2 Buxton
84D2 Buy
88C2 Buynaksk
69D3 Buzău
18C2 Buzançais
70A2 Buzet
67E4 Buziaş
85F3 Buzuluk
60B3 Bydgoszcz
47B6 Bygland
47B5 Bykle
49D2 Byn
47A5 Byrkjedal
51E4 Byske
63E3 Bytča
63E2 Bytom
60B2 Bytów
88B2 Bzipi

C

20C4 Cabanes
26B2 Cabeza
26B3 Cabra
71F3 Čačak
26A1 Caceres
25A4 Cacîlhas
21E2 Cadaqués
22A1 Cadas de Reyes
63E3 Čadca
19B4 Cadillac
26A4 Cádiz
15D3 Caen
10C1 Caernarvon
32B2 Cagli
29B6 Cagliari
7B5 Caher
7A5 Cahirciveen
19C4 Cahors
71E3 Čajniče
37E3 Čakovek
28B3 Calacuccia
68A4 Calafat
20A2 Calahorra
15F1 Calais
20B3 Calamocha
69D3 Călăraşi
21E4 Cala Ratjada
27E3 Calasparra
20B3 Calatayud
24A3 Caldas da Rainha
68B3 Călimăneşti
7B5 Callan
9B4 Callander
27F2 Calpe
30C4 Caltagirone
30C4 Caltanissetta
68C4 Călugăreni

39F3	Deggendorf
12B3	Deinze
68A1	Dej
12C1	De Kooy
72B3	Delčevo
34B1	Delémont
76B1	Delfi
12B2	Delft
12D1	Delfzil
40B2	Delmenhorst
70B2	Delnice
49D3	Delsbo
72B4	Demir Kapija
73F3	Demirköy
41E2	Demmin
12B2	Den Haag
12C1	Den Helder
27F2	Denia
12C1	Den Oever
12A3	De Panne
11D4	Deptford
88C2	Derbent
11D2	Derby
73E3	Dereköy
6C2	Derrybeg
76B2	Dervenakia
76B2	Dervenion
71D2	Derventa
35D3	Desenzano
74C3	Deskati
41E4	Dessau
67E4	Deta
37E3	Deutschlandsberg
20A1	Deva E
67F3	Deva R
12D2	Deventer
73D3	Devin
59D4	Diagučiai
75F1	Didymontichon
17C4	Die
40B1	Die (I.)
38C2	Dieburg
38A2	Diekirch
40B3	Diepholz
15E2	Dieppe
12C3	Diest
17C5	Digne
16B2	Digoin
16C2	Dijon

50C4	Dikanäs
72B2	Dimitrovgrad YU
73D3	Dimitrovgrad BG
72B1	Dimovo
14C3	Dinan
13C4	Dinant
14C3	Dinard
7A4	Dingle
8C2	Dingwall
39D3	Dinkelsbühl
88B1	Divnoye
49F1	Djäkneboda
71F4	Djakovica
71D1	Djakovo
4B2	Djúpavik
5E3	Djúpivogur
70C1	Djurdjevac
71E3	Djurdj Tara
87C4	Dneprodzerzhinsk
87C4	Dnepropetrovsk
86B2	Dno
35E1	Dobbiaco
59B4	Dobele
71D2	Doboj
67F3	Dobra
61D2	Dobre Miasto
67F4	Dobreta Turnu Severin
73F1	Dobrich
63E1	Dobrodzień
86C3	Dobrush
85G2	Dobryanka
77F2	Dodekanissos (I.)
72A3	Doganović
46C3	Dokka
16C2	Dole
10C2	Dolgellau
72A2	Dolievac
87C4	Dolinskaya
72B2	Dolni Lom
63F3	Dolný Kubín
64B2	Domaradz
62B3	Domažlice
46C2	Dombås
66B3	Dombóvár
15D3	Domfront
34B2	Domodossola
74C3	Domokos
38B4	Donaueschingen
39D3	Donauwörth

70C3 Duvno
61D2 Dylewo
47B4 Dyranut
84D2 Dzerzhinsk U
86B3 Dzerzhinsk RF
87C4 Dzhankoy
85H3 Dzhetygara
61D2 Działdowo

E

11E4 Eastbourne
11F2 East Dereham
11E2 East Retford
42C2 Ebeltoft
37D2 Ebensee
41E3 Eberswalde-Finow
33D4 Eboli
78B2 Eceabat
75E1 Echinos
13C5 Echternach
26B3 Écija
40C1 Eckernförde
44A3 Ed
12C2 Edam
74C2 Edessa
9C4 Edinburgh
73E3 Edirne
35D2 Edolo
46B1 Edöy
45E1 Edsbo
45D3 Edsbruk
69E3 Eforie
67D1 Eger
47A6 Egersund
39E3 Eggenfelden
5E2 Egilsstadhir
18D3 Égletons
38C4 Ehingen
36B2 Ehrwald
47B4 Eidfjord
46B3 Eidsbugarden
47D4 Eidsvoll
46A2 Eikefjord
41E4 Eilenburg
40C4 Einbeck
12C3 Eindhoven
36D3 Eisen
39D1 Eisenach
41F3 Eisenhüttenstadt
37F2 Eisenstadt
39D1 Eisfeld
59C6 Eišiškes
41D4 Eisleben
20B2 Ejea de los Caballeros
76C2 Ejina
76B1 Ejion
56C4 Ekenäs
78B2 Eksemil
44B1 Ekshärad
44C4 Eksjö
26B3 El Arahal
74C3 Elasson
28C2 Elba (I.)
22B2 El Barco
22C4 El Barco de Avila
74B2 Elbasani
60C2 Elblag
22B4 El Bodón
23E3 El Burgo de Osma
27F3 Elche
27D2 Elche de la Sierra
75E2 Eleftherupolis
59B4 Eleja
84C2 Elektrostal
73D2 Elena
23D4 El Escorial
22B1 El Ferrol del Caudillo
46D2 Elgå
8C2 Elgin
20C2 El Grado
73E2 Elhovo
9C4 Elie
57D3 Elimäki
88B1 Elista
61E2 Ełk
8D3 Ellon
23E4 El Molar
40C2 Elmshorn
46B1 Elnesvågen
23D4 El Pardo
26A4 El Puerto de Santa Maria
26A3 El Ronquillo
27F2 El Saler
50B3 Elsfjord
58C2 Elva
25C4 Elvas
46D3 Elversum

44C1	Fagersta	36C3	Ferleiten
67E3	Fåget	32C2	Fermo
11F2	Fakenham	22C3	Fermoselle
73E2	Fakija	7B5	Fermoy
15D3	Falaise	35E3	Ferrara
69D1	Fălciu	25B5	Ferreira
61D3	Falenty	69E3	Feteşti
43D1	Falkenberg	16B3	Feurs
9C4	Falkirk	35D3	Fidenza
44B3	Falköping	74A2	Fieri
10A4	Falmouth	19D4	Figeac
20C3	Falset	24B3	Figueira da Foz
42C4	Falster (I.)	21E2	Figueres
43D3	Falsterbo	9D6	Filey
65E4	Fălticeni	68B4	Filiaşi
44C1	Falun	76B3	Filiatra
32B1	Fano	74B4	Filipias
42A3	Fano (I.)	44C2	Filipstad
32B3	Fara	27D4	Fiñana
44A3	Färgelanda	48B1	Fines
49D3	Färila	50B2	Finneld
42A3	Färjestaden	50B3	Finneld
74C3	Farkadon	46D3	Finnskog
11D4	Farnham	52B3	Finnsnes
25B6	Faro	44C3	Finspång
45E3	Fårösund	41E4	Finsterwalde
74C3	Farsala	8A3	Fionnphort
47A6	Farsund	28C1	Firenze
33F4	Fasano	16B3	Firminy
87B3	Fastov	10B2	Fishguard
24B3	Fatima	74B4	Fiskardon
50B4	Fättjaure	52B1	Fiskeboll
69D3	Fåurei	31D3	Fiumefreddo
50B2	Fauske	32B3	Fiumicino
16C1	Fayl-Billot	47A4	Fjaera
15E2	Fécamp	51D1	Fjällåsen
82D2	Fedovo	48C3	Fjällnäs
83K1	Fedulki	49D1	Fjällsjö
41D1	Fehmarn (I.)	42B1	Fjerritslev
21E4	Felanitx	50C4	Flandberg
36A3	Feldkirch	4A1	Flateyri
36D3	Feldkirchen	46B2	Flatmark
35D4	Felina	9C6	Fleetwood
11F3	Felixstowe	47A6	Flekkefjord
44C2	Fellingsbro	45D2	Flen
67D3	Felnac	40C1	Flensburg
35E2	Feltre	15D3	Flers
87D4	Feodosiya	47C4	Flesberg
75F1	Fere	19C5	Fleurance

26B2 Fuente-Ovejuna
20B3 Fuentes de Ebro
38C1 Fulda
48C4 Fulunäs
19C4 Fumel
24C3 Fundão
41E2 Fürstenberg
37E3 Fürstenfeld
39E3 Furth im Walde
49D4 Furudal
39D4 Füssen
67D2 Füzesabony
42B3 Fyn (I.)
47B5 Fyresdal

G

61D3 Gąbin
73D2 Gabrovo
15E3 Gacé
71D4 Gacko
48C1 Gäddede
41D2 Gadebusch
68C3 Găești
32C4 Gaeta
84B2 Gagarin
19C5 Gaillac
8B2 Gairloch
9C4 Galashiels
69E2 Galați
84D2 Galich
31F1 Gallipoli
51E2 Gällivare
49D2 Gällö
7B4 Galway
54B4 Gamlakarleby
45D4 Gamleby
53E1 Gamylk
39E3 Ganacker
20C3 Gandesa
27F2 Gandia
53F2 Gandvik
17B5 Ganges
16A3 Gannat
17C4 Gap
72B2 Gara Dragoman
41D3 Gardelegen
35D3 Gardone
53D2 Gargia Fjellstue
59A5 Gargždai
35E3 Garibaldi
59C6 Garliava
39D4 Garmisch-Partenkirchen
7A5 Garries Bridge
27E4 Garrucha
9C6 Garstang
8B2 Garve
61E4 Garwolin
84B2 Gatchina
52B1 Gausvika
19B6 Gavarnie
24B3 Gavião
45D1 Gävle
77D1 Gavrion
83G2 Gayny
60C1 Gdańsk
86B2 Gdov
60B1 Gdynia
42C4 Gedser
12C3 Geel
38A1 Geilenkirchen
47B4 Geilo
46B2 Geiranger
38C3 Geislingen
30C4 Gela
40A4 Geldern
78B2 Gelibolu
73D3 General-Nikolaevo
73F1 General-Toševo
34A2 Genève
87C4 Genichesk
34C4 Genova
12B3 Gent
41D3 Genthin
84C3 Georgiu-Dezh
88B2 Georgiyevsk
39E1 Gera
13D6 Gérardmer
27D4 Gérgal
56A4 Geta
72B4 Gevgelija
68C1 Gheorgheni
68A1 Gherla
28B3 Ghisoni
26A4 Gibraltar
38C1 Giessen
40C3 Gifhorn
72C1 Gigen

46A2 Hareid
47C4 Harestua
58C3 Hargla
56B3 Harjavalta
66B4 Harkány
12C1 Harlingen
43E2 Härlunda
55E3 Härmä
73E3 Harmanli
49E2 Härnösand
20A1 Haro
9C6 Harrogate
52B1 Harstad
37E2 Hartberg
57D2 Hartola
11F3 Harwich
73D3 Haskovo
43E3 Hasle
46D3 Hasmar
43D2 Hässelholm
12C3 Hasselt
11E4 Hastings
52C2 Hasvik
67F3 Haţeg
50B3 Hattfjelldal
55F4 Hatuvaara
66C2 Hatvan
47A5 Haugesund
56C3 Hauho
47B5 Haukeligrend
47B4 Haukeliseter
54C3 Haukipudas
57D2 Haukivnori
55D1 Hautajärvi
41D3 Havelberg
10B3 Haverfordwest
62C3 Havlíčkúv Brod
53D1 Havöysund
78B1 Havsa
9C4 Hawick
78B1 Hayrabolu
6B3 Headford
8A2 Hebrides (I.)
45D1 Heby
38C3 Hechingen
12C3 Hechtel
44C1 Hedemora
51F2 Hedenäset
48C3 Hedeviken
49E1 Hednäs
40C1 Heide
38C2 Heidelberg
39D3 Heidenheim
38C3 Heilbronn
36C3 Heiligenblut
40C4 Heiligenstadt
4B4 Heimaey
48A2 Heimdal
57E1 Heinåvesi
57D3 Heinola
46B3 Helgheim
40B1 Helgoland (I.)
4B4 Hella
47A6 Helleland
27E2 Hellín
4A3 Hellissandur
12C3 Helmond
8C2 Helmsdale
41D3 Helmst
Helsingfors = Helsinki
43D2 Helsingør
57D4 Helsinki
10A4 Helston
58A2 Heltermaa
45E4 Hemse
46B3 Hemsedal
19A5 Hendaye
12D2 Hengelo
48B1 Hening
14B4 Hennebont
71E4 Herceg Novi
10C3 Hereford
40B3 Herford
42B2 Herning
26B1 Herrera del Duque
23D2 Herrera de Pisuerga
22C4 Hervas
41E4 Herzberg
40C4 Herzberg
15E2 Hesdin
47A6 Heskestad
67D2 Heves
9C5 Hexham
37D2 Hieflau
55E3 Hietaperä
58A2 Hiiuma (I.)
20B3 Hijar
12D1 Hijkersmilde

44B2	Karlstad
44C2	Karmansbo
73E2	Karnobat
41D2	Karow
77F3	Kárpathos (I.)
74C3	Karpenision
85G2	Karpinsk
82E2	Karpogory
54C4	Kärsämäki
58D3	Kärsava
86B2	Kärsava
49D4	Karsjö
56C1	Karstula
85H3	Kartaly
60B1	Kartuzy
51F2	Karungi
54B2	Karunki
56B2	Karvia
57E1	Karvio
77D1	Karystos
84C2	Kashin
84D3	Kasimov
	Kaskinen = Kaskö
56A2	Kaskö
58C1	Käsmu
77F4	Kásos (I.)
40C4	Kassel
78B1	Kastanee
38B2	Kastellaun
77D4	Kastellion
74B2	Kastoria
76A2	Katakolon
74C2	Katerini
72B3	Katlanovo
76B2	Kato Klitoria
75D1	Kato Nevrokopion
63E2	Katowice
45D2	Katrineholm
51D4	Kattisavan
56B2	Kauhajoki
56B1	Kauhava
59C6	Kaunas
46B3	Kaupanger
56B1	Kaustinen
53D3	Kautokeino
74A2	Kavaja
75E1	Kavala
73F1	Kavarna
87D4	Kavkaz

74B4	Kavos
85E1	Kazan
73D2	Kazanlâk
83G2	Kazhim
67D1	Kazincbarcika
59B6	Kazlų Rūda
77D2	Kea
77D2	Kea (I.)
52B4	Kebnekaise
66C3	Kecel
66C2	Kecskemét
59C5	Kédiniai
76A2	Kefallinia
4A4	Keflavik
58B1	Keila
58C3	Keipene
57D1	Keitele
8C2	Keith
59B4	Kekava
74B3	Këlcyra
55D1	Kelloselkä
59B5	Kelmé
9C4	Kelso
82C2	Kem
54C2	Kemi
55D1	Kemijärvi
39D2	Kemnath
39D4	Kempten
9C6	Kendal
7A5	Kenmare
63E1	Kepno
75E2	Keramoti
74B3	Kerasona
57D4	Kerava
87D4	Kerch
83G2	Kerki
74B3	Kerkyra
74A3	Kerkyra (I.)
53E4	Kersilö
57E1	Kesälahti
78B1	Keşan
73D2	Kesarevo
6C3	Kesh
56B2	Keskikyla
58B3	Kesterciems
55D3	Kestilä
9C5	Keswick
66B3	Keszthely
61D1	Kętrzyn

67E1 Kisvárda
57F1 Kitee
55D1 Kitka
51F1 Kittilä
36C2 Kitzbühel
39D2 Kitzingen
55D4 Kiuruvesi
56C1 Kivijärvi
55F4 Kivivaara
87C3 Kiyev
85G2 Kizel
82E2 Kizema
88C2 Kizlyar
50B1 Kjerringöy
52A4 Kjöfsvik
53E1 Kjöllefjord
72B3 Kjustendil
71D2 Kladanj
48A2 Klaebu
36D3 Klagenfurt
59A5 Klaipėda
44B1 Klarabro
62B3 Klatovy
47A5 Klepp
40A4 Kleve
73E1 Kliment
50B4 Klimpfjall
84C2 Klin
45E4 Klintehamn
84B3 Klintsy
72C2 Klisura
40B1 Klixbüll
70C2 Ključ
63D2 Klodzko
47D4 Klöfta
72A1 Klokočevac
63E1 Kluczbork
72C1 Kneža
70C3 Knin
37D2 Knittelfeld
72B2 Knjazevac
12B3 Knokke
84D2 Knyazhevo
61E2 Knyszyn
70A1 Kobarid
43D3 København
38B1 Koblenz
86A3 Kobrin
72B3 Kočani
70B1 Kočevje
82C2 Kochkoma
83J1 Kochmes
61E4 Kock
73E1 Kočmar
82E2 Kodima
37E3 Köflach
42C3 Køge
58C1 Kohtla-Järve
43D1 Köinge
53D1 Kokelv
71E3 Kokin Brod
54C2 Kokkokylä
54B4 Kokkola
59C4 Koknese
61F4 Kołacze
54B1 Kolari
71E4 Kolašin
64B1 Kolbuszowa
42B3 Kolding
58C2 Kolga-Jaani
62C2 Kolin
58A3 Kolka
61E2 Kolno
60C4 Koło
41F1 Kołobrzeg
84D2 Kologriv
84C2 Kolomna
87A4 Kolomyya
84B2 Kolpino
50A4 Kolvereid
53F1 Komagvær
63E4 Komárno
66B2 Komarom
87D4 Kommunarsk
75E1 Komotini
44B3 Kömpannebro
51E2 Kompelusvaara
82C2 Kondopoga
47C5 Kongsberg
53E1 Kongsfjord
50A4 Kongsmoen
47D4 Kongsvinger
41E3 Königs Wusterhausen
60C4 Konin
71D3 Konjic
57D1 Konnevesi
82E2 Konosha
87C3 Konotop

40A4	Krefeld
87C4	Kremenchug
37E1	Krems
83G1	Krestovka
59A5	Kretinga
63E1	Kreznice
47B6	Kristiansand
43E2	Kristianstad
46B1	Kristiansund
44C2	Kristinehamn
56A2	Kristinestad
	Kristūnankaupunki = Kristinestad
77D4	Kríti (I.)
72B3	Kriva Palanka
70A2	Krk (I.)
63E2	Krnov
76B3	Krokee
50B4	Kroken
48C2	Krokom
4B2	Króksfjardharnes
50B2	Krokstranda
54B4	Kronoby
82B2	Kronshtadt
88B1	Kropotkin
60C3	Krośniewice
64B2	Krosno
60A4	Krosno Odrzańskie
60B4	Krotoszyn
39D4	Krumbach
73E3	Krumovgrad
59B4	Kruopiai
63F4	Krupina
73F2	Kruševac BG
72A2	Kruševac YU
59C6	Krvonis
87D5	Krymsk
64B2	Krynica
88C2	Kuba
73E1	Kubrat
72A1	Kučevo
59B6	Kudirkos
36C2	Kufstein
56C2	Kuhmoinen
55E3	Kuhomo
55E3	Kuivajärvi
54C2	Kuivaniemi
58B2	Kuivastu
74B1	Kukësi

72B1	Kula BG
71E1	Kula YU
72C4	Kulata
59A4	Kuldiga
56B3	Kullaa
55D2	Kuloharju
72B3	Kumanovo
85G3	Kumertau
44C2	Kumla
70B1	Kumrovec
54C2	Kuna
58C1	Kunda
44B4	Kungäl
44B4	Kungsbacka
85G2	Kungur
67D2	Kunhegyes
56B1	Kuni
67D3	Kunszentmárton
38C3	Künzelsau
55D2	Kuolio
57D1	Kuopio
56B1	Kuortane
57D2	Kuortti
59C4	Kupiskis
87D4	Kupyansk
58A2	Kuressaare
61F2	Kurianka
56B2	Kurikka
84D2	Kurlovski
61E4	Kurów
52C4	Kurravaard
59B5	Kuršėnai
84C3	Kursk
55D1	Kursu
72A2	Kursumlija
54B1	Kurtakko
55D2	Kurtti
56C2	Kuru
55E2	Kurvinen
88A1	Kushchevskaya
88B2	Kutaisi
60C3	Kutno
53E3	Kuttura
63D3	Kúty
55D2	Kuusamo
57D3	Kuusankoski
85G2	Kuyeda
82C1	Kuzerka
71E2	Kuzmin

43E2	Lönsboda	62C1	Luban
50B2	Lönsdal	41F3	Lübben
16C2	Lons-le-Saunier	41D2	Lübeck
56C3	Loppi	60C3	Lubień
83G2	Lopydino	62C1	Lubin
26B3	Lora del Rio	61E4	Lublin
27E3	Lorca	63E1	Lubliniec
14B4	Lorient	87C4	Lubny
17B4	Loriol	28C1	Lucca
38B4	Lörrach	26B3	Lucena
49D3	Los	20B4	Lucena del Cid
27E3	Los Dolores	17C4	Luc-en-Diois
70A2	Losinj	64A3	Lučenec
70A2	Losinj (I.)	33D3	Lucera
26C1	Los Navalmorales	61E4	Łucka
26A2	Los Santos	41E4	Luckau
46D3	Löten	41E3	Luckenwalde
18C2	Lothiers	18B2	Luçon
14C4	Loudéac	38A1	Lüdenscheid
18B2	Loudun	44C1	Ludvika
7B4	Loughrea	38C3	Ludwigsburg
16C2	Louhans	38B2	Ludwigshaufen
6A3	Louisburgh	41D2	Ludwigslust
82C1	Loukhi	58D3	Ludza
55D2	Loukusa	86B2	Luga
25B6	Loulé	34C2	Lugano
62B2	Louny	87D4	Lugansk
19B6	Lourdes	22B1	Lugo E
24A3	Lourinhã	35E4	Lugo I
11E2	Louth	67E3	Lugoj
15E3	Louviers	72C2	Lukovit
51E4	Lövånger	61E3	Łuków
49D1	Lovberga	84D2	Lukoyanov
73D2	Loveč	51E3	Lulea
35D2	Lovere	78C1	Lüleburgaz
	Loviisa = Lovisa	51D2	Luleluspen
22B2	Lovios	20B1	Lumbier
57D3	Lovisa	22B3	Lumbrales
52B3	Lövli	45E4	Lummelunda
50C2	Lövnäs	8C3	Lumsden
62B2	Lovos	68C1	Lunca de Jos
82C1	Lovozero	43D3	Lund
41E3	Löwenberg	46B3	Lunde
11F3	Lowestoft	47D4	Lundersaeter
61D4	Łowicz	40C2	Lüneburg
71E2	Loznica	13D6	Lunéville
23E4	Lozoyuela	86B3	Luninets
22C1	Luanco	56C3	Luopioinen
22C1	Luarca	68A3	Lupeni

6C2	Malin	20A3	Maranchón
6B2	Malin More	18B2	Marans
78B1	Malkara	25A4	Marateca
73F2	Malko Tǎrnovo	77F1	Marathókampos
8B3	Mallaig	76C1	Marathon
6B3	Mallaranny	26B4	Marbella
21E4	Mallorca (I.)	38C1	Marburg
7B5	Mallow	48C2	Marby
10C2	Mallwyd	13C4	Marche
48B1	Malm	26B3	Marchena
51D2	Malmberget	51E2	Mårdsel
13C4	Malmédy	18B3	Marennes
45D2	Malmköping	18C3	Mareuil
43D3	Malmö	11F4	Margate
85F2	Malmyzh	33E4	Margherita
46A2	Malöy	67E2	Marghita
44B2	Malsjö	42B2	Mariager
31F4	Malta	44C4	Mariannelund
59D4	Malta LR	62A2	Mariánské Lázne
9D6	Malton	37E2	Mariazell
44B1	Malung	42C4	Maribo
85F2	Mamadysh	37E3	Maribor
69E3	Mamaia	45D2	Mariefred
15E4	Mamers	56A4	Mariehamn
74A1	Mamurasi	44B3	Mariestad
21E4	Manacor	59B6	Marijampolė
26C3	Mancha Real	31E2	Marina di Catanzaro
11D1	Manchester	31E3	Marina di Monasterace
47B6	Mandal	24A3	Marinha Grande
29B5	Mándas	87D4	Mariupol'
31F1	Manduria	58B2	Märjamaa
35D3	Manerbio	43D2	Markaryd
33E3	Manfredonia	11D2	Market Harborough
69E4	Mangalia	11E2	Market Rasen
38C2	Mannheim	85E3	Marks
17C5	Manosque	39D2	Marktredwitz
21D3	Manresa	11D3	Marlborough
23D2	Mansilla	19B4	Marmande
18B3	Mansle	78C1	Marmaraereglisi
15F3	Mantes	16C2	Marnay
35D3	Mantova	30B4	Marsala
57D3	Mäntsälä	17C6	Marseille
56C2	Mänttä	13C5	Mars-la-Tour
84D2	Manturovo	45E2	Märsta
57D2	Mäntyharju	34A2	Martigny
55D2	Mäntyjärvi	17B5	Martigues
56B3	Mäntyluoto	63E3	Martin
27D2	Manzanares	29B4	Martis
23D4	Maqueda	26C3	Martos

30C4 Modica
37E2 Mödling
46C3 Moely
9C4 Moffat
24C2 Mogadouro
86C3 Mogilev
87B4 Mogilev Podolskiy
25C6 Moguer
66C3 Mohács
63D2 Mohelnice
24C2 Moimenta da Beira
68C1 Moinești
50B3 Mo i Rana
58C2 Mõisaküla
65D4 Moiseiu
19C5 Moissac
33F4 Mola di Bari
10C1 Mold
64B3 Moldava
46B1 Molde
67E4 Moldova Nouă
65E3 Moldovița
59C5 Molėtal
33E4 Molfetta
20A3 Molina de Aragón
44B2 Molkom
44B4 Mölndal
86B3 Molodechno
22C2 Mombuey
73D3 Momčilgrad
42B3 Mommark
6C3 Monaghan
29B6 Monastir
34B3 Moncalieri
24B1 Monção
82C1 Monchegorsk
40A4 Mönchengladbach
25A5 Monchique
22B1 Mondoñedo
34B4 Mondovi
76C3 Monemvasia
25B4 Monforte
22B2 Monforte de Lemos
24C3 Monfortinho
61E2 Mońki
10C3 Monmouth
33F4 Monopoli
66C2 Monor
19C4 Monpazier
20B3 Monreal del Campo
13B4 Mons
35E3 Monselice
43F1 Mönsterås
25B4 Montagril
20B3 Montalban
27D1 Montalbo
32A3 Montalto
13A6 Montargis
19C5 Montauban
16B1 Montbard
21D3 Montblanch
16B3 Montbrison
13B4 Montcornet
19B5 Mont-de-Marsan
27E2 Montealegre
34B4 Monte Carlo
32B3 Montefiascone
35D4 Montefiorino
17B4 Montélimar
25B4 Montemor-o-Novo
32A2 Montepulciano
35E2 Montereale
13A6 Montereau
24B3 Monte Redondo
32B3 Monterosi
31D1 Montesano
29B4 Monti
13B6 Montier
13C6 Montigny-le-Roi
19C6 Mont-Louis
18D2 Montluçon
16A2 Montmarault
13C5 Montmédy
13B5 Montmirail
18C2 Montmorillon
26C3 Montoro
17B5 Montpellier
15E2 Montreuil
18B1 Montreuil-Bellay
34A2 Montreux
8C3 Montrose
15D3 Mont-Saint-Michel
34C3 Monza
20C2 Monzón
66B2 Mór
26C1 Mora E
48C4 Mora S
25B4 Móra

20B4	Mora de Rubielos	32B2	Muccia
62C3	Moravské Budějovice	75F2	Mudros
63D2	Moravský Beroun	82D2	Mudyuga
42A3	Mörbylånga	20B1	Mugaire
84D3	Mordovo	39E4	Mühldorf
61E3	Mordy	54C3	Muhos
20C4	Morella	55F4	Mujejärvi
16C2	Morez	27E3	Mula
14A3	Morgat	40C4	Mülhausen
13D5	Morhange	38B4	Mülheim
51E2	Morjärv	16D1	Mulhouse
14B3	Morlaix	8A3	Mull (I.)
44B4	Mörlanda	7C4	Mullingar
31D1	Mormanno	85E3	Mullovka
26B3	Morón	44B4	Mullsjö
9D5	Morpeth	56C2	Multia
50C1	Mörsvik	41F3	Müncheberg
18B1	Mortagne	39E4	Munchen
15E3	Mortagne	38C1	Münchhausen
15D3	Mortain	40C4	Münden
34C3	Mortara	47A4	Mundheim
82E1	Morzhovets (I.)	27D2	Munera
38C3	Mosbach	20B3	Muniesa
	Moscow = Moskva	44A3	Munkedal
50B3	Mösjöen	44B2	Munkfors
52A2	Moskenesöya (I.)	40B4	Münster
51D3	Moskosel	53D4	Muodoslomp
84C2	Moskva	53D4	Muonio
66B2	Mosonmagyaróvár	85E2	Murashi
47C5	Moss	17A4	Murat
62B2	Most	78C1	Muratlı
71D3	Mostar	29B6	Muravera
27D1	Mota	27E3	Murcia
23D3	Mota del Marqués	14B3	Mur-de-Bretagne
44C3	Motala	78C1	Mürefte
27E1	Motilla del Palancar	19C5	Muret
26C4	Motril	82C1	Murmansk
16A2	Moulins	84D2	Murom
25B5	Moura	22A1	Muros
25B5	Mourão	60B3	Murowana-Goślina
55D1	Mourujärvi	34A1	Murten
17C5	Moustiers-Sante-Marie	55E2	Murtovaara
6C2	Moville	68B2	Murtu
8B3	Moy	37E2	Mürzzuschlag
88B2	Mozdok	19B4	Mussidan
86B3	Mozyr	58C2	Mustla
70C2	Mrkonjićgrad	58C1	Mustvee
61D4	Mszczonów	57F1	Mutalahti
84C3	Mtsensk	54C1	Muurola

83J1	Muzhi
77E2	Mykonos (I.)
56B4	Mynämäki
52B1	Myre
75E2	Myrna
47D5	Mysen
64A2	Myślenice
41F2	Myslibórz Soldin
78B3	Mystegna
61D2	Myszyniec
78B3	Mytilene
	Mytilini = Lesvos
84C2	Mytishchi
63F3	Mýtna

N

56B4	Naantali
55F4	Naarva
7C4	Naas
85F2	Naberezhnyye Chelny
63D2	Náchod
67E3	Nädab
67D3	Nädlac
82C2	Nadvoitsy
42C3	Næstved
76B1	Nafpaktos
76C2	Nafplion
85F2	Nagorskoye
66B3	Nagyatád
66B3	Nagykanisa
66C2	Nagykörös
8C2	Nairn
88C3	Nakhichevan
42C3	Nakskov
88B2	Nalchik
48B1	Namsos
13C4	Namur
13C6	Nancy
18A1	Nantes
16C3	Nantua
32C4	Napoli
17A6	Narbonne
46D2	Narbuvoll
31F1	Nardò
73D3	Narečenski bani
32B3	Narni
56A2	Närpes
	Närpiö = Närpes

53F4	Naruska
57E4	Narva
83G1	Naryan Mar
48C2	Näs
44C1	Nås
49D2	Nåsåker
68B1	Näsäud
71D1	Našice
44C4	Nässjö
51E2	Nattavaara
36B3	Nauders
41E3	Nauen
39E1	Naumburg
74C2	Nausa
51D2	Nautelaur
26C1	Navahermosa
23D4	Navalcarnero
22C4	Navalmoral
26B1	Navalvillar
84B3	Navlya
77E2	Naxos
77E2	Naxos (I.)
24A3	Nazaré
84D3	Nazarovka
74C2	Nea Alexandria
76C2	Nea Epidavros
75D2	Nea Mudania
74C2	Neapolis
10C3	Neath
46D3	Nedreberg
52C4	Nedre Soppero
87D5	Neftegorsk
72B1	Negotin
72B4	Negotino
67F1	Negreşti
69E4	Negru Vodă
68C2	Nehoiaşu
53F2	Neiden
43E3	Neksø
84B2	Nelidovo
59D5	Nemenčinė
13A6	Nemours
7B4	Nenagh
74C3	Neon Monastirion
62B3	Nepomuk
19B5	Nérac
84D2	Nerekhta
59C4	Nereta
18D2	Néris

34C4	Nervi	7C5	New Ross
46B3	Nes	6D3	Newry
47C4	Nes	8C3	Newtonmore
47C4	Nesbyen	9B5	Newton Stewart
73F2	Nesebär	6C2	Newton Stewart
47A5	Nesflaten	10C2	Newtown
5F2	Neskaupstadhur	84D2	Neya
50B3	Nesna	87C3	Nezhin
46B1	Nesset	42B1	Nibe
86A3	Nesterov	31E2	Nicastro
47A4	Nesttun	17D5	Nice
41E2	Neubrandenburg	59D4	Nicgale
34A1	Neuchâtel	37F2	Nickelsdorf
13C6	Neufchâteau F	30C4	Nicosia
13C4	Neufchâteau B	61D2	Nidzica
15E2	Neufchâtel	61E4	Niedrzwica Duza
37D1	Neufelden	63D2	Niemcza
40C2	Neuhaus	40C3	Nienburg
39F3	Neuhaus	41F4	Niesky
39D3	Neumarkt	60C3	Nieszawa
40C1	Neumünster	75D2	Nigrita
37E2	Neunkirchen A	12C2	Nijmegen
38B2	Neunkirchen D	82C1	Nikel
41E3	Neuruppin	74C2	Niki
39D2	Neuses	51D4	Niknoret
40A4	Neuss	87C4	Nikolayev
40C3	Neustadt	85E3	Nikolayevskiy
18B2	Neuville	85E2	Nikolsk
86B2	Nevel	73D1	Nikopol BG
50B3	Nevernes	87C4	Nikopol U
16A2	Nevers	71E4	Nikšic
71D3	Nevesinje	55F4	Nilsiä
88B2	Nevinnomyssk	17B5	Nîmes
11E2	Newark	18B2	Niort
11D3	Newbury	72A2	Niš
6D3	Newcastle	24B3	Nisa
9D5	Newcastle upon Tyne	64B1	Nisko
9B5	New Galloway	55D1	Nissinvaara
11E4	Newhaven	63E4	Nitra
11E1	New Holland	54C4	Nivala
11E2	New Hunstanton	84D2	Nizhniy Novgorod
11E3	Newmarket	85G2	Nizhniy Tagil
10C3	Newport GB	85G2	Nizhnyaya Tura
11D4	Newport GB	4A4	Njardhvikur
6B3	Newport IRE	52C2	Njeamonjáiku
8C3	Newport-on-Tay	49E3	Njurunda
10A4	Newquai	52B2	nKvalöy (l.)
10B2	New Quay	35D3	Nogara
11E4	New Romney	19B5	Nogaro

15E4	Nogent-le-Rotrou
13B6	Nogent-sur-Seine
18A1	Noirmoutier
56C3	Nokia
85E1	Nolinsk
15E3	Nonancourt
83G1	Nonburg
12C2	Noordwijk aan Zee
56B3	Noormarkku
49D4	Nopplkoski
44C2	Nora
49E1	Nordanås
46B2	Nordberg
40A2	Norden D
51D3	Norden S
46A2	Nordfjordeid
50B1	Nordfold
48A1	Nord Fröya
41D4	Nordhausen
40A3	Nordhorn
48C1	Nordli
39D3	Nördlingen
49F1	Nordmaling
52C2	Nordreisa
50A3	Nordvik
47C4	Nore
47A4	Norheimsund
11E2	Norman Cross
44B4	Norra Unnaryd
49D1	Norrby
42A3	Nørre Nevel
42B1	Nørresundby
42A1	Nørre Vorupør
45D3	Norrköping
45E2	Norrtälje
51D4	Norsjö
18A1	Nort
9D6	Northallerton
11D3	Northampton
9C4	North Berwick
40C4	Northeim
8A2	North Uist (I.)
11F2	North Walsham
11F2	Norwich
83F2	Noshul
39F1	Nossen
79B4	Notii Sporades
31D4	Noto
47C5	Notodden
11D2	Nottingham
63E4	Nová Baňa
70C2	Nova Gradiška
34C3	Novara
73E2	Nova Zagora
82C3	Novaya Ladoga
27F3	Novelda
63E4	Nové Zámky
84B2	Novgorod
86C3	Novgorod Severskiy
67D3	Novi Kneževac
37F3	Novi Marof
73E1	Novi Pazar BG
71F3	Novi Pazar YU
71E1	Novi Sad
87C4	Novoalekseyevka
84D3	Novoanninskiy
87D4	Novocherkassk
87D4	Novofedorovka
87B3	Novograd Volynskiy
86B3	Novogrudok
70B1	Novo Mesto
63E3	Novo Mesto nad Váh
84C3	Novomoskovsk RF
87D4	Novomoskovsk U
13A5	Novon
87D5	Novorossiysk
74A2	Novosela
72C3	Novo Selo
87D4	Novoshakhtinsk
85E3	Novouzensk
85F2	Novo-Vyatsk
70C1	Novska
62B1	Nový Bor
60A4	Nowa Sól
60C2	Nowe
61D4	Nowe Miasto
41F2	Nowogard
64A2	Nowy Sącz
64A2	Nówy Targ
14C4	Nozay
67E3	Nucet
20A3	Nuevalos
27F1	Nules
56C4	Nummi
53D3	Nunnanen
29B5	Nuoro
57D2	Nurmaa
55F4	Nurmes

55F4	Nurmijärvi
39D2	Nürnberg
54C2	Nuupas
49E1	Nyåker
83J2	Nyaksimvol
82E2	Nyandoma
83G1	Nyashabozh
46D3	Nybergsund
42C3	Nyborg
43E2	Nybro
67D1	Nyékládháza
67E1	Nyírbátor
67E1	Nyíregyháza
56B1	Nykarleby
42C2	Nykøbing
42B2	Nykøbing
42C4	Nykøbing
45D3	Nyköping
49E1	Nyliden
62C2	Nymburk
45E2	Nynäshamn
17C5	Nyons
53F2	Nyrud
63D2	Nysa
46B2	Nysaetri
44B2	Nysäter
42C4	Nysted
82E2	Nyuksenitsa

O

69D2	Oancea
47A5	Oanes
8B3	Oban
59D4	Obeliai
36C3	Oberdrauburg
39D4	Oberstdorf
37E2	Oberwart
60B3	Oborniki
84C3	Oboyan
82E2	Obozerskiy
71E2	Obrenovac
70B3	Obrovac
73F2	Obzor
27D1	Ocaña
88B2	Ochamchire
49D4	Ockelbo
68C2	Ocland
47A4	Odda

42B2	Odder
25A5	Odeceixe
25A5	Odemira
42B3	Odense
44C3	Ödeshög
87C4	Odessa
69D2	Odobeşti
68C2	Odorheiu Secuiesc
71E1	Odžaci
39E1	Oelsnitz
38B3	Offenburg
59C4	Ogre
70B2	Ogulin
72A4	Ohrid
54C2	Oijärvi
57D3	Oitti
10B4	Okehampton
85G2	Okhansk
78C1	Oklalı
47A4	Oknarvik
48B1	Oksdol
52C2	Öksfjord
85F3	Oktyabrskiy
70C2	Okučani
4C1	Ólafsfjördhur
42A3	Öland (I.)
29B4	Olbia
46B2	Olden
41D1	Oldenburg
40B2	Oldenburg
12D2	Oldenzaal
52C2	Olderdalen
61E1	Olecko
83F2	Olema
47A5	Ölen
63D1	Oleśnica
63E1	Olesno Rosenberg
25B6	Olhão
54C2	Olhava
25C4	Olivenza
63F2	Olkusz
23D3	Olmedo
43E2	Olofström
63D2	Olomouc
82C2	Olonets
19B5	Oloron-Sainte-Marie
21E2	Olot
71D3	Olova
38B1	Olpe

85F3 Perevolotskiy
87C3 Pereyaslav-Khmelnitskiy
56C1 Perho
18C3 Perigueux
68B4 Perişoru
41D2 Perleberg
71F1 Perlez
85G2 Perm
74B3 Përmeti
72B3 Pernik
56C4 Perniö
37E2 Pernitz
13A4 Péronne
17A6 Perpignan
14B3 Perros-Guirec
8C3 Perth
32B2 Perugia
87C4 Pervomaysk
85G2 Pervouralsk
32B1 Pesaro
32C3 Pescara
74B1 Peshkopija
68A3 Peşteana-Jiu
72C3 Peštera
84C2 Pestovo
54C2 Petäjäskoski
11E2 Peterborough
8D2 Peterhead
11D4 Petersfield
78B3 Petra
30C4 Petralia
72C3 Petrič
68A3 Petrila
70C1 Petrinja
86B2 Petrodvorets
68A3 Petroşeni
72A1 Petrovac
71E4 Petrovac
85E3 Petrovsk
82C2 Petrozavodsk
19A5 Peyrehorade
17C5 Peyrolles
17A5 Pézanas
83G2 Pezmog
38C3 Pforzheim
13D6 Phalsbourg
13B4 Philippeville
39F3 Philippsreut
34C3 Piacenza
35D3 Piádena
61F4 Piask
68C1 Piatra Neamţ
9D6 Pickering
33D4 Piedimonte
26C2 Piedrabuena
22B1 Piedrafita
22C4 Piedrahita
23D4 Piedralaves
57D1 Pieksämaki
55D4 Pielavesi
18C3 Pierre-Buffière
63E3 Piest'any
Pietarsaari = Jakobstad
35E2 Pieve di Cadore
35D4 Pievepelago
56C1 Pihtipudas
60B3 Piła
55D4 Piipola
84B2 Pikalevo
64B2 Pilzno
73F3 Pınarhisar
82E2 Pinega
34B3 Pinerolo
4A2 Pingeyri
24C2 Pinhel
27E2 Pinoso
86B3 Pinsk
55D2 Pintamo
83F2 Pinyug
28C2 Piombino
61D4 Piotrków
Piræus = Pireus
70A2 Piran
76C2 Pireus
38B3 Pirmasens
39F1 Pirna
72B2 Pirot
55D1 Pirttikoski
87C3 Piryatin
28C1 Pisa
73D1 Pisanec
62B3 Písek
19B4 Pissos
28C1 Pisto
61E2 Pisz Johannisburg
51E3 Piteå
68B3 Piteşti
13A6 Pithiviers

8C3	Pitlochry
62B2	Pizeň
31E2	Pizzo
75F2	Pláka
71F1	Plandište
22C4	Plasencia
39E3	Platting
41D2	Plau
39E1	Plauen
71F4	Plav
59C4	Plaviņas
84C3	Plavsk
15D4	Plélan-le-Grand
68A4	Pleniţa
82E2	Plesetsk
86B3	Pleshchenitsy
60B4	Pleszew
72C1	Pleven
70B2	Plitvice
71E3	Pljevlja
71D4	Ploče
60C3	Płock
14C4	Ploërmel
68C3	Ploiești
16D1	Plombières
40C1	Plön
61D3	Płońsk
41F2	Płoty
73D3	Plovdiv
59A5	Plungė
10B4	Plymouth
60A3	Pniewy
21D2	Pobla de Segur
67E2	Pocsaj
62C2	Poděbrady
71E4	Podgorica
73D3	Podkova
75E2	Podochorion
84C2	Podolsk
82C2	Podporozhye
71D1	Podravska Slatina
71E3	Podromanija
72A2	Podujevo
28C2	Poggibonsi
74B2	Pogradeci
56C2	Pohja
54C2	Pohjaslahti
63D3	Pohořelice
68B1	Poiana Stampei

68C1	Poiana Teiului
68B3	Poina Tîrgu
18C2	Poitiers
15E2	Poix
63E1	Pojeczno
53E4	Pokka
23D1	Pola de Laviana
22C1	Pola de Lena
23D1	Pola de Siero
60A2	Polanów
51E2	Polcirkeln
60A2	Połczyn Zdroj
16C2	Poligny
21E3	Pollensa
86B2	Polotsk
73E2	Polski Gradec
87C4	Poltava
83F2	Polunochnoye
57E1	Polvijarvi
82C1	Polyarnyy
75D2	Polyjiros
74C2	Polykastron
24B3	Pombal
8C1	Pomona
22C2	Ponferrada
82E1	Ponoy
18B3	Pons
24B3	Pontão
16C2	Pontarlier
28C1	Pontassieve
16A3	Pontaumur
14C4	Pontchâteau
16C3	Pont-d'Ain
24B1	Ponte de Barca
24B1	Ponte de Lima
28C1	Pontedera
25B4	Ponte de Sor
13C5	Pont-è-Mousson
35E2	Ponte nelle Alpi
22A2	Pontevedra
13B5	Pontfaverger
14B4	Pontivy
14B4	Pont-l-Abbé
13A5	Pontoise
15D3	Pontorson
34C4	Pontremoll
35D2	Pontresina
17B5	Pont-Saint-Esprit
10C3	Pontypridd

71E2	Ražana
72A2	Razbojna
73E1	Razgrad
72C3	Raziog
11D3	Reading
82C2	Reboly
40A4	Recklinghausen
60A3	Recz
14C4	Redon
22A2	Redondela
25B4	Redondo
10A4	Redruth
39F3	Regen
39E3	Regensburg
31D3	Reggio Calabria
35D3	Réggio nell Emilia
68B1	Reghin
25B5	Reguengos
11E4	Reigate
13B5	Reims
52A2	Reine
23E1	Reinosa
52B2	Reinöya (I.)
54C4	Reisjärvi
55D4	Remeskylä
16D1	Remiremont
17B5	Remoulins
46D3	Rena
75D2	Rendina
40C1	Rendsburg
14C4	Rennes
53E3	Repojoki
53D1	Repvåg
27E1	Requena
72A1	Resavica
67E4	Reşiţa
13B5	Rethel
77D4	Rethimnon
66C2	Rétság
21D3	Reus
38C3	Reutlingen
85G2	Revda
13C5	Revigny
35E3	Revigo
4B3	Reykjavik
59D4	Rēzekne
10C2	Rhayader
40B3	Rheine
	Rhodes = Ródos

8A3	Rhum (I.)
73E2	Riš
68C2	Rişnov
23D1	Riaño
23E3	Riaza
22B2	Ribadavia
22C2	Ribadelago
22C1	Ribadeo
23D1	Ribadesella
21E2	Ribas
42B3	Ribe
30B4	Ribera
41E1	Ribnitz-Damgarten
32B1	Riccione
36C2	Ried
59A5	Rietavas
32B3	Rieti
58B3	Riga
55E3	Riihilahti
56C3	Riihimäki
58B1	Riisipere
70A2	Rijeka
72C3	Rilski Manastir
64A3	Rimavská-Sobota
35E4	Rimini
69D2	Rîmnicu Sărat
68B3	Rîmnicu Vîlcea
47C5	Rinde
46C3	Ringebu
42A2	Ringkøbing
42C3	Ringsted
52B2	Ringvassöya (I.)
69D1	Rînzeşti
16A3	Riom
24A3	Rio Maior
67E2	Rîpa
21E2	Ripoll
71E4	Risan
50C4	Risbäck
48C4	Risberg
19B5	Riscle
47C6	Risör
58B1	Risti
57D2	Ristiina
55D3	Ristijärvi
51E2	Risträsk
35D2	Riva
47C4	Rjukan
16B3	Roanne

78C1 Saray
29A5 Sardegna
Sardinia = Sardegna
34C1 Sargans
20C2 Sariñena
78D1 Sarıyer
14C2 Sark (I.)
67E2 Sarkad
57E2 Särkisalmi
78C2 Şarköy
19C4 Sarlat
67F4 Sarmizegetusa
48C4 Särna
87B3 Sarny
47D5 Sarpsborg
23E2 Sarracin
13D6 Sarrebourg
13D5 Sarreguemines
13D5 Sarre-Union
22B1 Sarria
20B4 Sarrión
28B3 Sartène
66A2 Sárvár
35D4 Sarzana
66B3 Sásd
84D3 Sasovo
29A4 Sassari
41E1 Sassnitz
35D4 Sasso
44C1 Säter
67D1 Sátoraljaújhely
67E1 Satu Mare
47A5 Sauda
4C2 Saudharkrókur
16B2 Saulieu
58C3 Saulkrasti
17C5 Sault
18B1 Saumur
55E3 Saunajärvi
17B4 Sauvetat
65F3 Säven
34B3 Savigliano
67E3 Săvirşin
57E2 Savitaipale
71E4 Šavnik
34B4 Savona
57E2 Savonlina
57E1 Savonranta
44C4 Sävsjö
53F4 Savukoski
50C3 Saxnäs
55F4 Säyneinen
31E1 Scanzano
9D6 Scarborough
38C4 Schaffhausen
38B1 Schameder
36C1 Schärding
37E2 Scheibbs
36D3 Scheifling
40C4 Scherfede
12B2 Scheveningen
35E2 Schio
13D6 Schirmech
69D1 Schitu Duca
39E1 Schleiz
40C1 Schleswig
38C2 Schlüchtern
39D4 Schongau
12B2 Schouwen (I.)
37E1 Schrems
39D3 Schrobenhausen
38C3 Schwäbisch Hall
39E3 Schwandorf
37F2 Schwechat
41F2 Schwedt
39D2 Schweinfurt
41D2 Schwerin
34C1 Schwyz
30B4 Sciacca
10A4 Scilly Is.
68A3 Scoarta
11F3 Scole
9C6 Scotch Corner
8B1 Scourie
8C1 Scrabster
11E1 Scunthorpe
9D5 Seaham
68A2 Sebeş
64B3 Sečovce
59A4 Seda
13C5 Sedan
78B2 Şeddülbahir
59B5 Šeduva
15E3 Sées
40C4 Seesen
68B4 Segarcea
27F1 Segorbe
23D4 Segovia

24C3	Segura	9C6	Settle
56B1	Seinäjoki	25A4	Setúbal
61E1	Sejny	29B5	Seui
52C2	Sekkemo	87C5	Sevastopol'
39D2	Selb	83F1	Severnyy
48B2	Selbu	82D2	Severodvinsk
11D1	Selby	82C1	Severomorsk
13D6	Sélestat	53F2	Sevettijärvi
67E2	Seleuş	26A3	Sevilla
4B4	Selfoss	73D2	Sevlievo
47B5	Seljord	5E2	Seydhisfjördhur
9C4	Selkirk	13B5	Sézanne
49E2	Selsjön	68C2	Sfîntu Gheorghe
49E2	Seltjärn	10C4	Shaftesbury
85F2	Selty	85E2	Shakhunya
37E2	Semmering	9C5	Shap
63E4	Senec	85F3	Sharlyk
63E3	Senica	85E2	Sharya
32C1	Senigallia	83G1	Shchelyayur
70B2	Senj	11D1	Sheffield
52B3	Senja (I.)	88C2	Sheki
13A5	Senlis	82E2	Shenkursk
29B6	Senorbì	87B3	Shepetovka
13A6	Sens	10C3	Shepton Mallet
67D3	Senta	12C3	S-Hertogenbosch
21D2	Seo de Urgel	8D2	Shetland Is.
60B2	Sępólno	8B2	Shiel Bridge
23E3	Sepulveda	74A1	Shkodra
22C4	Sequeros	86C6	Shostka
63E4	Sered'	87C4	Shpola
85E1	Sergach	10C2	Shrewsbury
85F3	Sergiyevsk	85E1	Shumerlya
77D2	Serifos (I.)	84D2	Shuya
85H2	Serov	59B5	Šiauliai
25B5	Serpa	70C3	Šibenik
84C3	Serpukhov	68B2	Sibiu
31E3	Serra	30B4	Sicilia
34C3	Serravalle		Sicily = Sicilia
75D1	Serre	71E2	Šid
17C4	Serres	49E2	Sidensjö
24B3	Sertã	75D1	Sidirokastron
74C3	Servia	61E3	Siedlce
25A4	Sesimbra	38B1	Siegburg
51F3	Seskarön (I.)	38B1	Siegen
34C2	Sesto Calende	61E3	Siemiatycze
34A3	Sestriere	28C2	Siena
34C4	Sestri Levante	64C1	Sieniawa
59C5	Šeta	54B1	Sieppijärvi
17A5	Sète	60C4	Sieradz

60C3	Sierpe	31D4	Siracusa
34B2	Sierre	65E3	Siret
77D2	Sifnos (I.)	67E3	Siria
82C1	Sig	53E4	Sirkka
17A6	Sigean	54B1	Sirkka
65D3	Sighetu Marmaţ	59C5	Širvintos
68B2	Sighişoara	70C1	Sisak
4C1	Siglufjördhur	17C5	Sisteron
38C4	Sigmaringen	77F4	Sitia
45D2	Sigtuna	21D3	Sitges
23E4	Sigüenza	12C3	Sittard
58C3	Sigulda	55D2	Sivikko
54C3	Siikajoki	83J1	Sivomaskinskiy
57D1	Siilinjärvi	82E2	Siya
49F1	Sikeå	42C3	Sjaelland (I.)
51E3	Sikfors	71F3	Sjenica
51D3	Sikselet	46C3	Sjoa
51D3	Siksjön	43D3	Sjobo
59B5	Šilalė	46D3	Sjömoen
29A6	Siliqua	42B2	Sjørup
78C1	Silivri	50B4	Sjoutnäs
42B2	Silkeborg	46C3	Skåbu
44B2	Sillerud	42B3	Skaerbaek
59A5	Šilutė	42C1	Skagen
34C2	Silvaplana	64A2	Skalbmierz
25A6	Silves	53D2	Skaldi
68A2	Simeria	42B2	Skanderborg
87C5	Simferopol'	47A4	Skånevik
72C3	Simitli	44C3	Skänninge
67E2	Simläul-Silvaniei	43D3	Skanör
38B2	Simmern	44B3	Skara
45D3	Simonstorp	49E1	Skarda
57E2	Simpele	47D4	Skarnes
43E3	Simrishamn	45D1	Skärplinge
58C1	Simuna	64A1	Skarżysko Kamienna
68C3	Sinaia	59B5	Skaudvilė
68A1	Sincraiu Almaşului	59D4	Škaune
25A5	Sines	45E1	Skebo
54C1	Sinettä	11E2	Skegness
38C4	Singen	51E4	Skellefteå
46C1	Singsås	44B4	Skene
29B4	Siniscola	7A5	Skibbereen
70C3	Sinj	52C3	Skibotn
67D3	Sinnicolau Mare	47C5	Skien
25A4	Sintra	44C4	Skillingaryd
38B1	Sinzig	9C6	Skipton
66B3	Siófok	42B2	Skive
34B2	Sion	42A2	Skjern
73D2	Šipka	50B2	Skjerstad

46B2	Skodje
49E2	Skog
53D2	Skoganvarre
53F2	Skogly
48B2	Skogn
75E3	Skopelos
72A3	Skopje
60C2	Skórcz
47D4	Skotterud
44B3	Skövde
51E2	Skröven
59D4	Skrudallena
59A4	Skrunda
47A5	Skudeneshamn
59A4	Skuodas
53E1	Sküppagurra
43D3	Skurup
45D1	Skutskär
52A4	Skutvik
60A3	Skwierzyna
8A2	Skye (I.)
75E3	Skyrós
75E3	Skyrós (I.)
49D2	Skyttmon
42C3	Slagelse
51D3	Slagnäs
71D4	Slano
86B2	Slantsy
62B2	Slaný
68B4	Slatina
67E4	Slatina Timiş
53D1	Slätten
86C3	Slavgorod
63D3	Slavkov
71D1	Slavonska Požega
71D2	Slavonski Brod
87D4	Slavyansk
60A2	Sławno
11E2	Sleaford
54C4	Slevi
8B2	Sligachan
6B3	Sligo
45E4	Slite
73E2	Sliven
85F2	Slobodskoy
69D3	Slobozia
64A2	Słomniki
37E3	Slovenska Bistrica
41F3	Słubice
70B2	Slunj
60B1	Słupsk
86B3	Slutsk
43D1	Smålandsstenar
59B5	Smalininkai
71F2	Smederevs Palanka
71F2	Smederovo
44C1	Smedjebacken
87C4	Smela
58C3	Smiltene
68C4	Smirdioasa
73E2	Smjadovo
46B1	Smöla (I.)
84B3	Smolensk
73D3	Smoljan
86B3	Smorgon
48B1	Snåsa
12C1	Sneek
7A5	Sneem
62C3	Soběslav
61D3	Sochaczew
87D5	Sochi
53E4	Sodankyla
49E4	Söderhamn
45D2	Södertalje
72C2	Sofija
82C1	Sofporog
47A6	Sogndal
46B3	Sogndalsfjora
13B4	Soignies
56C1	Soini
13B5	Soissons
72A2	Soko Banja
84D2	Sokol
61F2	Sokołka
62A2	Sokolov
64B1	Sokołow
61E3	Sokołów Podlaski
23E1	Solarès
49E1	Solberg
36B3	Sölden
69D1	Soleşti
82E2	Solginskiy
84D2	Soligalich
85G2	Solikamsk
85F3	Sol-Iletsk
49E2	Solleftea
21E3	Sóller
46C2	Sollia

34B1	Solothurn	19C4	Souillac
21D2	Solsona	18A3	Soulac-sur-Mer
45D4	Solstadsström	11D4	Southampton
66C3	Solt	11E3	Southend-on-Sea
40C2	Soltau	10B3	South Molton
43E2	Sölvesborg	10C1	Southport
46D2	Sömådal	9D5	South Shields
16B2	Sombernon	8A2	South Uist (I.)
71E1	Sombor	11F3	Southwold
56C3	Somero	16A2	Souvigny
50C1	Sommarset	68B1	Sovata
60C3	Sompolno	69D2	Soveja
42B3	Sønderborg	31E2	Soverato
41D4	Sondershausen	31E2	Soveria
34C2	Sondrio	85E2	Sovetsk
55D4	Sonkajärvi	73F2	Sozopol
53D4	Sonkamoutka	13C4	Spa
38C1	Sontra	11E2	Spalding
20C2	Sopeira	76B2	Sparti
60B1	Sopot	8B3	Spean Bridge
72A4	Sopotnica	38B3	Speyer
66A2	Sopron	31E2	Spezzano
32C3	Sora	37E3	Spielfeld
27D4	Sorbas	34B1	Spiez
45D3	Sörderköping	34B4	Spigno
29B5	Sorgono	33E4	Spinazzola
20A2	Soria	64A3	Spišská-Nova Ves
48C1	Söril	8C3	Spital of Glenshee
42C3	Sorø	36D3	Spittal
85F3	Sorochinsk	46B2	Spjelkavik
87B4	Soroki	70C3	Split
52C1	Söroya (I.)	34C2	Splügen
52B3	Sorreisal	59D4	Špogi
33D4	Sorrento	32B2	Spoleto
50C3	Sorsele	35D2	Spondigna
21D2	Sort	41F4	Spremberg
82C2	Sortavala	71E1	Srbobran
52B1	Sortland	73D2	Sredec
48C3	Sörvatnet	60B4	Śrem
46D2	Sörvika	60B4	Środa
83G2	Sosnogorsk	71F1	Srpska Crnja
82C2	Sosnovo	40C2	Stade
82C1	Sosnovyy	38A1	Stadtky
63F2	Sosnowiec	40A3	Stadtlohn
85H2	Sosva	8B2	Staffin
87D4	Sosyka	11D2	Stafford
55E3	Sotkamo	87D4	Stakhanov
47A4	Sotra (I.)	48C1	Stallvika
77D4	Souda	50C4	Stalon

11E2 Stamford
49D1 Stamsele
52A2 Stamsund
47D4 Stange
72C3 Stanke Dimitrov
64A1 Starachowice
64A2 Stará Lubovňa
71E2 Stara Pazova
84B2 Staraya Russa
73D2 Stara Zagora
41F2 Stargard Szczciński
72B4 Stari Dojran
84B2 Staritsa
39D4 Starnberg
60C2 Starogard
73F1 Staro Orjahovo
84C3 Staryy Oskol
64A1 Staszów
47A5 Stavanger
12C1 Staveren
88B1 Stavropol'
75E1 Stavrupolis
61E2 Stawiski
31E1 Stazione di Nova Siri
47B5 Steane
73E1 Stefan Karadža
43D3 Stege
36B3 Steinach
47A4 Steinberg bru
48B1 Steinkjer
13C5 Stenay
41D3 Stendal
58B3 Stende
50C4 Stensele
51D2 Stenträsk
88C3 Stepanakert
85G3 Sterlitamak
63D2 Šternberk
60B4 Stęszew
37D2 Steyr
44C4 Stigamo
45D3 Stigtomta
72A3 Štimlje
72B4 Štip
9B4 Stirling
52C2 Stjernöya
48B2 Stjördalshalsen
48C4 Stöa
49E3 Stocka
37E1 Stockerau
45E2 Stockholm
11D1 Stockport
9D5 Stockton
49D3 Stöde
11D2 Stoke on Trent
52B1 Stokmarknes
71D4 Stolac
44B1 Stöllet
75D3 Stomion
8D3 Stonehaven
11D3 Stony Stratford
50B4 Stora Blåsjön
46C1 Storås
56A4 Storby
46C1 Stören
52C3 Storfjord
53E1 Storfjordbotn
44C2 Storfors
50B2 Storjord
48B2 Storlien
8B1 Stornoway
48A2 Storodden
83G2 Storozhevsk
48C3 Storsätern
48C2 Storsjö
50C4 Storuman
45D1 Storvik
42B2 Støvring
73F1 Stožer
6C2 Strabane
72B3 Stracin
62B3 Strakonice
41E1 Stralsund
46B2 Stranda
45D2 Strängäs
6D3 Strangford
9B5 Stranraer
38B3 Strasbourg
36C2 Strasswalchen
11D3 Stratford-on-Avon
49E4 Stråtjära
39E3 Straubing
52A4 Straumsnes
39D1 Straussfurt
68A4 Strehaia
58C3 Strenči
34B2 Stresa
62B2 Stříbro

50B3	Strimasund	32C3	Sulmona
76C1	Strofylia	39E2	Sulzbach-Rosenberg
31D2	Stromboli (I.)	8D2	Sumburgh
8B2	Stromeferry	66B3	Sümeg
51E4	Strömfors	73E1	Sumen
49E2	Strömnäs	88C2	Sumgait
8C1	Stromness	63D2	Šumperk
44A3	Strömstad	87C3	Sumy
49D1	Strömsund	45D2	Sundbyborg
11D3	Stroud	9D5	Sunderland
42A2	Struer	45E4	Sundre
72A4	Struga	49E3	Sundsvall
72B4	Strumica	29A5	Suniy
46B2	Stryn	76C2	Sunion
87A4	Stryy	49E4	Sunnäsbruk
60A3	Strzelce Krajeńskie	44C1	Sunnasjö
63E1	Strzelce Opolskie	46C2	Sunndalsora
60B3	Strzelno	44B2	Sunne
64B2	Strzyzow	58C3	Suntaži
36A3	Stuben	57D1	Suolahti
46D1	Stugudal	53D2	Suolovuopmi
49D2	Stugun	55E3	Suomussalmi
63E4	Štúrovo	57D1	Suonenjoki
38C3	Stuttgart	50C1	Suorva
49D3	Styggberg	82C2	Suoyarvi
4A2	Stykkishólmur	53E2	Supru
59D4	Subate	85E3	Sura
32C3	Subiaco	72B3	Surdulica
66C3	Subotica	18B2	Surgères
65E3	Suceava	21D3	Suria
70C3	Sučevići	46C1	Surnadalsöra
63F2	Sucha	34A3	Susa
60B2	Suchorze	70C3	Šušica
11E3	Sudbury	60C2	Susz
4A1	Sudhureyri	11E2	Sutterton
27F2	Sueca	11D2	Sutton Coldfield
75F1	Suflion	61E1	Suwałki
68A3	Sugag	49D4	Svabensverk
70C1	Suhopolje	43E3	Svaneke
13B5	Suippes	51F2	Svanstein
55D4	Sukeva	53F2	Svanvik
84C3	Sukhinichi	51E1	Svappavaara
88B2	Sukhumi	47A5	Svartevatn
47A5	Suldal	50B2	Svartisdalen
60A4	Sulechów	51E3	Svartlá
69F2	Sulina	53F1	Svartnes
40B3	Sulingen	87D4	Svatovo
50C2	Sulitjelma Sulicielbma	59C5	Svědasai
57E2	Sulkava	48C3	Sveg

44A3	Tanum
62C1	Tanvald
31D3	Taormina
58C1	Tapa
51D2	Tarajaure
27D1	Tarancon
31E1	Taranto
16B3	Tarare
19C6	Tarascon
83F1	Tarasova
27E2	Tarazona
20B2	Tarazona
8A2	Tarbert
19B5	Tarbes
9B4	Tarbet
71D3	Tarčin
51E1	Tarendö
73E1	Târgovište
26A4	Tarifa
42A2	Tarm
50B3	Tärnaby
64B1	Tarnobrzeg
73D2	Târnovo
64A2	Tarnów
63E1	Tarnowskie Góry
45D1	Tärnsjö
10C2	Tarporley
32A3	Tarquinia
21D3	Tarragona
21D3	Tarrega
19A5	Tartas
58C2	Tartu
35F2	Tarvisio
67E2	Tăşnad
66B2	Tatabánya
59C5	Taujėnai
10C4	Taunton
59B5	Tauragė
20B2	Tauste
25B6	Tavira
10B4	Tavistock
88B2	Tbilisi
60C2	Tczew
69D2	Tecuci
9D5	Teeside
39E4	Tegernsee
68A2	Teiuş
72B1	Tekija
78C1	Tekirdağ

88C2	Telavi
68B1	Telciu
72C2	Teliš
59B5	Telšiai
27D1	Tembleque
54C3	Temmes
29B4	Tempio
41E2	Templin
56C4	Tenala
10B3	Tenby
17D5	Tende
53E4	Tepasto
74A3	Tepelena
62B2	Teplice
51F1	Tepsal
32C2	Teramo
12C1	Terchelling (I.)
67E4	Teregova
61F3	Terespol
30C4	Termini
33D3	Termoli
32B3	Terni
87B4	Ternopol
32C4	Terracina
29A5	Terralba
31E1	Terranova
21D3	Terrassa
19C4	Terrasson
29B5	Tertenia
20B4	Teruel
73E1	Tervel
59B4	Tërvete
57D1	Tervo
54C2	Tervola
41E2	Teterow
72A3	Tetovo
29A6	Teulada
56B2	Teuva
12C1	Texel (I.)
16D1	Thann
75E2	Thasos
75E2	Thasos (I.)
74A1	Thelhi
19C4	Thenon
75D2	Thessaloniki
11E3	Thetford
29A5	Thiesi
13C5	Thionville
77E3	Thira

W

COLLINS GEM

Other Gem titles that may interest you include:

Gem World Atlas
A compact yet comprehensive atlas of the world, fully updated to show the new political boundaries of the emergent European republics **£3.50 net**

Gem Atlas of Britain
A handy, pocket-sized atlas of Britain featuring over sixty town and city centre plans **£3.50 net**

Gem Flags
An up-to-date, fully illustrated guide to the flags of the world, explaining the origins, history and significance of the flags of over 200 countries
£3.50 net

Gem Basic Facts Geography
One of a range of illustrated dictionaries in key school subjects, this book explains the essential terms and concepts in geography and so is invaluable for exam revision **£2.99 net**